Goethean Science

D1252848

Goethean Science

by

Rudolf Steiner

2005
MERCURY PRESS
Chestnut Ridge, New York

In the collected edition of Rudolf Steiner's works in German, the
volume containing the German text is entitled *Goethes Natur-
wissenschaftliche Schriften, Einleitungen*, (Vol. I in the Biblio-
graphic Survey). It was originally published as introductions to
Goethe's Natural-Scientific Works in *Kürschner's Deutsche National Literatur*, edited by Rudolf Steiner, with introductions,
footnotes, and annotations in four volumes, 1883-1897.

Also translated as *Goethe the Scientist*.

This translation into English was made by William Lindeman

Copyright © 1988 by William Lindeman

Cover: Graphic form by Rudolf Steiner (originally as a study for
the book *Truth and Science*).

Layout and lettering, Peter Stebbing.

Library of Congress Cataloging-in-Publication Data
Steiner, Rudolf, 1861-1925.
Goethean Science
1. Goethe, Johann, Wolfgang von, 1749-1832-
Knowledge-Science. I. Title.
Library of Congress Catalog Card Number: 88-061734
ISBN 978-0-936132-92-1 (pbk.)

All rights reserved. No part of this book may be repro-
duced in any form without written permission of the
publisher, except for brief quotations embodied in critical reviews or articles.

Printed & Published in the USA by
MERCURY PRESS
Fellowship Community
241 Hungry Hollow Road
Chestnut Ridge, N.Y. 10977
(845) 425-9357
www.fellowshipcommunity.org
mercurypress@fellowshipcommunity.org

Contents

I

Introduction

On August 18, 1787, Goethe wrote to Knebel from Italy: "To judge by the plants and fish I have seen in Naples and Sicily, I would, if I were ten years younger, be very tempted to make a trip to India, *not in order to discover something new, but in order to contemplate in my own way what has already been discovered.*" In these words is to be found the point of view from which we have to look at Goethe's scientific works. With him it is never a matter of discovering new facts, but rather of opening up a *new point of view*, of looking at nature in a particular way. It is true that Goethe made a number of great single discoveries, such as the intermaxillary bone, the vertebral theory of the skull in osteology, the common identity of all plant organs with the leaf in botany, etc. But we have to regard as the life and soul of all these individual cases the magnificent view of nature by which they are carried; in the study of organisms we have to fix our attention above all on a magnificent discovery that overshadows everything else: *that of the being of the organism itself.* Goethe has set forth the principle by which an organism is what it presents itself to be; he sets forth the causes whose results appear to us in the manifestations of life; he sets forth, in fact, everything we can ask about the manifestations of life from a point of view concerned with principles.[1]

From the beginning, this is the goal of all his striving with respect to the organic natural sciences; in his pursuit of this goal, those particular discoveries arose for him as though of themselves. He had to find them if he did not want to be hindered in his further striving. Natural science before him – which did not know the essential being of life phenomena, and which simply investigated organisms as compositions of parts, according to outer characteristics, just as one does with inorganic things – often had, along its way, to give these particulars an incorrect interpretation, to present them in a false light. One cannot of course see any such error in the particulars themselves. But we will recognize this only after we have first understood the organism, since the particulars in themselves, considered separately, do not bear within themselves the principle that explains them. They can be explained only by the nature of the whole, because it is *the whole* that gives them being and significance. Only after Goethe had discovered precisely this nature of the whole did these erroneous interpretations become evident to him; they could not be reconciled with his theory of living beings; they contradicted it. If he wanted to go further on his way, he would have to clear away such preconceptions. This was the case with the intermaxillary bone. Certain facts that are of value and interest only if one possesses just such a theory as that of the vertebral nature of the skull bone were unknown to that older natural science. All these hindrances had to be cleared away by means of individual discoveries. These, therefore, never appear in Goethe's case as ends in themselves; they must always be made in order to confirm a great thought, to confirm that *central discovery*. The fact cannot be denied that Goethe's contemporaries came to the same observations sooner or later, and that all of them would perhaps be known today even without Goethe's efforts; but even less can the fact be denied that no one until now has expressed his great discovery, encompassing all organic nature, independently of him in such an exemplary way[2] – in fact, we still lack an even partially satisfactory appreciation of his discovery. Basically it does not matter whether Goethe was the first to discover a certain fact or only rediscovered it; the fact first gains its true significance through the way he fits it into his view of nature. This is what has been overlooked until now. The particular facts have been overly emphasized and this has led to polemics. One has indeed often pointed to Goethe's conviction about the consistency of nature, but one did not recognize that the main thing, in organic science for example, is to show what the nature is of that which maintains this consistency. If one calls it the *typus*, then one must say in what the being of the *typus* consists in Goethe's sense of the word.

The significance of Goethe's view about plant metamorphosis does not lie, for example, in the discovery of the individual fact that leaf, calyx, corolla, etc., are identical organs, but rather in the magnificent building up in thought of a living whole of mutually interacting formative laws; this building up proceeds from his view of plant metamorphosis, and determines out of itself the individual details and the individual stages of plant development. The greatness of this idea, which Goethe then sought to extend to the animal world also, dawns upon one only when one tries to make it alive in one's spirit, when one undertakes to rethink it. One then becomes aware that this thought is the very nature of the plant itself translated into the idea and living in our mind just as it lives in the object; one observes also that one makes an organism alive for oneself right into its smallest parts, that one pictures it not as a dead, finished object, but rather as something evolving, becoming, as something never at rest within itself.

As we now attempt, in what follows, to present more thoroughly everything we have indicated here, there will become clear to us at the same time the true relationship of the Goethean view of nature to that of our own age, and especially to the theory of evolution in its modern form.

How Goethe's Theory of Metamorphosis Arose

If one traces the history of how Goethe's thoughts about the development of organisms arose, one can all too easily become doubtful about the part one must ascribe to the early years of the poet, i.e., to the time before he went to Weimar. Goethe himself attached very little value to the natural-scientific knowledge he had in that period: "I had no idea what external nature actually means and not the slightest knowledge about its so-called three kingdoms." On the basis of this statement, one usually thinks that his natural-scientific reflections began only after his arrival in Weimar. Nevertheless, it seems advisable to go back still further if one does not want to leave the whole spirit of his views unexplained. The enlivening power that guided his studies in the direction we want to describe later already manifests itself in earliest youth.

When Goethe entered the University of Leipzig, that spirit was still entirely dominant in natural-scientific endeavors which is characteristic of a great part of the eighteenth century, and that sundered the whole of science into two extremes that one felt no need to unite. At one extreme there stood the philosophy of Christian Wolff (1679-1754), which moved entirely within an abstract element; at the other stood the individual branches of science that lost themselves in the outer description of endless details, and that lacked any effort to seek out a higher principle within the world of their particular objects of study. Wolff's kind of philosophy could not find its way out of the sphere of his general concepts into the realm of immediate reality, of individual existence. There the most obvious things were treated with all possible thoroughness. One discovered that a *thing* is a something that has no contradiction in itself, that there are finite and infinite substances, etc. But if one approached the things themselves with these generalities, in order to understand their life and working, one stood there completely at a loss; one could find no application of those concepts to the world in which we live and which we want to understand. The things themselves, however, that surround us were described in rather non-principle terms, purely according to their looks, according to their outer features. On the one hand, there was a science of principles that lacked living content, that did not delve lovingly into immediate reality; on the other hand, a science without principles, lacking all ideal content; each confronted the other without mediation; each was unfruitful for the other. Goethe's healthy nature found itself repelled in the same way by both kinds of one-sidedness;[3] in his opposition to them, there developed within him the mental pictures that later led him to that fruitful grasp of nature in which idea and experience comprehensively interpenetrate each other, mutually enliven one another, and become one whole.

The concept, therefore, that those two extremes could grasp the least emerged for Goethe as the very first: *the concept of life.* When we look at a living being according to its outer manifestation, it presents itself to us as a number of particulars manifesting as its members or organs. The description of these members, according to form, relative position, size, etc., can be the subject of the kind of extensive exposition to which the second of the two sciences we named devoted itself. But one can also describe in this same way any mechanical construction out of inorganic parts. One forgot completely that the main thing to keep in mind about the organism is the fact that here the outer manifestation is governed by an inner principle, that the whole works in every organ. That outer manifestation, the spatial juxtaposition of its parts, can also be observed after its life is destroyed, because it does still remain for a time. But what we have before us as a dead organism is in reality no longer an organism. That principle has disappeared that permeated all the particulars. *In opposition to that way of looking at things that destroys life in order to know life, Goethe early on established the possibility and need of a higher way.* We see this already in a letter of July 14, 1770 from his Strassburg period, in which he speaks of a butterfly: "The poor creature trembles in the net, rubs off its most beautiful colors; and even if one captures it unharmed, it still lies there finally stiff and lifeless; the corpse is not the whole creature; something else belongs to it, a main part, and in this case as in every other, a most major main part: its *life.*" The words in *Faust* [Part 1, Study] also have their origin, in fact, from this same view:

> Who'll know aught living and describe it well,
>
> Seeks first the spirit to expel.
>
> He then has the component parts in hand
>
> But lacks, alas! the spirit's bond.[4]

As one would fully expect from a nature like Goethe's, however, he did not stop with the negation of a view, but rather sought to develop his own view more and more; and we can very often find already in the indications we have about his thinking from 1769-1775 the germs of his later works. He was developing for himself the idea of a being in which each part enlivens the other, in which one principle imbues all the particulars. We read in *Faust* [Part I, Night]:

> Into the whole how all things blend,
>
> Each in the other working, living!

And in *Satyros*[Act 4]:

> How from no-thing the primal thing arose,
>
> How power of light through the night did ring,
>
> Imbuing the depths of the beings all;
>
> Thus welled up desiring's surge.
>
> And the elements disclosed themselves,
>
> With hunger into one another poured,
>
> *All-imbuing all-imbued.*

This being is conceived of as subject to continuous changes in time, but in all the stages of these changes only *one* being is always manifesting itself, a being that asserts itself as what endures, as what is constant within the change. About this primal thing (*Urding*), it is further stated in *Satyros*:

> And rolling up and down did go
> The all and one eternal thing,
> *Ever changing ever constant*!

Compare with this what Goethe wrote in 1807 as an introduction to his theory of metamorphosis: "But if we look at all forms, especially the organic ones, we find that nowhere is there anything enduring, anything at rest, anything complete, but rather it is far more the case that everything is in continuous motion and flux." Over against this flux, Goethe there sets up the idea – or "a something held fast in the world of experience only for the moment" – as that which is *constant*. From the above passage from *Satyros*, one can see clearly enough that the foundation for Goethe's morphological ideas had already been laid before he came to Weimar.

But we must firmly bear in mind that this idea of a living being is not applied right away to any single organism, but rather the entire universe is pictured as such a living being. What moves Goethe to this view, of course, is to be sought in his alchemical studies with Fraulein von Klettenberg and in his reading of Theophrastus Paracelsus after his return from Leipzig (1768-69). Through one experiment or another, one sought to hold fast that principle that permeates the entire universe, to make it manifest within a substance.[5] Nevertheless, this way of looking at the world, which borders on the mystical, represents only a passing episode in Goethe's development, and soon gives way to a healthier and more objective way of picturing things. But his view of the entire world as one great organism, as we find this indicated in the passages from *Faust* and from *Satyros* cited above, still stands until about 1780, as we shall see later from his essay on *Nature*. This view confronts us once more in *Faust*, at that place where the earth spirit is represented as that life principle that permeates the universal organism [Part I, Night]:

In the tides of life, in actions' storm,

Up and down I wave,

To and fro weave free,

Birth and the grave,

An infinite sea,

A varied weaving,

A radiant living.

As definite views were thus developing in Goethe's mind, there came into his hand in Strassburg a book that sought to propound a worldview that was the exact antithesis of his own. It was Holbach's *Système de la Nature.*[6] Whereas until then he had only had to censure the fact that one described what is alive as though it were a mechanical accumulation of individual things, now he could get to know, in Holbach, a philosopher who really regarded what is alive as a mechanism. What, in the former case, sprang merely from an inability to know life down into its roots here leads to a dogma pernicious to life. In *Poetry and Truth*, Goethe says about this: "One matter supposedly exists from all eternity, and has moved for all eternity, and now with this motion supposedly brings forth right and left and on all sides, without more ado, the infinite phenomena of existence. We would indeed have been satisfied with this, if the author had really built up the world before our eyes out of his moving matter. But he might know as little about nature as we do, for as soon as he has staked up a few general concepts, he leaves nature at once, in order to transform what appears as something higher than nature, or as a higher nature in nature, into a nature that is material, heavy, moving, to be sure, but still without direction or shape, and he believes that he has gained a great deal by this." Goethe could find nothing in this except "moving matter," and in opposition to this, his concepts about nature took ever clearer form. We find these brought together and presented in his essay *Nature*, written about 1780. Since, in this essay, all Goethe's thoughts about nature – which until then we only find in scattered indications – are gathered together, it takes on special significance. The idea here confronts us of a being that is caught up in constant change and yet remains thereby ever the same: "All is new and ever the old." "She (nature) transforms herself eternally, and there is within her no moment of standing still," but "her laws are immutable." We will see later that Goethe seeks the *one* archetypal plant within the endless multitude of plant forms. We also find this thought indicated here already: "Each of her (nature's) works has its own being, each of her manifestations has the most isolated concept, and yet all constitute *one*." Yes, even the position he took later with respect to exceptional cases – namely, not to regard them simply as mistakes in development, but rather to explain them out of natural laws – is already very clearly expressed here: "Even the most unnatural is nature," and "her exceptions are rare."

We have seen that Goethe had already developed for himself a definite concept of an organism before he came to Weimar. For, even though the above-mentioned essay *Nature* was written only long after his arrival there, it still contains for the most part earlier views of Goethe. He had not yet applied this concept to any particular genus of natural objects, to any individual beings. In order to do this he needed the concrete world of living beings within immediate reality. A reflection of nature, passed through the human mind, was absolutely not the element that could stimulate Goethe. His botanical conversations with Hofrat Ludwig in Leipzig remained just as much without any deeper effect as the dinner conversations with medical friends in Strassburg. With respect to scientific study, the young Goethe seems altogether to be like Faust, deprived of the freshness of firsthand beholding of nature, who expresses his longing for this in the words [Part I, Night]:

> Ah! Could I but on mountain height
> Go onward in thy [the moon's] lovely light,
> With spirits hover round mountain caves,
> Weave over meadows thy twilight laves…

It seems a fulfillment of this longing when, with his arrival in Weimar, he is permitted "to exchange chamber and city air for the atmosphere of country, forest, and garden."

We have to regard as the immediate stimulus to his study of plants the poet's occupation of planting the garden given him by Duke Karl August. The acceptance of the garden by Goethe took place on April 21, 1776, and his diary, edited by R. Keil, informs us often from then on about Goethe's work in this garden, which becomes one of his favorite occupations. An added field for endeavors in this direction was afforded him by the forest of Thüringen, where he had the opportunity of acquainting himself also with the lower organisms in their manifestations of life. The mosses and lichens interest him especially. On October 31, 1778, he requests of Frau von Stein mosses of all sorts, with roots and damp, if possible, so that they can propagate themselves. We must consider it as highly significant that Goethe was already then occupying himself with this world of lower organisms and yet later derived the laws of plant organization from the higher plants. As we consider this fact, we should not attribute it, as many do, to Goethe's underestimation of the significance of less developed beings, but rather to his fully conscious intention.

From then on Goethe never leaves the plant realm. It is very possible that he took up Linnaeus' writings already quite early. We first hear of his acquaintance with them in letters to Frau von Stein in 1782.

Linnaeus' endeavor was to bring a systematic overview into knowledge of the plants. A certain sequence was to be discovered, in which every organism has a definite place, so that one could easily find it at any time, so that one would have altogether, in fact, a means of orientation within the unlimited number of particulars. To this end the living beings had to be examined with respect to their degree of relatedness to each other and accordingly be arranged together in groups. Since the main point to all this was to know every plant and easily to find its place within the system, one had to be particularly attentive to those characteristics that distinguish one plant from another. In order to make it impossible to confuse one plant with another, one sought out primarily those distinguishing traits. In doing so, Linnaeus and his students regarded external traits – size, number, and location of individual organs – as characteristic. In this way, the plants were indeed ordered sequentially, but just as one could also have ordered a number of inorganic bodies: according to characteristics taken, not from the inner nature of the plant, but from visual aspects. The plants appear in an external juxtaposition, without any inner necessary connection. Because of the significant concept he had of the nature of a living being, Goethe could not be satisfied by this way of looking at things. No effort was made there to seek out the essential being of the plant. Goethe had to ask himself the question: In what does that "something" consist that makes a particular being of nature into a plant? He had to recognize further that this something occurs in all plants in the same way. And yet the endless differentiation of the individual beings was there, needing to be explained. How does it come about that that oneness manifests itself in such manifold forms? These must have been the questions that Goethe raised in reading Linnaeus' writings, for he says of himself after all: "What he – Linnaeus – sought forcibly to keep apart had to strive for unity in accordance with the innermost need of my being."

Goethe's first acquaintance with Rousseau's botanical endeavors falls into about the same period as that with Linnaeus. On June 16, 1782, Goethe writes to Duke Karl August: "Among Rousseau's works there are some most delightful letters about botany, in which he presents this science to a lady in a most comprehensible and elegant way. It is a real model of how one should teach and it supplements *Emile*. I use it therefore as an excuse to recommend anew the beautiful realm of the flowers to my beautiful lady friends." Rousseau's botanical endeavors must have made a deep impression on Goethe. The emphasis we find in Rousseau's work upon a nomenclature arising from the nature of the plants and corresponding to it, the freshness of his observations, his contemplation of the plants for their own sake, apart from any utilitarian considerations – all this was entirely in keeping with Goethe's way. And something else the two had in common was the fact that they had come to study the plant, not for any specific scientific purposes, but rather out of general human motives. The same interest drew them to the same thing.

Goethe's next intensive observations in the plant world occur in the year 1784. Wilhelm Freiherr von Gleichen, called Russwurm, had published back then two works dealing with research of lively interest to Goethe: *The Latest News from the Plant Realm* and *Special Microscopic Discoveries about Plants Flowers and Blossoms, Insects, and other Noteworthy Things.* Both works dealt with the processes of plant fertilization. Pollen, stamens, and pistil were carefully examined and the processes occurring there were portrayed in beautifully executed illustrations. Goethe now repeated these investigations. On January 12, 1785, he writes to Frau von Stein: "A microscope is set up in order, when spring arrives, to re-observe and verify the experiments of von Gleichen, called Russwurm." During the same spring he also studies the nature of the seed, as a letter to Knebel on April 2, 1785 shows: "I have thought through the substance of the seed as far as my experiences reach." For Goethe, the main thing in all these investigations is not the individual details; the goal of his efforts is to explore the essential being of the plant. On April 8, 1785, he reports to Merck that he "had made nice discoveries and *combinations*" in botany. The term "combinations" also shows us here that his intention is to construct for himself, through thinking, a picture of the processes in the plant world. His botanical studies now drew quickly near to a particular goal. To be sure, we must also now bear in mind that Goethe, in 1784, had already discovered the intermaxillary bone, which we will later discuss in detail, and that this discovery had brought him a significant step closer to the secret of how nature goes about its forming of organic beings. We must, moreover, bear in mind that the first part of Herder's *Ideas on the Philosophy of History*[9] was completed in 1784 and that conversations between Goethe and Herder on things of nature were very frequent at that time. Thus, Frau von Stein reports to Knebel on May 1, 1784: "Herder's new book makes it likely that we were first plants and animals ... Goethe is now delving very thoughtfully into these things, and everything that has once passed through his mind becomes extremely interesting." We see from this the nature of Goethe's interest at that time in the greatest questions of science. Therefore his reflections upon the nature of the plant and the combinations he made about it during the spring of 1785 seem quite comprehensible. In the middle of April of this year he goes to Belvedere expressly for the purpose of finding a solution to his doubts and questions, and on June 15, he communicates to

Frau von Stein: "I cannot express to you how legible the book of nature is becoming for me; my long efforts at spelling have helped me; now suddenly it is working, and my quiet joy is inexpressible." Shortly before this, in fact, he wants to write a short botanical treatise for Knebel in order to win him over to this science.[10] Botany draws him so strongly that his trip to Karlsbad, which he begins on June 20, 1785 in order to spend the summer there, turns into a journey of botanical study. Knebel accompanied him. Near Jena, they meet a seventeen-year-old youth, Friedrich Gottlieb Dietrich, whose specimen box showed that he was just returning from a botanical excursion. We hear more in detail about this interesting trip from Goethe's *History of my Botanical Studies*[11] and from some reports of Ferdinand Cohn in Breslau, who was able to borrow them from one of Dietrich's manuscripts. In Karlsbad then, botanical conversations quite often afford pleasant entertainment. Back home again, Goethe devotes himself with great energy to the study of botany; in connection with Linnaeus' *Philosophia Botanica*, he makes certain observations about mushrooms, mosses, lichens, and algae, as we see from his letters to Frau von Stein. Only now, after he himself has already thought and observed a great deal, does Linnaeus become more useful to him; in Linnaeus he finds enlightenment about many details that help him forward in his combinations. On November 9, 1785, he reports to Frau von Stein: "I continue to read Linnaeus; I have to; I have no other book. It is the best way to read a book thoroughly, a way I must often practice, especially since I do not easily read a book to the end. This one, however, is not principally made for reading, but rather for review, and it serves me now excellently, since I have thought over most of its points myself." During these studies it becomes ever clearer to him, *that it is after all only one basic form that manifests in the endless multitude of single plant individuals; this basic form itself was also becoming ever more perceptible to him*; he recognized further, *that within this basic form, there lies the potential for endless transformation, by which manifoldness is created out of oneness*. On July 9, 1786, he writes to Frau von Stein: "*It is a becoming aware of the ... form with which nature is always only playing as it were, and in playing brings forth its manifold life*." Now the most important thing of all was to develop this lasting, this constant element, this archetypal form with which nature, as it were, plays – to develop it in detail into a plastic configuration. In order to do this, one needed an opportunity to separate what is truly constant and enduring in the form of plants from what is changing and inconstant. For observations of this kind, Goethe had as yet explored too small an area. He had to observe one and the same plant under different conditions and influences; for only through this does the changeable element really become visible. In plants of different kinds this changeable element is less obvious. The journey to Italy that Goethe had undertaken from Karlsbad on September 3 and that gave him such happiness brought him all this. He made many observations already with respect to the flora of the Alps. He found here not merely new plants that he had never seen before, but also plants he knew already, *but changed.* "Whereas in lower-lying regions, branches and stems were stronger and thicker, the buds closer to each other, and the leaves broad, higher in the mountains, branches and stems became more delicate, the buds moved farther apart so that there was more space between nodes, and the leaves were more lance-shaped. I noticed this in a willow and in a gentian, and convinced myself that it was not because of different species, for example. Also, near the Walchensee I noticed longer and more slender rushes than in the lowlands."[12] Similar observations occurred repeatedly. By the sea near Venice, he discovers different plants that reveal characteristics that only the old salt of the sandy ground, but even more the salty air, could have given them. He found a plant there that looked to him like "our innocent coltsfoot, but here it was armed with sharp weapons, and the leaf was like leather, as were the seedpods and the stems also; everything was thick and fat."[13] Goethe there regarded all the outer characteristics of the plant, everything belonging to the visible aspect of the plant, as inconstant, as changing. From this he drew the conclusion that the essential being of the plant, therefore, does not lie in these characteristics, but rather must be sought at deeper levels. It was from observations similar to these of Goethe that Darwin also proceeded when he asserted his doubts about the constancy of the outer forms of genera and species. But the conclusions drawn by the two men are utterly different. Whereas Darwin believes the essential being of the organism to consist in fact only of these outer characteristics, and, from their changeability draws the conclusion that there is therefore nothing constant in the life of the plants, Goethe goes deeper and draws the conclusion that if those outer characteristics are not constant, then the constant element must be sought in something else that underlies those changeable outer aspects. It becomes Goethe's goal to develop this something else, whereas Darwin's efforts go in the direction of exploring and presenting the specific causes of that changeability. Both ways of looking at things are necessary and complement one another. It is completely erroneous to believe that Goethe's greatness in organic science is to be found in the view that he was a mere forerunner of Darwin. Goethe's way of looking at things is far broader; it comprises two aspects: 1. the *typus*, i.e., the lawfulness manifesting in the organism, the animalness of the animal, the life that gives form to itself out of itself, that has the power and ability – through the possibilities lying within it – to develop itself in manifold outer shapes (species, genera); 2. the interaction of the organism with inorganic nature and of the organisms with each other (adaptation and the struggle for existence). Darwin developed only the latter aspect of organic science. One cannot therefore say that Darwin's theory is the elaboration of Goethe's basic ideas, but rather that it is merely the elaboration of one aspect of his ideas. Darwin's theory looks only at those facts that cause the world of living beings to evolve in a certain way, but does not look at that "something" upon which those facts act determinatively. If only the one aspect is pursued, then it can also not lead to any complete theory of organisms; essentially, this must be pursued in the spirit of Goethe; the one aspect must be complemented and deepened by the other aspect of his theory. A simple comparison will make the matter clearer. Take a piece of lead; heat it into liquid form; and then pour it into cold water. The lead has gone through two states, two stages, one after the other; the first was brought about by the higher temperature, the second by the lower. Now the form that each stage takes does not depend only on the nature of warmth, but also depends quite essentially on the nature of the lead. A different body, if subjected to the same media, would manifest quite different states. Organisms also allow themselves to be influenced by the media surrounding them; they also, affected by these media, assume different states and do so, in fact, totally in accordance with their own nature, in accordance with that being which makes them organisms. And one does find this being in Goethe's ideas. Only someone who is equipped with an understanding for this being will be capable of grasping why organisms respond (react) to particular causes in precisely one way and in no other. Only such a person will be capable of correctly picturing to himself the changeability in the manifest forms of organisms and the related laws of adaptation and of the struggle for existence.[14]

Goethe's thought about the archetypal plant (*Urpflanze*) takes on ever clearer and more definite shape in his mind. In the botanical garden in Padua (*Italian Journey*, September 27, 1786), where he goes about in a vegetation strange to him, "The thought becomes ever more alive to him that one could perhaps develop for oneself all the plant shapes out of one shape." On November 17, 1786, he writes to Knebel: "My little bit of botany is for the first time a real pleasure to have, in these lands where a happier, less intermittent vegetation is at home. I have already made some really nice general observations whose consequences will also please you." On February 19, 1787 (see *Italian Journey*), he writes in Rome that he is on his way "to discovering beautiful new relationships showing how nature achieves something tremendous that looks like nothing: out of the simple to evolve the most manifold." On March 25, he asks that Herder be told that he will soon be ready with his archetypal plant. On April 17 (see *Italian Journey*) in Palermo, he writes down the following words about the archetypal plant: "There must after all be such a one! How would I otherwise know that one formation or another is a plant, if they were not all formed according to the same model." He had in mind the complex of developmental laws that organizes the plant, that makes it into what it is, and through which, with respect to a particular object of nature, we arrive at the thought, "This is a plant": all that is the archetypal plant. As such, the archetypal plant is something ideal, something that can only be held in thought; but it takes on shape, it takes on a certain form, size, color, number of organs, etc. This outer shape is nothing fixed, but rather can suffer endless transformations, which are all in accordance with that complex of developmental laws and follow necessarily from it. If one has grasped these developmental laws, this archetypal picture of the plant, then one is holding, in the form of an idea, that upon which nature as it were founds every single plant individual, and from which nature consequentially derives each plant and allows it to come into being. Yes, one can even invent plant shapes, in accordance with this law, which could emerge by necessity from the being of the plant and which could exist if the necessary conditions arose for this. Thus Goethe seeks, as it were, to copy in spirit what nature accomplishes in the forming of its beings. On May 17, 1787, he writes to Herder: "Furthermore, I must confide to you that I am very close to discovering the secret of plant generation and organization, and that it is the simplest thing one could imagine ... The archetypal plant will be the most magnificent creation in the world, for which nature itself will envy me. With this model and the key to it, one can then go on inventing plants forever that must follow lawfully; that means: which, even if they don't exist, still could exist, and are not, for example, the shadows and illusions of painters or poets but rather have an inner truth and necessity. The same law can be applied to all other living things." A further difference between Goethe's view and that of Darwin emerges here, especially if one considers how Darwin's view is usually propounded.[15] It assumes that outer influences work upon the nature of an organism like mechanical causes and change it accordingly. For Goethe, the individual changes are the various expressions of the archetypal organism that has within itself the ability to take on manifold shapes and that, in any given case, takes on the shape most suited to the surrounding conditions in the outer world. These outer conditions merely bring it about that the inner formative forces come to manifestation in a particular way. These forces alone are the constitutive principle, the creative element in the plant. Therefore, on September 6, 1787 (*Italian Journey*), Goethe also calls it a *hen kai pan (a one and all)* of the plant world.

If we now enter in detail into this archetypal plant itself, the following can be said about it. The living entity is a self-contained whole, which brings forth its states of being from out of itself. Both in the juxtaposition of its members and in the temporal sequence of its states of being, there is a reciprocal relationship present, which does not appear to be determined by the sense-perceptible characteristics of its members, nor by any mechanical-causal determining of the later by the earlier, but which is governed by a higher principle standing over the members and states of being. The fact that one particular state is brought forth first and another one last is determined in the nature of the whole; and the sequence of the intermediary states is also determined by the idea of the whole; what comes before is dependent upon what comes after, and vice versa; in short, within the living organism, there is *development* of one thing out of the other, a transition of states of being into one another; no finished, closed-off existence of the single thing, but rather continuous *becoming*. In the plant, this determination of each individual member by the whole arises insofar as every organ is built according to the same basic form. On May 17, 1787 (*Italian Journey*), Goethe communicates these thoughts to Herder in the following words: "It became clear to me, namely, that within that organ (of the plant) that we usually address as leaf, there lies hidden the true Proteus that can conceal and manifest itself in every shape. Any way you look at it, the plant is always only leaf, so inseparably joined with the future germ that one cannot think the one without the other." Whereas in the animal that higher principle which governs every detail appears concretely before us as that which moves the organs and uses them in accordance with its needs, etc., the plant is still lacking any such *real* life principle; in the plant, this life principle still manifests itself only in the more indistinct way that all its organs are built according to the same formative type – in fact, that the whole plant is contained as possibility in every part and, under favorable conditions, can also be brought forth from any part. This becomes especially clear to Goethe in Rome when Councillor Reiffenstein, during a walk with him, broke off a branch here and there and asserted that if it were stuck in the ground it would have to grow and develop into a whole plant. The plant is therefore a being that successively develops certain organs that are all – both in their interrelationships and in the relationship of each to the whole – built according to one and the same idea. Every plant is a harmonious whole composed of plants.[16] When Goethe saw this clearly, his whole remaining concern was with the individual observations that would make it possible to set forth in detail the various stages of development that the plant brings forth from itself. For this also, what was needed had already occurred. We have seen that in the spring of 1785 Goethe had already made a study of seeds; on May 17, 1787, from Italy, he announces to Herder that he has quite clearly and without any doubt found the point where the germ (*Keim*) lies. That took care of the first stage of plant life. But the unity of structure in all leaves also soon revealed itself visibly enough. Along with numerous other examples showing this, Goethe found above all in fresh fennel a difference between the lower and upper leaves, which nevertheless are always the same organ. On March 25 (*Italian Journey*), he asks Herder to be informed that his theory about the cotyledons was already so refined that one could scarcely go further with it. Only one small step remained to be taken in order also to regard the petals, the stamens, and the pistil as metamorphosed leaves. The research of the English botanist Hill could lead to this; his research was becoming more generally known at that time, and dealt with the transformation of individual flower organs into other ones.

As the forces that organize the being of the plant come into actual existence, they take on a series of structural forms in space. Then it is a question of the living concept that connects these forms backwards and forwards.

When we look at Goethe's theory of metamorphosis, as it appears to us in the year 1790, we find that for Goethe this concept is one of alternating expansion and contraction. In the seed, the plant formation is most strongly contracted (concentrated). With the leaves, there follows the first unfolding, the first expansion of the formative forces. That which, in the seed, is compressed into a point now spreads out spatially in the leaves. In the calyx, the forces again draw together around an axial point; the corolla is produced by the next expansion; stamens and pistil come about through the next contraction; the fruit arises through the last (third) expansion, whereupon the whole force of plant life (its entelechy) conceals itself again, in its most highly concentrated state, in the seed. Although we now can follow nearly all the details of Goethe's thoughts on metamorphosis up to their final realization in the essay that appeared in 1790, it is not so easy to do the same thing with the concept of expansion and contraction. Still one will not go wrong in assuming that this thought, which anyway is deeply rooted in Goethe's spirit, was also woven by him already in Italy into his concept of plant formation. Since a greater or lesser spatial development, which is determined by the formative forces, is the content of this thought, and since this content therefore consists in what the plant presents directly to the eye, this content will certainly arise most easily when one undertakes to draw the plant *in accordance with the laws of natural formation*. Goethe found now a bush-like carnation plant in Rome that showed him metamorphosis with particular clarity. He writes about this: "Seeing no way to preserve this marvelous shape, I undertook to draw it exactly, and in doing so attained ever more insight into the basic concept of metamorphosis." Perhaps such drawings were often made and this could then have led to the concept we are considering.

In September 1787, during his second stay in Rome, Goethe expounds the matter to his friend Moritz; in doing so he discovers how alive and perceptible the matter becomes through such a presentation. *He always writes down* how far they have gotten. To judge by this passage and by a few other statements of Goethe's, it seems likely that the writing down of his theory of metamorphosis – at least aphoristically – occurred already in Italy. He states further: "Only in this way – through presenting it to Moritz – could I get something of my thoughts down on paper." There is now no doubt about the fact that this work, in the form in which we now have it, was written down at the end of 1789 and the beginning of 1790; but it would be difficult to say how much of this latter manuscript was a mere editing and how much was added then. A book announced for the next Easter season, which could have contained something of the same thoughts, induced him in the autumn of 1789 to take his thoughts in hand and to arrange for their publication. On November 20, he writes to the Duke that he is spurred on to write down his botanical ideas. On December 18, he sends the manuscript already to the botanist Batsch in Jena for him to look over; on the 20th, he goes there himself in order to discuss it with Batsch ; on the 22nd, he informs Knebel that Batsch has given the matter a favorable reception. He returns home, works the manuscript through once more and then sends it to Batsch again, who returns it to him on January 19, 1790. Goethe himself has recounted in detail the experiences undergone by the handwritten manuscript as well as by the printed edition. Later, in the section on "The Nature and Significance of Goethe's Writings on Organic Development," we will deal with the great significance of Goethe's theory of metamorphosis, as well as with the detailed nature of this theory.

III

How Goethe's Thoughts on the Development of the Animals Arose

Lavater's great work *Physiognomical Fragments for Furthering Human Knowledge and Human Love*[17] appeared during the years 1775-1778. Goethe had taken a lively interest in it, not only through the fact that he oversaw its publication, but also by making contributions to it himself. But what is of particular interest now is that, within these contributions, we can already find the germ of his later zoological works.

Physiognomy sought, in the outer form of the human being, to know his inner nature, his spirit. One studied the human shape, not for its own sake, but rather as an expression of the soul. Goethe's sculptural spirit, born to know outer relationships, did not stop there. As he was in the middle of those studies that treated outer form only as a means of knowing the inner being, there dawned on him the independent significance of the former, the shape. We see this from his articles on animal skulls written in 1776 that we find inserted into the second section of the second volume of the *Physiognomical Fragments*. During that year, he is reading Aristotle on physiognomy, finds himself stimulated by it to write the above articles, but at the same time attempts to investigate the difference between the human being and the animals. He finds this difference in the way the whole human structure brings the head into prominence, in the lofty development of the human brain, toward which all the members of the body point, as though to their central place: "How the whole form stands there as supporting column for the dome in which the heavens are to be reflected." He finds the opposite of this now in animal structure. "The head merely hung upon the spine! The brain, as the end of the spinal cord, has no more scope than is necessary for the functioning of the animal spirits and for directing a creature whose senses are entirely within the present moment." With these indications, Goethe has raised himself above the consideration of the individual connections between the outer and inner being of man, to the apprehension of a great whole and to a contemplation of the form as such. He arrived at the view that the *whole* of man's structure forms the basis of his higher life manifestations, that within the particular nature of this whole, there lie the determining factors that place man at the peak of creation. What we must bear in mind above everything else in this is that Goethe seeks the animal form again in the perfected human one; except that, with the former, the organs that serve more the animal functions come to the fore, are, as it were, the point toward which the whole structure tends and which the structure serves, whereas the human structure particularly develops those organs that serve spiritual functions. We find here already: What hovers before Goethe as the animal organism is no longer this or that sense-perceptible real organism, but rather an ideal one, which, with the animals, develops itself more toward the lower side, and with man toward a higher one. Here already is the germ of what Goethe later called the *typus*, and by which he did not mean "any individual animal," but rather the "idea" of the animal. And even more: Here already we find the echo of a law that he enunciated later and that is very significant in its implications – to the effect, namely, "that diversity of form springs from the fact that a preponderance is granted to this or that part over the others." Here already, the contrast between animal and man is sought in the fact that an ideal form develops itself in two different directions, that in each case, one organ system gains a preponderance and the whole creature receives its character from this.

In the same year (1776), we also find, however, that Goethe becomes clear about the starting point for someone who wants to study the form of the animal organism. He recognized that the bones are the foundations of its formations, a thought he later upheld by definitely taking the study of bones as his starting point in anatomical work. In this year he writes down a sentence that is important in this respect: "The mobile parts form themselves according to them (the bones) – or better, *with* them – and come into play only insofar as the solid parts allow." And a further indication in Lavater's physiognomy ("It may already have been noticed that I consider the *bony system to be the basic sketch of the human being*, the skull to be the fundamental element of the bony system, and all fleshy parts to be hardly more than the color on this drawing.") may very well have been written under the stimulus of Goethe, who often discussed these things with Lavater. These views are in fact identical to indications written down by Goethe. But Goethe now makes a further observation about this, which we must particularly take into consideration: "This statement (that one can see from the bones, and indeed most strongly of all from the skull, how the bones are the foundations of the form) which here (with respect to the animals) is indisputable, will meet with serious contradiction *when applied to the dissimilarity of human skulls.*" What is Goethe doing here other than seeking the simpler animal again within the complex human being, as he later expressed it (1795)! From this we can gain the conviction *that the basic thoughts upon which Goethe's thoughts on the development of animal form were later to be built up had already established themselves in him out of his occupation with Lavater's physiognomy in the year 1776.*

In this year, Goethe's study of the particulars of anatomy also begins. On January 22, 1776, he writes to Lavater: "The duke had six skulls sent to me; have noticed some marvelous things that are at your honor's disposal, if you have not found them without me." His connections with the university in Jena gave him further stimulus to a more thorough study of anatomy. We find the first indications of this in the year 1781. In his diary, published by Keil, under the date October 15, 1781, Goethe notes that he went to Jena with old Einsiedel and studied anatomy there. At Jena there was a scholar who furthered Goethe's studies immensely: Loder. This same man then also introduces him further into anatomy, as Goethe writes to Frau von Stein on October 29, 1781,[18] and to Karl August on November 4.[19] To the latter he now also expressed his intention of "explaining the skeleton," to the "young people" in the Art Academy, and of "leading them to a knowledge of the human body." He adds: "I do it both for my sake and for theirs; the methods I have chosen will make them, over this winter, fully familiar with the basic pillars of the body." The entries in Goethe's diary show that he actually did give these lectures, ending them on January 16. There must have been many discussions with Loder about the structure of the human body during this same period. Under the date of January 6, the diary notes: "Demonstration of the heart by Loder." Just as we now have seen that in 1776 Goethe was already harboring far-reaching thoughts about the structure of animal organization, so we cannot doubt for a moment that his present thorough study of anatomy raised itself beyond the consideration of the particulars to higher points of view. Thus he writes to Lavater and Merck on November 14, 1781 that he is treating "bones as a text to which everything living and everything human can be appended." As we consider a text, pictures and ideas take shape in our spirit that seem to be called forth, to be created by the text. Goethe treated the bones as just such a text; i.e., as he contemplates them, thoughts arise in him about everything living and everything human. During these contemplations, therefore, definite ideas about the formation of the organism must have struck him. Now we have an ode by Goethe, from the year 1782, "The Divine," which lets us know to some extent how he thought at the time about the relationship of the human being to the rest of nature. The first verse reads:

> Noble be man,
> Helpful and good!
> For that *alone*
> Distinguishes him
> From all the beings
> That we know.

Having grasped the human being in the first two lines of this verse according to his spiritual characteristics, Goethe states that these alone distinguish him from all the other beings of the world. This "*alone*" shows us quite clearly that Goethe considered man, in his physical constitution, to be absolutely in conformity with the rest of nature. The thought, to which we already drew attention earlier, becomes ever more alive in him, that one basic form governs the shape of the human being as well as of the animals, that the basic form only mounts to such perfection in man's case that it is capable of being the bearer of a free spiritual being. With respect to his sense-perceptible characteristics, the human being must also, as the ode goes on to state:

> By iron laws
> Mighty, eternal
> His existence's
> Circle complete.

But in man these laws develop in a direction that makes it possible for him to do the "impossible":

> He distinguishes,
> Chooses and judges;
> He can the moment
> Endow with duration.

Now we must also still bear in mind that while these views were developing ever more definitely in Goethe, he stood in lively communication with Herder, who in 1783 began to write his *Ideas on a Philosophy of the History of Mankind.* This work might also be said to have arisen out of the discussions between these two men, and many an idea must be traced back to Goethe. The thoughts expressed here are often entirely Goethean, although stated in Herder's words, so we can draw from them a trustworthy conclusion about Goethe's thoughts at that time.

Now in the first part of his book, Herder holds the following view about the nature of the world. A principle form must be presupposed that runs through all beings and realizes itself in different ways. "From stone to crystal, from crystal to metals, from these to plant creation, from plants to animal, from it to the human being, we saw the *form of organization ascend,* and saw along with it the forces and drives of the creature diversify and finally all unite themselves in the form of man, insofar as this form could encompass them." The thought is perfectly clear: An ideal typical form, which as such is not itself sense-perceptibly real, realizes itself in an endless number of spatially separated entities with differing characteristics all the way up to man. At the lower levels of organization, this ideal form always realizes itself in a particular direction; the ideal form develops in a particular way according to this direction. When this typical form ascends as far as man, it brings together all the developmental principles – which it had always developed only in a one-sided way in the lower organisms and had distributed among different entities – in order to form one shape. From this, there also follows the possibility of such high perfection in the human being. In man's case, nature bestowed upon one being what, in the case of the animals, it had dispersed among many classes and orders. This thought worked with unusual fruitfulness upon the German philosophy that followed. To elucidate this thought, let us mention here the description that Oken later gave of the same idea. In his *Textbook of Natural Philosophy*[20], he says: "The animal realm is only *one* animal; i.e., it is the representation of animalness with all its organs existing each as a whole in itself. An individual animal arises when an individual organ detaches itself from the general animal body and yet carries out the essential animal functions. The animal realm is merely the dismembered highest animal: man. There is only one human kind, only one human race, only one human species, just because man is the whole animal realm." Thus there are, for example, animals in which the organs of touch are developed, whose whole organization, in fact, tends toward the activity of touch and finds its goal in this activity; and other animals in which the instruments for eating are particularly developed, and so forth; in short, with every species of animal, one organ system comes one-sidedly to the fore; the whole animal merges into it; everything else about the animal recedes into the background. Now in human development, all the organs and organ systems develop *in such a way* that one allows the other enough space to develop freely, that each one retires within those boundaries that seem necessarily to allow all the others to come into their own in the same way. In this way, there arises a harmonious interworking of the individual organs and systems into a harmony that makes man into the most perfect being, into the being that unites the perfections of all other creatures within itself. These thoughts now also formed the content of the conversations of Goethe with Herder, and Herder gives expression to them in the following way: that "the human race is to be regarded as *the great confluence of lower organic forces* that, in him, were to arrive at the forming of humanity." And in another place: "And so we can assume: *that man is a central creation among the animals, i.e., that he is the elaborated form in which the traits of all the species gather around him in their finest essence.*"

In order to indicate the interest Goethe took in Herder's work Ideas on a *Philosophy of the History of Mankind*, let us cite the following passage from a letter of Goethe to Knebel on December 8, 1783: "Herder is writing a philosophy of history, such as you can imagine, new from the ground up. We read the first chapters together the day before yesterday; they are exquisite ... world and natural history is positively rushing along with us now." Herder's expositions in Book 3, Chapter VI, and in Book 4, Chapter I, to the effect that the erect posture inherent in the human organization and everything connected with it is the fundamental prerequisite for his activity of reason – all this reminds us directly of what Goethe indicated in 1776 in the second section of the second volume of Lavater's *Physiognomical Fragments* about the generic difference between man and the animals, which we have already mentioned above. This is only an elaboration of that thought. All this justifies us, however, in assuming that in the main Goethe and Herder were in agreement all that time (1783ff.) with respect to their views about the place of the human being in nature.

But this basic view requires now that every organ, every part of an animal, must also be able to be found again in man, only pushed back within the limits determined by the harmony of the whole. To be sure, a certain bone, for example, must achieve a definite form in a particular species, must become predominant there, but this bone must also at least be indicated in all other species; it must in fact also not be missing in man. If, in a certain species, the bone takes on a form appropriate to it by virtue of its own laws, then, in man the bone must adapt itself to the whole, must accommodate its own laws of development to those of the whole organism. But it must not be lacking, if a split is not to occur in nature by which the consistent development of a type would be interrupted.

This is how the matter stood with Goethe, when all at once he became aware of a view that totally contradicted this great thought. The learned men of that time were chiefly occupied with finding traits that would distinguish one species of animal from another. The difference between animals and man was supposed to consist in the fact that the former have a little bone, the intermaxillary bone, between the two symmetrical halves of the upper jaw, which holds the upper incisors and supposedly is lacking in man. In the year 1782, when Merck was beginning to take a lively interest in osteology and was turning for help to some of the best-known scholars of that time, he received from one of them, the distinguished anatomist Sömmerring, on October 8, 1782, the following information about the difference between animal and man: "I wish you had consulted Blumenbach on the subject of the intermaxillary bone, which, other things being equal, is the only bone that all the animals have, from the ape on, including even the orangutan, but that is *never found in man*; except for this bone, there is nothing keeping you from being able to transfer everything man has onto the animals. I enclose therefore the head of a doe in order to convince you that this *os intermaxillare* (as Blumenbach calls it) or *os incisivum* (as Camper calls it) is present even in animals having no incisors in the upper jaw." Although Blumenbach found in the skulls of unborn or young children a trace *quasi rudimentum* of the *ossis intermaxillaris* – indeed, had once found in one such skull two fully separated little kernels of bone as actual intermaxillary bones – still he did not acknowledge the existence of any such bone. He said about this: "There is a world of difference between it and the true *osse intermaxillari*." Camper, the most famous anatomist of the time, was of the same view. He referred to the intermaxillary bone, for example, as having "never been found in a human being."[21] Merck held Camper in the deepest admiration and occupied himself with his writings.

Not only Merck, but also Blumenbach and Sömmerring were in communication with Goethe. His correspondence with Merck shows us that Goethe took the deepest interest in Merck's study of bones and shared his own thoughts about these things with him. On October 27, 1782, he asked Merck to write him something about Camper's *incognitum*,[22] and to send him Camper's letters. Furthermore, we must note a visit of Blumenbach in Weimar in April, 1783. In September of the same year, Goethe goes to Göttingen in order to visit Blumenbach and all the professors there. On September 28, he writes to Frau von Stein: "I have decided to visit all the professors and you can imagine how much running about it requires to make the rounds in a few days." He goes up to Kassel where he meets with Forster and Sömmerring. From there he writes to Frau von Stein on October 2: "I am seeing very fine and good things and am being rewarded for my quiet diligence. The happiest news is that I can now say that I am on the right path and from now on nothing is lost."

It is in the course of these activities that Goethe must first have become aware of the prevailing views about the intermaxillary bone. To his way of looking at things, these views must right away have seemed erroneous. The typical basic form, according to which all organisms must be built, would thereby be destroyed. For Goethe, there could be no doubt that this part, which to a more or less developed degree is to be found in all higher animals, must also have its place in the development of the human form, and would only recede in man because the organs of food-intake in general recede before the organs serving mental functions. By virtue of his whole spiritual orientation, Goethe could not think otherwise than that an intermaxillary bone must also be present in man. It was only a matter of proving this empirically, of finding what form this bone takes in man and to what extent it adapts itself to the whole of his organism. He succeeded in finding this proof in the spring of 1784, together with Loder, with whom he compared human and animal skulls in Jena. On March 27, he reported the matter to both Frau von Stein[23] and to Herder.[24]

Now this individual discovery, compared to the great thought by which it is sustained, should not be overvalued: for Goethe also, its value lay only in the fact that it cleared away a preconception that seemed to hinder his ideas from being consistently pursued right into the farthest details of an organism. Goethe also never regarded it as an individual discovery, but always only in connection with his larger view of nature. This is how we must understand it when, in the above-mentioned letter to Herder, he says: "It should heartily please you also, for it is like

the keystone to man; it is not lacking; it is there too! And how!"
And right away he reminds his friend of the wider perspective:
"I thought of it also in connection with your whole picture, how
beautiful it will be there." For Goethe, it could make no sense to
assert that the animals have an intermaxillary bone but that man
has none. If it lies within the forces that shape an organism to
insert an intermediary bone between the two upper jaw bones of
animals, then these same forces must also be active in man, at
the place where that bone is present in animals, and working in
essentially the same way except for differences in outer manifestation. Since Goethe never thought of an organism as a dead,
rigid configuration, but rather always as going forth out of its
inner forces of development, he had to ask himself: What are
these forces doing within the upper jaw of man? It could definitely not be a matter of whether the intermaxillary is present or
not, but only of what it is like, of the form it has taken. And this
had to be discovered empirically.

The thought of writing a more comprehensive work on nature now made itself felt more and more in Goethe. We can conclude this from different things he said. Thus he writes to Knebel
in November 1784, when he sends him the treatise on his discovery: "I have refrained from showing yet the result, to which
Herder already points in his ideas, which is, namely, that one
cannot find the *difference between man and animal in the details.*" Here the important point is that Goethe says he has refrained from showing the basic thought yet; he wants to do this
therefore later, in a larger context. Furthermore, this passage
shows us that the basic thoughts that interest us in Goethe above
all – the great ideas about the animal *typus* – were present long
before that discovery. For, Goethe admits here himself that indications of them are already to be found in Herder's ideas; the
passages, however, in which they occur were written before the
discovery of the intermaxillary bone. *The discovery of the intermaxillary bone is therefore only a result of these momentous
views.* For people who did not have these views, the discovery
must have remained incomprehensible. They were deprived of
the only natural, historic characteristic by which to differentiate
man from the animals. They had little inkling of those thoughts
that dominated Goethe and that we earlier indicated: that the

elements dispersed among the animals unite themselves in the *one* human form into a harmony; and thus, in spite of the similarity of the individual parts, they establish a difference in the whole that bestows upon man his high rank in the sequence of beings. They did not look at things ideally, but rather in an externally comparative way; and for this latter approach, to be sure, the intermaxillary bone was not there in man. They had little understanding for what Goethe was asking of them: to see with the *eyes of the spirit*. That was also the reason for the difference in judgment between them and Goethe. Whereas Blumenbach, who after all also saw the matter quite clearly, came to the conclusion that "there is a world of difference between it and the true "*osse intermaxillari*," Goethe judged the matter thus: How can an outer diversity, no matter how great, be explained in the face of the *necessary inner* identity? Apparently Goethe wanted to elaborate this thought now in a consistent manner and he did occupy himself a great deal with this, particularly in the years immediately following. On May 1, 1784, Frau von Stein writes to Knebel: "Herder's new book makes it likely that we were first plants and animals ... Goethe is now delving very thoughtfully into these things, and each thing that has once passed through his mind becomes extremely interesting." To what extent there lived in Goethe the thought of presenting his views on nature in a larger work becomes particularly clear to us when we see that, with every new discovery he achieves, he cannot keep from expressly raising the possibility to his friends of extending his thoughts out over the whole of nature. In 1786, he writes to Frau von Stein that he wants to extend his ideas – about the way nature brings forth its manifold life by playing, as it were, with one main form – "out over all the realms of nature, out over its whole realm." And when in Italy the idea of metamorphosis in the plants stands plastically in all its details before his spirit, he writes in Naples on May 17, 1787: "The same law can be applied ... to everything living." The first essay in *Morphological Notebooks* (1817)[25] contains the words: "May that, therefore, which I often dreamed of in my youthful spirit as a book now appear as a sketch, even as a fragmentary collection." It is a great pity that such a work from Goethe's hand did not come about. To judge by everything we have, it would have been a creation far surpassing everything of this sort that has been done in recent times. It would have become a canon from which every endeavor in the field of natural science would have to take its start and against which one could test the spiritual content of such an endeavor. The deepest philosophical spirit, which only superficiality could deny to Goethe, would have united with a loving immersion of oneself into what is given to sense experience; far from any one-sided desire to found a system purporting to encompass all beings in one general schema, this endeavor would grant every single individual its rightful due. We would have had to do here with the work of a spirit in whom no one individual branch of human endeavor pushes itself forward at the expense of all the others, but rather in whom the totality of human existence always hovers in the background when he is dealing with one particular area. Through this, every single activity receives its rightful place in the interrelationships of the whole. The objective immersing of oneself into the observed objects brings it about that the human spirit fully merges with them, so that Goethe's theories appear to us, not as though a human spirit abstracted them from the objects, but rather as though the objects themselves formed these theories within a human spirit who, in beholding, forgets *himself.* This strictest objectivity would make Goethe's work the most perfect work of natural science; it would be an ideal for which every natural scientist would have to strive; for the philosopher, it would be an archetypal model of how to find the laws of *objective contemplation of the world.* One can conclude that the epistemology now arising everywhere as a philosophical basic science will be able to become fruitful only when it takes as its starting point Goethe's way of thinking and of looking at the world. In the *Annals* of 1790, Goethe himself gives the reason why this work did not come about: "The task was so great that it could not be accomplished in a scattered life."

If one proceeds from this standpoint, the individual fragments we have of Goethe's natural science take on immense significance. We learn to value and understand them rightly, in fact, only when we regard them as going forth from that great whole.

In the year 1784, however, merely as a kind of preliminary exercise, the treatise on the intermaxillary bone was to be produced. To begin with, it was not to be published, for Goethe writes of it to Sömmerring on March 6, 1785: "Since my little treatise is *not entitled at all to come before the public and is to be regarded merely as a rough draft*, it would please me very much to hear anything you might want to share with me about this matter." Nevertheless it was carried out with all possible care and with the help of all the necessary individual studies. At the same time, help was enlisted from young people who, under Goethe's guidance, had to carry out osteological drawings in accordance with Camper's methods. On April 23, 1784, therefore, he asks Merck for information about these methods and has Sömmerring send him Camperian drawings. Merck, Sömmerring, and other acquaintances are asked for skeletons and bones of every kind. On April 23, he writes to Merck that it would please him very much to have the following skeletons: "…a myrmecophaga, bradypus, lion, tiger, or similar skeletons." On May 14, he asks Sömmerring for the skull of his elephant skeleton and of the hippopotamus, and on September 16, for the skulls of the following animals: "wildcat, lion, young bear, incognitum, anteater, camel, dromedary, sea lion." Individual items of information are also requested from his friends: thus from Merck the description of the palatal part of his rhinoceros and particularly the explanation as to "how the rhinoceros horn is actually seated upon the nasal bone." At this time, Goethe is utterly absorbed in his studies. The elephant skull mentioned above was sketched by Waitz from many sides by Camper's methods, and was compared by Goethe with a large skull in his possession and with other animal skulls, since he discovered that in this skull most of the sutures were not yet grown together. In connection with this skull, he makes an important observation. Until then one assumed that in all animals merely the incisors were embedded in the intermaxillary bone, and that the canine teeth belonged to the upper jaw bone; only the elephant was supposed to be an exception. In it, the canine teeth were supposed to be contained in the intermaxillary bone. This skull now shows him also that this is not the case, as he states in a letter to Herder. His osteological studies accompany him on a journey to

Eisenach and to Braunschweig that Goethe undertakes during that summer. On the second trip, in Braunschweig, he wants "to look into the mouth of an unborn elephant and to carry on a hearty conversation with Zimmermann." He writes further about this fetus to Merck: "I wish we had in our cupboard the fetus they have in Braunschweig: it would be quickly dissected, skeletized, and prepared. I don't know what value such a monster in spirits has if it is not dismembered and its inner structure explained." From these studies, there then emerges that treatise that is reported in Volume I of the natural-scientific writings in Kürschner's *National Literature*. Loder was very helpful to Goethe in composing this treatise. With his assistance, a Latin terminology comes into being. Moreover, Loder prepares a Latin translation. In November 1784, Goethe sends the treatise to Knebel and already on December 19 to Merck, although only shortly before (on December 2) he believes that not much will come of it before the end of the year. The work was equipped with the necessary drawings. For Camper's sake, the Latin translation just mentioned was included. Merck was supposed to send the work on to Sömmerring. The latter received it in January 1785. From there it went to Camper. When we now take a look at the way Goethe's treatise was received, we are confronted by a quite unpleasant picture. At first no one has the organ to understand him except Loder, with whom he had worked, and Herder. Merck is pleased by the treatise, but is not convinced of the truth of what is asserted there. In the letter in which Sömmerring informs Merck of the arrival of the treatise, we read: "Blumenbach already had the main idea. In the paragraph that begins 'Thus there can be no doubt,' he [Goethe] says 'since the rest of them (the edges) are grown together'; the only trouble is that these edges were never there. I have in front of me now jawbones of embryos, ranging from three months of age to maturity, and no edge was ever to be seen toward the front. And to explain the matter by the pressure of bones against each other? Yes, if nature works like a carpenter with hammer and wedges!" On February 13, 1785, Goethe writes to Merck: "I have received from Sömmerring a very frivolous letter. He actually wants to talk me out of it. Oh my!" – And Sömmerring writes to Merck on May 11, 1785: "Goethe, as I can see from his letter yesterday, still does not want to abandon his idea about the *ossis intermaxillaris*."

And now Camper.[26] On September 16, 1785, he communicates to Merck that the accompanying tables were not drawn at all according to his methods. He in fact found them to be quite faulty. The outer aspect of the beautiful manuscript is praised and the Latin translation is criticized – in fact, the advice is even given to the author that he brush up on his Latin. Three days later, he writes that he has made a number of observations about the intermaxillary bone, but that he must continue to maintain that man has no intermaxillary bone. He agrees with all of Goethe's observations except the ones pertaining to man. On March 21, 1786, he writes yet again that, out of a great number of observations, he has come to the conclusion: *the intermaxillary bone does not exist in man.* Camper's letters show clearly that he could go into the matter with the best possible will, but was not able to understand Goethe at all.

Loder at once saw Goethe's discovery in the right light. He gives it a prominent place in his anatomical handbook of 1788 and treats it from now on in all his writings as a fully valid fact of science about which there cannot be the least doubt.

Herder writes about this to Knebel: "Goethe has presented me with his treatise on the bone; it is very simple and beautiful; the human being travels *the true path of nature* and fortune comes to meet him." Herder was in fact able to look at the matter with the "spiritual eye" with which Goethe saw it. Without this eye, a person could do nothing with this matter. One can see this best from the following. Wilhelm Josephi (instructor at the University of Göttingen) writes in his *Anatomy of the Mammals*[27] in 1787: "The *ossa intermaxillaria* is also considered to be one of the main characteristics differentiating the apes from man; yet, according to my observation, the human being also has such as *ossa intermaxillaria*, at least in the first months of his life, but it has usually grown together very early – already in the mother's womb, in fact – with the true upper jaw bones, especially in its external appearance, so that often no noticeable trace remains of it at all." Goethe's discovery is, to be sure, also fully stated here, not as one demanded by the consistent realization of the *typus*, however, but rather as the expression of fact directly visible to the eye. If one relies only upon the latter, then, to be sure, it depends only upon a happy chance whether or not one finds precisely such specimens in which one can see the matter exactly. But if one grasps the matter in Goethe's ideal way, then these particular specimens serve merely as confirmation of the thought, are there merely to demonstrate *openly* what nature otherwise conceals; but the idea itself can be found in any specimen at all; every specimen reveals a particular case of the idea. In fact, if one possesses the idea, one is able through it to find precisely those cases in which the idea particularly expresses itself. Without the idea, however, one is at the mercy of chance. One sees, in actuality, that after Goethe had given the impetus by his great thought, one then gradually became convinced of the truth of his discovery through observation of numerous cases.

Merck, to be sure, continued to vacillate. On February 13, 1785, Goethe sends him a split-open upper jawbone of a human being and one of a manatee, and gives him points of reference for understanding the matter. From Goethe's letter of April 8, it appears that Merck was won over to a certain extent. But he soon changed his mind again, for on November 11, 1786, he writes to Sömmerring: "According to what I hear, Vicq d'Azyr has actually included *Goethe's so-called discovery* in his book."

Sömmerring gradually abandoned his opposition. In his book *On the Structure of the Human Body*[28] he says: "Goethe's ingenious attempt in 1785, out of comparative osteology, to show, with quite correct drawings, that man has the intermaxillary bone of the upper jaw in common with the other animals, deserved to be publicly recognized."

To be sure, it was more difficult to win over Blumenbach. In his *Handbook of Comparative Anatomy*[29] in 1805, he still stated the opinion that man has no intermaxillary bone. In his essay *Principles of Zoological Philosophy*, written in 1830-32, however, Goethe can already speak of Blumenbach's conversion. After personal communication, he came over to Goethe's side. On December 15, 1825, in fact, he presents Goethe with a beautiful example that confirmed his discovery. A Hessian athlete sought help from Blumenbach's colleague Langenbeck for an "*os intermaxillare* that was prominent in a quite animal-like way." We still have to speak of later adherents of Goethe's ideas. But it should still be mentioned here that M.J. Weber succeeded, with diluted nitric acid, in separating from an upper jawbone an intermaxillary bone that had already grown into it.

Goethe continued his study of bones even after completion of this treatise. The discoveries he was making at the same time in botany enliven his interest in nature even more. He is continually borrowing relevant objects from his friends. On December 7, 1785, Sömmerring is actually annoyed "that Goethe is not sending him back his heads." From a letter of Goethe's to Sömmerring on June 8, 1786 we learn that he still even then had skulls of his.

In Italy also, his great ideas accompanied him. As the thought of the archetypal plant took shape in his spirit, he also arrives at concepts about man's form. On January 20, 1787, Goethe writes in Rome: "I am somewhat prepared for anatomy and have acquired, though not without effort, a certain level of knowledge of the human body. Here, through endless contemplation of statues, one's attention is continuously drawn to the human body, but in a higher way. The purpose of our medical and surgical anatomy is merely to know the part, and for this a stunted muscle will also serve. But in Rome, the parts mean nothing unless at the same time they present a noble and beautiful form.

In the big hospital of San Spirito, they have set up for artists a very beautifully muscled body in such a way that the beauty of it makes one marvel. It could really be taken for a flayed demigod, a Marsyas.

It is also the custom here, following the ancients, to study the skeleton not as an artificially arranged mass of bones but rather with the ligaments still attached, from which it receives some life and movement."

The main thing for Goethe here is to learn to know the laws by which nature forms organic *shapes* – and especially human ones – and to learn to know the tendency nature follows in forming them. On the one hand, Goethe is seeking within the series of endless plant shapes the archetypal plant with which one can endlessly invent more plants that must be consistent, i.e., that are fully in accordance with that tendency in nature and that would exist if suitable conditions were present; and on the other hand, Goethe was intent, with respect to the animals and man, upon "discovering the ideal characteristics" that are totally in accord with the laws of nature. Soon after his return from Italy, we hear that Goethe is "industriously occupied with anatomy," and in 1789, he writes to Herder: "I have a newly discovered *harmoniam naturae* to expound." What is here described as newly discovered may be a part of his vertebral theory about the skull. The completion of this discovery, however, falls in the year 1790. What he knew up until then was that all the bones that form the back of the head represent three modified spinal vertebrae. Goethe conceived the matter in the following way. The brain represents merely a spinal cord mass raised to its highest level of perfection. Whereas in the spinal cord those nerves end and begin that serve primarily the lower organic functions, in the brain those nerves begin and end that serve higher (spiritual) functions, pre-eminently the sense nerves. In the brain there only appears in a developed form what already lies indicated in the spinal cord as possibility. The brain is a fully developed spinal cord; the spinal cord a brain that has not yet fully unfolded. Now the vertebrae of the spinal column are perfectly shaped in conformity with the parts of the spinal cord; the vertebrae are the organs needed to enclose them. Now it seems probable in the highest degree, that if the brain is a spinal cord raised to its highest potentiality, then the bones enclosing it are also only more highly developed vertebrae. The whole head appears in this way to be prefigured in the bodily organs that stand at a lower level. The forces that are already active on lower levels are at work here also, but in the head they develop to the highest potentiality lying within them. Again, Goethe's concern is only to find evidence as to how the matter actually takes shape in accordance with sense-perceptible reality. Goethe says that he recognized this relationship very soon with respect to the bone of the back of the head, the occiput, and to the posterior and anterior sphenoid bones; but that – during his trip to northern Italy when he found a cracked-open sheep's skull on the dunes of the Lido – he recognized that the palatal bone, the upper jaw, and the intermaxillary bone are also modified vertebrae. This skull had fallen apart so felicitously that the individual vertebrae were distinctly recognizable in the individual parts. Goethe showed this beautiful discovery to Frau von Kalb on April 30, 1790 with the words: "Tell Herder that I have gotten one whole principle nearer to animal form and to its manifold transformations, and did so through the most remarkable accident."

This was a discovery of the most far-reaching significance. It showed that all the parts of an organic whole are identical with respect to idea, that "inwardly unformed" organic masses open themselves up outwardly in different ways, and that it is one and the same thing that – at a lower level as spinal cord nerve and on a higher level as sense nerve – opens itself up into the sense organ, that takes up, grasps, and apprehends the outer world. This discovery revealed every living thing in its power to form and give shape to itself from within outward; only then was it grasped as something *truly living*. Goethe's basic ideas, also in relation to animal development, had now attained their final form. The time had come to present these ideas in detail, although he had already planned to do this earlier, as Goethe's correspondence with F.H. Jacobi shows us. When he accompanied the Duke, in July 1790, to the Silesian encampment, he occupied himself primarily there (in Breslau) with his studies on animal development. He also began there really to write down his thoughts on this subject. On August 31, 1790, he writes to Friedrich von Stein: "In all this bustle, I have begun to write my treatise on the development of the animals."

In a comprehensive sense, the idea of the animal *typus* is contained in the poem "Metamorphosis of the Animals," which first appeared in 1820 in the second of the morphological notebooks. During the years 1790-95, Goethe's primary natural-scientific work was with his color theory. At the beginning of 1795, Goethe was in Jena, where the brothers von Humboldt, Max Jacobi, and Schiller were also present. In this company, Goethe brought forward his ideas about comparative anatomy. His friends found his presentations so significant that they urged him to put his ideas down on paper. It is evident from a letter of Goethe to the elder Jacobi that Goethe complied with this urging right away, while still in Jena, by dictating to Max Jacobi the outline of a comparative osteology that is printed in the first volume of Goethe's natural-scientific writings in Kürschner's *Na-*

tional Literature. In 1796, the introductory chapters were further elaborated. These treatises contain Goethe's basic views about animal development, just as his writing, *"An Attempt to Explain the Metamorphosis of the Plant,"*[30] contains his basic views on plant development. Through communication with Schiller – since 1794 – Goethe came to a turning point in his views, in that from now on, with respect to his own way of proceeding and of doing research, he began to observe himself, so that his way of viewing things became for him an *object of study*. After these historical reflections, let us now turn to the nature and significance of Goethe's views on the development of organisms.

IV

The Nature and Significance of Goethe's Writings on Organic Development

The great significance of Goethe's morphological works is to be sought in the fact that in them the theoretical basis and method for studying organic entities are established, and this is a *scientific deed of the first order*.

If one is to do justice to this rightly, one must above all bear in mind the great difference existing between the phenomena of inorganic nature and those of organic nature. A phenomenon of the first kind, for example, is the impact of two elastic balls upon one another. If one ball is at rest and the other ball strikes it from a certain direction and with a certain velocity, then the first ball is likewise given a certain direction and velocity. If it is a matter then of *comprehending* such a phenomenon, this can be achieved only by our transforming into concepts what is directly there for the senses. We would succeed in this to the extent that nothing of a sense-perceptibly real nature remained that we had not permeated conceptually. We see one ball approach and strike the other, which then goes on moving. We have *comprehended* this phenomenon when, from the mass, direction, and velocity of the first ball, and from the mass of the second, we can determine the direction and velocity of the second ball; when we see that under the given conditions this phenomenon must *necessarily* occur. But this means nothing other than: that which offers itself to our senses must appear as a *necessary consequence* of what we have to postulate ideally beforehand. If this is the case, then we can say that concept and phenomenon coincide. *There is nothing in the concept that is not also in the phenomenon, and nothing in the phenomenon that is not also in the concept.* Now we must take a closer look into those relationships out of which a phenomenon of inorganic nature occurs as a necessary consequence. The important fact arises here that the sense-perceptible processes of inorganic nature are determined by factors that likewise belong to the sense world. In our example, mass, velocity, and direction – i.e., exclusively factors belonging to the sense world – come into consideration. Nothing further arises as a determining factor for the phenomenon. It is only the directly sense-perceptible factors that determine *one another*. A conceptual grasp of such processes is therefore nothing other than a tracing of something sense-perceptibly real back to something sense-perceptibly real. Spatial-temporal relationships, mass, weight, or sense-perceptible forces such as light or warmth call forth phenomena that themselves belong in the same category. A body is heated and increases thereby in volume; the heating and the expanding both belong to the sense world; both the cause and the effect do so. We therefore do not need to go outside the sense world at all in order to comprehend such processes. We merely trace, *within* the sense world, one phenomenon back to another. When we therefore explain such a phenomenon, i.e., want to permeate it conceptually, we do not need to take up into the concept any elements other than those that are observably *perceptible* to our senses. We can observe everything that we want to comprehend. And the congruence of perception (phenomenon) and concept consists in this. Nothing in the processes remains obscure to us, because we know the relationships from which they follow. With this, we have elaborated upon the character of inorganic nature and have shown at the same time to what extent we can explain inorganic nature *out of itself*, without going out of or beyond it. Now one has never doubted this explainability, ever since one first began to think about the nature of these things. One has not, to be sure, always gone through the above train of thought from which the possibility of a congruence of concept and perception follows; but still one has never hesitated to explain phenomena out of the nature of their own being in the way indicated.[31]

But matters were different, *up until Goethe*, with respect to the phenomena of the *organic* world. In the case of an organism, sense-perceptible factors appear – form, size, color, warmth conditions of an organ, for example – that are not determined by factors of the same kind. One cannot say of the plant, for example, that the size, form, location, etc., of the roots determine the sense-perceptible factors of the leaf or blossom. A body for which this were the case would not be an organism but rather a machine. It must be admitted that all the sense-perceptible factors of a living being do not manifest as a result of other sense-perceptible factors,[32] as is the case with inorganic nature. On the contrary, in an organism, all sense-perceptible qualities manifest as the result of a factor that is no longer *sense-perceptible*. They manifest as the result of a higher unity hovering over the sense-perceptible processes. It is not the shape of the root that determines that of the trunk, nor the trunk's shape that determines that of the leaf, and so on; rather, all these forms are determined by something standing over them that itself is not again a form observable by the senses; these forms do exist for one another, but not as a result of one another. They do not mutually determine one another, but rather are all determined by something else. Here we cannot trace what we perceive with our senses back to other sense-perceptible factors; we must take up, into the concept of the processes, elements that do not belong to the world of the senses; *we must go out of and beyond the sense world. Observation* no longer suffices; we must grasp *the unity* conceptually if we want to explain the phenomena. Because of this, however, a separation occurs between observation and concept; they no longer seem to coincide with each other; the concept hovers over what is observed. It becomes difficult to see the connection. Whereas in inorganic nature concept and reality were one, here they seem to diverge and actually to belong to two different worlds. The observation that offers itself directly to the senses no longer seems to bear within itself its own basis, its own being. The object does not seem explainable out of itself, but rather from something else. Because the object appears in a way not governed by the laws of the sense world, but is there for the senses nevertheless, appears to the senses, it is then as though we stood here before an insoluble contradiction in nature, as though a chasm existed between inorganic phenomena, which are comprehensible through themselves, and organic beings, in which an intrusion into the laws of nature occurs, *in which universally valid laws seem suddenly to be broken. Up until Goethe*, in fact, science generally considered this chasm to exist; he was the first to succeed in speaking the word that solved the riddle. Before him, one thought that only inorganic nature was explainable out of itself; man's ability to know ceases when confronted by organic nature. One can best estimate the greatness of the deed Goethe accomplished when one considers that the great reformer of philosophy in recent time, Kant, not only shared completely in that old error, but even sought, in fact, to find a scientific foundation for the view that the human spirit will never succeed in explaining organic entities. He saw the possibility, to be sure, of an intellect – of an *intellectus archetypus*, of an intuitive intellect – to which it would be granted to see into the relationship of concept and reality in organic beings just as it does in inorganic things; only, he denied to man himself the possibility of any such intellect (*Verstand*).[33] For Kant, it is supposedly characteristic of the human intellect that it can think of the unity, the concept of a thing, only as resulting from the interaction of its parts – as an analytical generalization gained by a process of abstraction – but not in such a way that each individual part manifests as the outflow of a definite concrete (synthetical) unity, of a concept in an intuitive form. For this reason, it is also supposedly impossible for the intellect to explain organic nature, because organic nature would have to be thought of, indeed, as working from the whole into the parts. Kant says about this: "It is characteristic of our intellect, therefore, with respect to our power of judgment, that it does not determine knowledge through itself, does not determine what is particular through what is general, and that therefore the particular cannot be traced back to the general."[34] According to this, we would therefore have to renounce all knowledge, with regard to organic entities, of the necessary connection between the idea of the whole – which can only be thought – and what manifests to our senses in space and time. According to Kant, we must limit ourselves to the recognition that such a connection exists; but the logical challenge to know how the general thought, the idea, steps out of itself and manifests itself as sense-perceptible reality, this supposedly cannot be fulfilled with respect to organisms. Rather we would have to assume that concept and reality confront each other here without mediation; and that some influence lying outside them both creates them in somewhat the same way a person, according to an idea he has thought up, constructs some composite thing or other – a machine, for example. In this way the possibility of an explanation of the world of organisms was denied, its impossibility in fact seemingly proven.

This is how matters stood when Goethe undertook to devote himself to the organic sciences. But he entered into these studies after preparing himself for them in a most appropriate way, through repeated readings of the philosopher Spinoza.

Goethe took up Spinoza for the first time in the spring of 1774. In *Poetry and Truth*, he says of this, his first acquaintance with the philosopher: "That is, after vainly looking around in the whole world for a means of educating my strange being, I finally happened upon the *Ethics* of this man." In the summer of the same year, Goethe met with Friedrich Jacobi. The latter, who had come more thoroughly to terms with Spinoza – as his letters of 1785 about Spinoza's teachings show – was entirely qualified to lead Goethe more deeply into the essential nature of the philosopher. Spinoza was also very much discussed at that time, for in Goethe "everything was still in its first effects and counter effects, fermenting and seething." Somewhat later, he found a book in his father's library whose author heatedly opposed Spinoza, even distorting him, in fact, into a total caricature. This gave Goethe the stimulus to occupy himself seriously once more with the profound thinker. In Spinoza's writings he found elucidation on the deepest scientific questions that he was then capable of raising. In 1784, the poet reads Spinoza with Frau von Stein. On November 19, 1784, he writes to her: "I am bringing Spinoza along in Latin, in which everything is much clearer ..." The effect of this philosopher upon Goethe was now immense. Goethe himself was always clear about this. In 1816, he writes to Zelter: "Except for Shakespeare and Spinoza, I do not know that any departed soul has had such an effect upon me (as Linnaeus)." He regards Shakespeare and Spinoza therefore as the two spirits who have exerted the greatest influence on him. The manner in which this influence now manifested itself with respect to his studies of organic development becomes clearest to us if we consider a statement about Lavater from Goethe's *Italian Journey*; Lavater was also in fact a proponent of the view generally prevalent then that something living can arise only through an influence that does not lie in the nature of the entity itself, through a violation of the general laws of nature. Goethe then wrote the following words about this: "Recently I found, in a pitiful, apostolically monkish declamation of the Zurich prophet, the nonsensical words that *everything that has life lives by something outside itself.* Or it sounded something like that. Now a missionary can write down something like that, and when he is revising it no good spirit tugs at his sleeve." Now that is expressed entirely in the spirit of Spinoza. Spinoza makes a distinction between three kinds of knowledge. The first kind is that in which upon hearing or reading certain words we recall certain things and form certain mental pictures of these things that are similar to the pictures by which we represent the things to ourselves pictorially. The second kind of knowledge is that in which, out of sufficient mental pictures of the characteristics of things, we form general concepts for ourselves. The third kind of knowledge, however, is that in which we advance from an adequate picture of the real being of certain attributes of God to an adequate knowledge of the being of things. Spinoza calls this kind of knowledge *scientia intuitiva, knowledge in beholding.* This last, the highest kind of knowledge, is that for which Goethe strove. One must above all be clear about what Spinoza meant by this: The things are to be known in such a way that we recognize within their being certain attributes of God. Spinoza's God is the idea-content of the world, the driving principle that supports and carries everything. Now one can picture this either in such a way that one takes this principle to be an independent being – existing by itself, separated off from finite beings – that has these finite things outside itself, governs them, and causes them to interact. Or, on the other hand, one can picture this being as having merged into finite things in such a way that it is no longer over and outside them, but rather now exists only *within* them. This view in no way denies that primal principle; it acknowledges it entirely; only, it regards this principle as having been *poured out* into the world. The first view regards the finite world as a manifestation of the infinite, but this infinite remains with its own being intact; it relinquishes nothing of itself. It does not go out of itself; it remains what it was before it manifested itself. The second view also regards the finite world as a manifestation of the infinite, only it assumes that this infinite, in becoming manifest, has gone entirely out of itself, has laid itself, its own being and life, into its creation in such a way that it now exists only within *this creation*. Now since our activity of knowing is obviously a becoming aware of the essential being of things, and since this being can after all consist only in the involvement a finite being has in the primal principle of all things, our activity of knowing must then mean a becoming aware of that infinite within the things.[35] Now, as we have described above, it was readily assumed, before Goethe, with respect to inorganic nature, that one could explain it out of itself, that it carries within itself its own substantiation and essential being, but that this is not the case with organic nature. Here one could not know, within an object itself, that essential being which manifests itself within the object. One therefore assumed this being to be outside the object. In short: one explained organic nature according to the first view and inorganic nature according to the second. As we have seen, Spinoza had proven the necessity for a unified knowledge. He was too much the philosopher to have been able also to extend this theoretical requirement out over the specialized area of organic science. It remained for Goethe to do this now. Not only his statement about Spinoza quoted above, but also numerous others show us that Goethe adhered decisively to Spinoza's views. In *Poetry and Truth*: "Nature works according to laws that are eternal, necessary, and so divine that even the Divinity Himself could change nothing about them." And, in connection with Jacobi's book, *Of Divine Things and their Manifestation*,[36] Goethe remarks: "How could the book of such a beloved friend be welcome to me when I had to see developed in it the thesis that nature conceals God. With my pure, deep, inborn, and trained way of looking at things, which *had taught me absolutely to see God in nature, nature in God*, such that this way of picturing things constituted the foundation of my whole existence, would not such a peculiar, one-sidedly limited statement estrange me forever in spirit from this most noble man whose heart I revered and loved?" Goethe was completely conscious of the great step he was taking in science; he recognized that by breaking down the barriers between inorganic and organic nature and by consistently carrying through on Spinoza's way of thinking, he was giving science a significant turn. We find his knowledge of this fact expressed in his essay

Power to Judge in Beholding (Anschauende Urteilskraft). After he had found, in the *Critique of Judgment*, the Kantian establishment of the inability of the human intellect to explain an organism, as we described above, Goethe expresses his opposition to it in this way: "To be sure, the author (Kant) seems here to point to a divine intellect; but when we, in fact, lift ourselves in the moral sphere into a higher region through belief in God, virtue, and immortality and mean to draw near to the primal being, so likewise, in the intellectual realm, it could very well be the case that we would make ourselves worthy, through beholding an ever-creating nature, of participating spiritually in its productions. Since I had, after all, ceaselessly pressed on, at first unconsciously and out of an inner urge, toward that primal archetypal element, since I had even succeeded in building up a presentation of this that was in accordance with nature, nothing more could keep me then from courageously undertaking the *adventure of reason*, as the old man of Königsberg himself calls it."

The essential thing about a process of inorganic nature – a process belonging merely to the sense world, in other words – consists in the fact that it is caused and determined by another process that likewise belongs only to the sense world. Let us assume now that the causal process consists of the elements m, d, and v (mass, direction, and velocity of a moving elastic ball) and that the resulting process consists of the elements m', d', and v'; then what m, d, and v are will always determine what m', d', and v' are. If I now want to comprehend the process, I must represent the whole process, consisting of cause and effect, in one common concept. But this concept is not of such a sort that it could lie within the process itself and determine the process. The concept now brings both processes together into one common expression. It does not cause and determine. Only the objects of the sense world determine each other. The elements m, d, and v are elements that are also perceptible to the external senses. The concept appears there only in order to serve man's spirit as a means of drawing things together; it *expresses something* that is not ideally, conceptually real, but rather is sense-perceptibly real. And that something that it expresses is a sense-perceptible object. Knowledge of inorganic nature is based upon the possibility of grasping the outer world through the senses and of expressing its interactions through concepts. Kant saw the possibility of knowing things in *this* way as the only way man has. He called this thinking "*discursive*." *What* we want to know is an external perception; the concept, the unity that draws things together, is merely a means. But if we wanted to know organic nature, we would then have to consider the ideal element, the conceptual factor, not as something that expresses or signifies something else, but rather we would have to know the *ideal element as such*; it would have to have a content of its own, stemming from itself, and not from the spatial-temporal world of the senses. That unity which, in inorganic nature, man's spirit merely abstracts from the world, would have to build upon itself, would have to develop itself *out of its own self*, would have to be fashioned in accordance with its own being and not according to the influences of other objects. Man is supposedly denied the ability to apprehend such an entity as this that develops itself out of itself and that manifests itself out of its own power. Now what is necessary for such an apprehension? A power of judgment that can impart to a thought yet another substance (*Stoff*) than one merely taken up by the outer senses, a power of judgment that can apprehend not merely what is sense-perceptible, but also what is purely ideal, by itself, separated from the sense world. Now one can call a concept that is not taken from the sense world by abstraction, but rather has a content flowing out of itself and only out of itself, an "*intuitive concept*" and knowledge of this concept an "intuitive" one. What follows from this is clear: *An organism can be apprehended only in an intuitive concept*. Goethe shows, through what he does, that it is granted to the human being to know in this way.

What prevails in the inorganic world is the interaction of the parts of a series of phenomena; it is their reciprocal determining of each other. This is not the case in the organic world. There, one part of an entity does not determine the other, but rather the whole (the idea), out of itself and in accordance with its own being, determines each individual part. One can follow Goethe in calling this self-determining whole an "*entelechy*." An entelechy is therefore a power that, out of itself, calls itself into existence. What comes into manifestation also has a sense-perceptible existence, but this is determined by that entelechical principle. From this also arises the seeming contradiction. An organism determines itself out of itself, fashions its characteristics in accordance with a presupposed principle, and yet it is sense-perceptibly real. It has therefore arrived at its sense-perceptible reality in a completely different way than the other objects of the sense world; thus it seems to have arisen in an unnatural way. But it is also entirely explainable that an organism, in its externality, is just as susceptible to the influences of the sense world as is any other body. The stone falling from a roof can strike a living entity just as well as an inorganic object. An organism is connected with the outer world through its intake of nourishment, etc.; all the physical circumstances of the outer world affect it. Of course this can also occur only insofar as the organism is an object of the sense world, a spatial-temporal object. This object of the outer world then, this entelechical principle that has come into existence, is the outer manifestation of the organism. But since the organism is subject not only to its own laws of development but also to the conditions of the outer world, since it is not only what it should be in accordance with the being of the self-determining entelechical principle, but also is what other dependencies and influences have made it, therefore the organism never seems, as it were, to accord fully with itself, never seems obedient merely to its own being. Here human reason enters and forms for itself, *in idea*, an organism that is not in accordance with the influences of the outer world, but rather corresponds only to that entelechical principle. Every coincidental influence that has nothing to do with the organism *as such* falls away entirely here. This idea, now, that corresponds purely to what is organic in the organism is the idea of the archetypal organism; it is Goethe's *typus*. From this one can also see the great justification for this idea of the *typus*. This idea is not merely an *intellectual concept*; it is what is truly organic in every organism, without which an organism would not be one. This idea is, in fact, more real than any individual real organism, because it manifests itself in *every* organism. It also expresses the essential nature of an organism *more fully, more purely* than any individual, *particular* organism. It is acquired in an essentially different way than the concept of an inorganic process. This latter is drawn from, abstracted from, reality; it is not at work within reality; the idea of the organism, however, is active, is at work as entelechy within the organism; it is, in the form grasped by our reason, only the being of the entelechy itself. This idea does not draw the experience together; it *brings about* what is to be experienced. Goethe expresses this in the following words: "Concept is *summation*, idea is *result* of experience; to find the sum requires intellect; to grasp the result requires reason" (*Aphorisms in Prose*). This explains that kind of reality that belongs to the Goethean archetypal organism (archetypal plant or archetypal animal). This Goethean method is clearly the only possible one by which to penetrate into the essential nature of the world of organisms.

With respect to the inorganic, the fact should be regarded as essential that the phenomenon, in all its manifoldness, is not identical with the lawfulness that explains it, but rather points, merely, to this lawfulness as to something external to it. The observation (the material element of knowledge, given us by the outer senses) and the concept (the formal element, by which we recognize the observation as necessitated) confront each other as two elements that objectively require each other, it is true; but they do so in such a way that the concept does not lie within the individual parts of a series of phenomena themselves, but rather within a relationship of these parts to each other. This relationship, which brings the manifoldness into a unified whole, is founded *within the individual parts* of the given, but as a *whole* (as a unity) it does not come to real, concrete manifestation. Only the *parts* of this relationship come to outer existence – in the object. The unity, the concept, first comes to manifestation *as such* within our intellect. The intellect has the task of drawing together the manifoldness of the phenomenon; it relates itself to the manifoldness as its *sum*. We have to do here with a duality: with the manifold thing that we *observe*, and with the unity that we *think*. In organic nature the parts of the manifoldness of an entity do not stand in such an external relationship to each other. The unity comes into reality in the observed entity simultaneously with the manifoldness, as something identical with the manifoldness. The relationship of the individual parts of a phenomenal whole (an organism) has become a real one. It no longer comes to concrete manifestation merely within our intellect, but rather within the object itself, and in the object it brings forth the manifoldness out of itself. The concept does not have the role merely of summation, of being a combiner that has its object *outside* itself; the concept has become completely *one* with the object. What we observe is no longer different from that by which we think the observed; we are observing the concept as the idea itself. Therefore, Goethe calls the ability by which we comprehend organic nature the power to judge in beholding (*anschauende Urteilskraft*).

What explains (the formal element of knowledge, the concept) and what is explained (the material, the beheld) are identical. The idea by which we grasp the organic is therefore essentially different from the concept by which we explain the inorganic; the idea does not merely draw together – like a sum – a given manifoldness, but rather sets forth its own content out of itself. The idea is the *result* of the given (of experience), is concrete manifestation. Herein lies the reason why in inorganic natural science we speak of *laws* (natural laws) and explain the facts by them, and in organic nature, on the other hand, we do this by *types*. The law is not one and the same with the manifoldness of the observed that the law governs; the law stands over it; in the *typus*, however, the ideal element and the real element have become a unity; the manifoldness can be explained only as going forth from a point of the whole, the whole that is identical with the manifoldness.

In Goethe's knowledge of this relationship between the science of the inorganic and that of the organic lies what is so significant in his research. One is in error, therefore, when today one often explains his research as a forerunner of that monism which wants to found a unified view of nature – comprising both the organic and the inorganic – by endeavoring to trace what is organic back to the same laws (mechanical-physical categories and laws of nature) by which the inorganic is determined. We have seen how Goethe conceives a monistic view to be. The way he explains the organic is essentially different from the way he proceeds with respect to the inorganic. He wants to be sure that the mechanistic way of explaining things is strictly avoided with respect to what is of a higher nature (see his *Aphorisms in*

Prose). He criticizes Kieser and Link for wanting to trace organic phenomena back to inorganic activity.

What gave rise to the erroneous view about Goethe indicated above was the relationship into which he brought himself to Kant with respect to the possibility of a knowledge of organic nature. But when Kant asserts that our intellect is not able to explain organic nature, he certainly does not mean by this that organic nature rests upon mechanical lawfulness and that he is only unable to grasp it as resulting from mechanical-physical categories. For Kant, the reason for this inability lies, rather, precisely in the fact that our intellect can explain only mechanical-physical things and that the being of the organism is *not* of this nature. Were it so, then the intellect, by virtue of the categories at its command, could very well grasp its being. It is definitely not Goethe's thought now to explain the organic world as a mechanism *in spite of* Kant; but rather he maintains that we by no means lack the ability to know that higher kind of nature's working that establishes the essential being of the organic.

As we consider what has just been said, we are confronted right away by an essential difference between inorganic and organic nature. Since in inorganic nature any process whatever can cause another, and this in turn yet another, and so on, the sequence of occurrences seems nowhere to be a closed one. Everything is in continuous interaction, without any one particular group of objects being able to close itself off from the effects of others. The sequences of inorganic activity have nowhere a beginning nor an end; there is only a chance connection between one happening and the next. If a stone falls to earth, the effect it produces depends upon the chance form of the object on which it falls. It is a different matter now with an organism. Here the unity is primary. The entelechy, built upon itself, comprises a number of sense perceptible developmental forms of which one must be the first and another the last; in which one form can always only follow the other in an altogether definite way. The ideal unity puts forth out of itself a series of sense-perceptible organs in a certain sequence in time and in a particular spatial relationship, and closes itself off in an altogether definite way from the rest of nature. It puts forth its various states out of itself.

These can therefore also be grasped only when one studies the development of successive states as they emerge from an ideal unity; i.e., an organic entity can be understood only in its becoming, in its developing. An inorganic body is closed off, rigid, can only be moved from outside, is inwardly immobile. An organism is restlessness within itself, ever transforming itself from within, changing, producing metamorphoses. The following statements of Goethe refer to this: "Reason is oriented toward what is becoming, the intellect toward what has become; the former does not bother itself about purpose (*wozu*?); the latter does not ask about origin (*woher*?). Reason rejoices in development; intellect wishes to hold everything fixed in order to use it" (*Aphorisms in Prose*) and: "Reason has rulership only over what is living; the world that has already come about, with which geognosy concerns itself, is dead." (Ibid)

The organism confronts us in nature in two main forms: as plant and as animal, in a different way in each. The plant differs from the animal in its lack of any *real* inner life. This last manifests in the animal as sensation, arbitrary movement, etc. The plant has no such soul principle. It still consists entirely in its externality, in its *form.* By determining its life, as it were, out of one point, that entelechical principle confronts us in the plant in such a way that all its individual organs are formed according to the same developmental principle. The entelechy manifests here as the developmental force of the individual organs. These last are all fashioned according to one and the same developmental type; they manifest as modifications of *one* basic organ, as a repetition of this organ at different levels of development. What makes the plant into a plant, *a certain form-creating force*, is at work in every organ in the same way. Every organ appears therefore as *identical* to all the others and also to the whole plant. Goethe expresses this as follows: "I have realized, namely, that in that organ of the plant that we are usually accustomed to address as "leaf," the true Proteus lies hidden that can conceal and reveal itself in every formation. Anyway you look at it, the plant is always only leaf, so inseparably joined with the future germ (*Keim*) that one cannot think the one without the other." (*Italian Journey*) Thus the plant appears, as it were, composed of nothing but individual plants, as a complex individual consisting in turn of simpler ones. The development of the plant progresses therefore from level to level and forms organs; each organ is identical to every other, i.e., similar in formative principle, different in appearance. The inner unity spreads itself out, as it were, in the plant; it expresses itself in manifoldness, loses itself in this manifoldness in such a way that it does not gain – as the animal does, as we will see later – a concrete existence that is endowed with a certain independence and that, as a center of life, confronts the manifoldness of the organs and uses them as mediators with the outer world.

The question now arises: What brings about that difference in the appearance of plant organs that, according to their inner principle, are identical? How is it possible for developmental laws that all work according to *one* formative principle to bring forth at one time a leaf and at another a petal? In the case of plant life, which lies entirely in the realm of the external, this differentiation can also be based only upon external, i.e., spatial, factors. Goethe regards an alternating expansion and contraction as just such external factors. As the entelechical principle of plant life, working out from one point, comes into existence, it manifests itself as something spatial; the formative forces work in space. They create organs with definite spatial forms. Now these forces either concentrate themselves, they strive to come together, as it were, into one single point (this is the stage of contraction); or they spread themselves out, unfold themselves, seek in a certain way to distance themselves from each other (this is the stage of expansion). In the whole life of the plant, three expansions alternate with three contractions. Everything that enters as differentiation into the plant's formative forces – which in their essential nature are identical – stems from this alternating expansion and contraction. At first the whole plant, in all its potential, rests, *drawn together* into one point, in the seed (a). It then comes forth and unfolds itself, *spreads itself out* in leaf-formation (c). The formative forces thrust themselves apart more and more; therefore the lower leaves appear still raw, compact (cc'); the further up the stem they are, the more ribbed and indented they become. What formerly was still pressing together now separates (leaf d and e). What earlier stood at successive intervals (zz') from each other appears again in one point of the stem (w) in the calyx (f). This is the second contraction. In the corolla, an unfolding, a *spreading out*, occurs again. Compared with the sepals, the petals (g) are finer and more delicate, which can only be due to a lesser intensity at one point, i.e., be due to a greater extension of the formative forces. The next contraction occurs in the reproductive organs (stamens (h), and pistil (i)), after which a new expansion takes place in the fruiting (k). In the seed (a) that emerges from the fruit, the whole being of the plant again appears contracted to a point.[37]

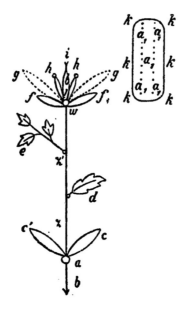

The whole plant represents only an unfolding, a realization, of what rests in the bud or in the seed as potentiality. Bud and seed need only the appropriate external influences in order to become fully developed plant forms. The only difference between bud and seed is that the latter has the earth directly as the basis of its unfolding, whereas the former generally represents a plant formation upon the plant itself. The seed represents a plant individuality of a higher kind, or, if you will, a whole cycle of plant forms. With the forming of every bud, the plant begins a new stage of its life, as it were; it regenerates itself, concentrates its forces in order to unfold them again anew. The forming of a bud is therefore an interruption of vegetation. The plant's life can contract itself into a bud when the conditions for actual real life are lacking, in order then to unfold itself anew when such conditions do occur. The interruption of vegetation in winter is based on this. Goethe says about this: "It is very interesting to observe how a vegetation works that is actively continued and uninterrupted by severe cold; here there are no buds, and one only learns now to comprehend what a bud is. What lies hidden in the bud where we are is open to the day there; what lies within the bud, therefore, is true plant life; only the conditions for its unfolding are lacking."

Goethe's concept of alternating expansion and contraction has met with especially strong opposition. All the attacks on it, however, originate from a misunderstanding. One believes that these concepts could be valid only if a physical cause could be found for them, only if one could demonstrate a way of working of the laws at work in the plant from which such expansion and contraction could proceed. This only shows that one is setting the matter down on its tip instead of its base. There is not something there that causes the contraction and expansion; on the contrary, everything else is the result of these; they cause a progressive metamorphosis from stage to stage. One is just not able to picture the concept in its own characteristic form, in its intuitive form; one requires that the concept represent the result of an external process. One can only think of expansion and contraction as caused and not as causing. Goethe does not look upon *expansion* and *contraction* as resulting from the nature of the inorganic processes occurring in the plant; rather he regards them as the way that inner entelechical principle shapes itself. He could therefore not view them as a sum, as a drawing together, of sense-perceptible processes and deduce them from such processes, but rather had to see them as proceeding from the inner unified principle itself.

The plant's life is maintained by metabolism. With respect to this, an essential difference sets in between those organs closer to the root – i.e., to that organ which sees to the taking in of nourishment from the earth – and those organs that receive the nourishment which has already passed through the other organs. The former appear directly dependent upon their external inorganic environment; the latter, on the other hand, upon the organic parts that precede them. Each subsequent organ thus receives nourishment prepared, as it were, for it by the preceding organ. Nature progresses from seed to fruit through a series of stages in such a way that what follows appears as the result of what precedes. And Goethe calls this progressing a *progressing upon a spiritual ladder*. Nothing more than what we have indicated lies in his words, "that an upper node – through the fact that it arises out of the preceding one and receives its sap indirectly through it – must receive its sap in a more refined and more filtered state, must also enjoy the effects of what the leaves have done with the sap in the meantime, must develop itself more finely and bring a finer sap to its leaves and buds." All these things become comprehensible when one applies to them the meaning intended by Goethe.

The ideas presented here are the elements inherent in the being of the archetypal plant – inherent in a way that conforms, in fact, only to this archetypal plant itself, and not as these elements manifest in any given plant where they no longer conform to their original state but rather to external conditions.

Something different occurs now, to be sure, in animal life. Life does not lose itself here in its external features, but rather separates itself, detaches itself from its corporeality and uses its corporeal manifestation only as a tool. It no longer expresses itself as the mere ability to shape an organism from within outward, but rather expresses itself within an organism as something that is still there besides the organism, as its ruling power. The animal appears as a self-contained world, a microcosm in a much higher sense than the plant. It has a center that each organ serves.

> Thus is every mouth adept at grasping the food
> That is right for the body, be now weak and toothless
> The jaw, or mighty with teeth; in every instance
> An adept organ conveys food to each member.
> Also every foot does move – be it long or a short one –
> All harmonious to the sense and need of the creature.

In the case of the plant, the whole plant is in every organ, but the life principle exists nowhere as a particular center; the identity of the organs lies in their being formed according to the same laws. In the case of the animal, every organ appears as coming from that center; the center shapes all organs in accordance with its own nature. The form of the animal is therefore the basis for its external existence. This form, however, is determined from within. The way an animal lives must therefore take its direction from those inner formative principles. On the other hand, the inner development in itself is unrestricted, free; within certain limits, it can adapt itself to outer influences; but this development is still determined by the inner nature of the *typus* and not by mechanical influences from outside. Adaptation cannot therefore go so far as to make an organism seem to be only a product of the outer world. Its development is restricted to certain limits.

These limits no god can extend; nature honors them;

For only thus restricted was ever the perfect possible.

If every animal being existed only in accordance with the principles lying within the archetypal animal, then they would all be alike. But the animal organism members itself into a number of organ systems, each of which can arrive at a definite degree of development. This is the basis now for a diverse evolution. Equally valid among the others as idea, one system can nevertheless push itself forward to a particular degree; it can use for itself the supply of formative forces lying within the animal organism and can deprive the other organs of it. The animal will thus appear as particularly developed in the direction of that organ system. Another animal will appear as developed in another direction. Herein lies the possibility for the differentiation of the archetypal organism in its transition to the phenomenal realm in genera and species.

The real (factual) causes of this differentiation, however, are still not yet given thereby. Here adaptation and the *struggle for existence* come into their own right – the former causing the organism to shape itself in accordance with the outer conditions surrounding it, the latter working in such a way that only those entities survive that are best adapted to existing conditions. Adaptation and the struggle for existence, however, could have absolutely no effect upon the organism if the constituting principle of the organism were not of such a kind that – while continuously maintaining its inner unity – it can take on the most manifold forms. The relationship of outer formative forces to this principle should in no way be regarded as one in which, for example, the former determine the latter in the same way one inorganic entity determines another. The outer conditions are, to be sure, the stimulus *for* the *typus* to develop in a certain form; but this form itself cannot be derived from the outer determining factors, but only from the inner principle. In explaining the form, one should always seek the outer factors, but one should not regard the form itself as resulting from *them*. Goethe would have rejected the derivation of the developmental forms of an organism from the surrounding outer world through mere causality, just as much as he rejected the teleological principle according to which the form of an organ is traced back to an external purpose it is to serve.

In the case of those organ systems of an animal in which what matters is more the external aspect of the structure – in the bones, for example – there that law which we saw in the plants appears again, as in the forming of the skull bones. Goethe's gift for recognizing the inner lawfulness in purely external forms manifests here quite especially.

The difference between plant and animal established by these views of Goethe might seem meaningless in face of the fact that modern science has grounds for justifiable doubt that there is any definite borderline between plant and animal. Goethe, however, was already aware of the impossibility of setting up any such borderline. In spite of this, there are specific definitions of plant and animal. This is connected with Goethe's whole view of nature. He assumes absolutely nothing *constant, fixed in the phenomenal realm*; for in this realm everything fluctuates in continuous motion. But the *essential being of a thing*, which can be held fast in a concept, cannot be derived from the fluctuating forms, but rather from certain *intermediary stages* at which this being can be observed. For Goethe's view, it is quite natural that one set up specific definitions and that these are nevertheless not held to in one's experience of certain transitional forms. In fact, he sees precisely in this the mobile life of nature.

With these ideas, Goethe established the theoretical foundations of organic science. He found the essential being of the organism. One can easily fail to recognize this if one demands that the *typus*, that self-constituted principle (entelechy), itself be explained by something else. But this is an unfounded demand, because the *typus*, held fast in its intuitive form, explains itself. For anyone who has grasped that "forming of itself in accordance with itself" of the entelechical principle, this constitutes the solution of the riddle of life. Any other solution is impossible, because this solution is the essential being of the thing itself. If Darwinism has to presuppose an archetypal organism, then one can say of Goethe that he discovered the essential being of that archetypal organism.[39] It is Goethe who broke with the mere juxtaposing of genera and species, and who undertook a regeneration of organic science in accordance with the essential being of the organism. Whereas the systems before Goethe needed just as many different concepts (ideas) as there were outwardly different species for which no intermediary existed, Goethe maintained that in idea all organisms are alike, that they are different only in their manifestation; and he explained why they are so. With this, the philosophical foundation for a scientific system of organisms was created. It was then only a matter of implementing this system. It would have to be shown how all real organisms are only manifestations of an idea, and *how* they manifest themselves in a given case.

The great deed thus accomplished for science was also widely acknowledged by those more educated in the field. The younger d'Alton writes to Goethe on July 6, 1827: "I would regard it as my greatest reward if Your Excellency, whom natural science has to thank not only for *a total transformation through magnificent perspectives and new views* in botany, but also for many first-rate contributions to the field of osteology, should recognize in the accompanying pages an endeavor worthy of praise." Nees von Esenbeck, on June 24, 1820, wrote: "In your book, which you called *An Attempt to Explain the Metamorphosis of Plants*, the plant has spoken about itself among us for the first time, and, in this beautiful anthropomorphism, also captivated me while I was still young." And finally Voigt, on June 6, 1831: "With lively interest and humble thanks I have received your little book on metamorphosis, which now so obligingly includes me historically also as one of the early adherents of this theory. It is strange: one is fairer toward animal metamorphosis – I do not mean the old metamorphosis of the insects, but rather the new kind about the vertebrae – than toward plant metamorphosis. Apart from the plagiarisms and misuses, the silent recognition of animal metamorphosis may rest on the belief that one was *risking less* there. For, in the skeleton the separate bones remain ever the same, whereas in botany, metamorphosis threatens to topple the whole terminology and consequently the *determining of species*, and there weak people are afraid, because they do not know where something like that might lead." Here there is complete understanding for Goethe's ideas. The awareness is there that a new way of viewing what is individual must take place; and the new systematics, the study of particulars, should only first proceed then from this new view. The self-supporting *typus* contains the possibility of assuming endlessly manifold forms as it enters into manifestation; and these forms are the object of our sense perception, are the genera and species of the organism living in space and time. Insofar as our spirit apprehends that general idea, the *typus*, it has grasped the whole realm of organisms in all its unity. When now our spirit *beholds* the development of the *typus* in each particular form of manifestation, this form becomes comprehensible to it; this form appears to our spirit as one of the stages, one of the metamorphoses, in which the *typus* realizes itself. And the nature of the systematics to be founded by Goethe was to consist in demonstrating these different stages. In the animal, as well as in the plant realm, there holds sway an ascending evolutionary sequence; organisms are divided into highly developed and undeveloped ones. How is this possible? It is characteristic of the ideal form of the *typus* of the organisms, in fact, that it consists of spatial and temporal elements. For this reason, it also appeared to Goethe as a *sensible-supersensible* form. It contains spatial-temporal forms as ideal perception (intuitive). When the *typus* now enters into manifestation, the truly (no longer intuitive) sense-perceptible form can correspond fully to that ideal form or not; the *typus* can come to its full development or not. The lower organisms are indeed lower through the fact that their form of manifestation does not fully correspond with the organic *typus*. The more that outer manifestation and organic *typus* coincide in a given entity, the more highly developed it is. This is the objective basis of an ascending evolutionary sequence. It is the task of any systematics to demonstrate this relationship with respect to the form of every organism. In arriving at the *typus*, the archetypal organism, however, no account can be taken of this; in arriving at the *typus* it can only be a matter of finding a form that represents the most perfect expression of the *typus*. Goethe's archetypal plant is meant to provide such a form.

One has reproached Goethe for taking no account of the world of cryptogamia in arriving at his *typus*. We have indicated earlier that this could only have been so out of the fullest consciousness, since he did occupy himself also with the study of these plants. This does have its objective basis, however. The cryptogamia are in fact those plants in which the archetypal plant only comes to expression in a highly one-sided way; they represent the idea of the plant in a one-sided sense-perceptible form. They can be judged according to the idea thus set up; but this idea itself only bursts forth fully in the phanerogamia.

But what is to be said here is that Goethe never accomplished this implementation of his basic thought, that he entered too little into the realm of the particular. Therefore all his works remain fragmentary. His intention of also shedding light here is shown by his words in the *Italian Journey* (September 27, 1786) to the effect that it will be possible, with the help of his ideas, "truly to determine genera and species, which until now has occurred in a very arbitrary way, it seems to me." He did not carry out this intention, did not make a specific presentation of the connection of his general thoughts to the realm of the particular, to the reality of the individual forms. This he himself regarded as a deficiency in his fragments; with respect to this he writes to Soret von de Candolle on June 28, 1828: "It is also becoming more and more clear to me how he regards my intentions, in which I am persisting and which, in my short *essay on metamorphosis, are stated definitely enough, it is true, but whose connection with botany based on perception does not emerge clearly enough, as I have known for a long time.*" This is certainly also the reason why Goethe's views were so misunderstood; they were misunderstood only because they were *not* understood at all.

In Goethe's concepts we also gain an ideal explanation for the fact, discovered by Darwin and Haeckel, that the developmental history of the individual represents a repetition of the history of the race. For, what Haeckel puts forward here cannot after all be taken for anything more than an unexplained fact. It is the fact that every individual entity passes, in a shortened form, through all those stages of development that paleontology also shows us as separate organic forms. Haeckel and his followers explain this by the law of heredity. But heredity is itself nothing other than an *abbreviated expression* for the fact just mentioned. The explanation for it is that those forms, as well as those of the individual, are the manifest forms of one and the same archetypal image that, in successive epochs, brings to unfoldment the formative forces lying within this image as potentiality. Every higher entity is indeed more perfect through the fact that, through the favorable influences of its environment, it is not hindered in the completely free unfolding of itself in accordance with its inner nature. If, on the other hand, because of certain influences, the individual is compelled to remain at a lower stage, then only some of its inner forces come to manifestation, and then that which is only a part of a whole in a more highly developed individual is this individual's whole. And in this way the higher organism appears in its development as composed of the lower organisms, or too the lower organisms appear in their development as parts of the higher one. In the development of a higher animal, we must therefore also see again the development of all the lower ones (biogenetic law). Just as the physicist is not satisfied with merely stating and describing facts, but also seeks out their *laws* – i.e., the concepts of the phenomena – so, for the person who wants to penetrate into the nature of organic entities, it also does not suffice for him merely to cite the facts of kinship, heredity, struggle for existence, etc.; but rather he wants to know the ideas underlying these things. We find this striving in Goethe. What Kepler's three laws are for the physicist, Goethe's ideas of the *typus* are for the organic scientist. Without them, the world is a mere labyrinth of facts for us. This has often been misunderstood. One declares that the concept of metamorphosis in Goethe's sense is merely a *picture* that basically occurs only in our intellect through abstraction. That Goethe was not clear about the fact that the concept of the transformation of leaves into flower organs makes sense only if the latter, the stamens, for example, were once real leaves. However, this turns Goethe's view upside down. A sense-perceptible organ is turned into a principally primary one and the other organ is then derived from it in a sense-perceptible way. Goethe never meant it this way. For him, what is first in time is absolutely not also first with respect to the idea, to the principle: It is not because the stamens were once true leaves that they are now related to the leaves; no, but rather because they are related ideally, in accordance with their inner nature, they appeared at one time as true leaves. The sense-perceptible transformation is only the result of the ideal relatedness and not the other way around. Today, it is an established empirical fact that all the lateral organs of the plant are identical; but why does one call them identical? According to Schleiden, because these *all* develop on the axis in such a way that they are pushed forth as lateral protuberances, in such a way that lateral cell formation remains only on the original body and that no new cells form on the tip that is formed first. This is a purely external relatedness, and one considers the idea of identity to be the result of this. Again the matter is otherwise for Goethe. For him the lateral organs are identical in their idea, in their inner being; therefore they also *manifest* outwardly as identical formations. For him, sense-perceptible relatedness is a result of inner, ideal relatedness. The Goethean conception differs from the materialistic one in the way it poses its questions; the two do not contradict one another; they complement one another. Goethe's ideas provide the foundation for the other view. Goethe's ideas are not merely a poetic foreshadowing of later discoveries but rather independent principle discoveries that have not by far been valued enough and upon which natural science will still draw for a long time. Even when the empirical facts that he used shall have been far surpassed, or in part even disproven, by more exact and detailed research, still the ideas he set up are fundamental once and for all for organic science, because they are independent of those empirical facts. Just as, according to Kepler's laws, every newly discovered planet must revolve around its star, so must every process in organic nature occur according to Goethe's ideas. Long before Kepler and Copernicus, people saw the occurrences in the starry heavens. These two first found the laws. Long before Goethe, people observed the realm of organic nature; Goethe found its laws. *Goethe is the Copernicus and Kepler of the organic world.*

One can also clarify for oneself the nature of the Goethean theory in the following way. Besides ordinary empirical mechanics, which only collects the facts, there is also a rational mechanics, which, from the inner nature of the basic mechanical principles, deduces the *a priori* laws as necessary ones. As empirical mechanics relates to rational mechanics, so the theories of Darwin, Haeckel, etc., relate to the rational organic science of Goethe. About this aspect of his theory, Goethe was not at once clear from the beginning. Later, to be sure, he expressed it quite emphatically. When he writes to Heinrich Wilhelm Ferdinand Wackenroder, on January 21, 1832: "Continue to acquaint me with everything that interests you; *it will connect somewhere with my reflections,*" he means by this only that he has found the basic principles of organic science from which everything else must be derived. At an earlier time, however, this all worked unconsciously in his spirit and he just treated the facts according to it.[40] It first became objectively clear to him through that first scientific conversation with Schiller that we will describe later. Schiller recognized right away the ideal nature of Goethe's archetypal plant and declared that no reality could be consistent with such a plant. This stimulated Goethe to think about the relationship of what he called "*typus*" to empirical reality. He encountered a problem here that belongs to the most significant problems of all human investigation: the problem of the relationship between idea and reality, between thinking and experience. *This* became ever clearer to him: No one single empirical object corresponds entirely to his *typus*; no entity of nature was identical to it. The content of the *typus* concept cannot therefore stem from the sense world as such, even though it is won in the encounter with the sense world. Its content must therefore lie within the *typus* itself; the idea of the archetypal entity could only be of a kind that, by virtue of a necessity lying within itself, develops a content out of itself that then in another form – in the form of a perception – manifests within the phenomenal world. It is interesting in this regard to see how Goethe himself, when meeting empirical natural scientists, stood up for the *rights of experience* and for keeping idea and object strictly separated. In 1786, Sömmerring sends him a book in which Sömmerring makes an attempt to discover the seat of the soul. In a letter that he sends to Sömmerring on August 28, 1796, Goethe finds that Sömmerring has woven too much metaphysics into his views; an idea about objects of experience has no justification if it goes beyond these, if it is not founded in the being of the object itself. With objects of experience, the idea is an organ for grasping, in its necessary interconnection, that which otherwise would be merely perceived in a blind juxtaposition and succession. But, from the fact that the idea is not allowed to bring anything new to the object, it follows that the object itself, in its own essential being, is something ideal and that empirical reality must have two sides: one, by which it is particular, individual, and the other by which it is ideal-general.

Association with contemporary philosophers and the reading of their works led Goethe to many points of view in this respect. Schelling's work *On the World-Soul*[41] and his *Sketch of a System of Natural Philosophy*[42] as well as Steffen's *Basic Features of a Philosophical Natural Science*[43] were fruitful for him. Also a great deal was talked through with Hegel. These stimuli finally led him to take up Kant again, with whom Goethe had already once occupied himself at Schiller's instigation. In 1817 (see his *Annals*) he takes a historical look at Kant's influence upon his ideas on nature and natural things. To these reflections, going to the core of science, we owe the following essays:

Fortunate Event (Glückliches Ereignis)
Power to Judge in Beholding (Anschauende Urteilskraft)
Reflection and Devotion (Bedenken and Ergebung)
Formative Impulse (Bildungstrieb)
Apologies for the Undertaking (Das Unternehmen wird entschuldigt)
The Purpose Introduced (Die Absicht eingeleitet)

The Content Prefaced (Der Inhalt bevorwortet)
History of My Botanical Studies (Geschichte meines botanischen Studiums)
How the Essay on the Metamorphosis of the Plants Arose (Entstehen des Aufsatzes über Die Metamorphose der Pflanzen)

All these essays express the thought already indicated above, that every object has two sides: the direct one of its manifestation (form of manifestation), and the second one that contains its *being*. In this way, Goethe arrives at the only satisfactory view of nature, which establishes the one truly objective method. If a theory regards the ideas as something foreign to the object itself, as something merely subjective, then it cannot profess to be truly objective if it ever uses the idea at all. But Goethe can maintain that he adds nothing to the objects that does not already lie in the objects themselves.

Goethe also pursued the detailed factual aspects of those branches of science to which his ideas were related. In 1795, he attended lectures by Loder on the ligaments; during this period, he did not at all lose sight of anatomy and physiology, which seems all the more important since it was precisely then that he was writing his lectures on osteology. In 1796 attempts were made to grow plants in darkness and under colored glass. Later on, the metamorphosis of insects was also investigated.

A further stimulus came from the philologist F.A. Wolf, who drew Goethe's attention to his namesake Wolff who, in his *Theoria Generationis*, had already expressed ideas in 1759 that were similar to those of Goethe on the metamorphosis of the plants. Goethe was moved by this fact to concern himself more deeply with Wolff, which he did in 1807; he discovered later, however, that Wolff, with all his acuity, was not yet clear on precisely the main points. Wolff did not yet know the *typus* as something nonsense-perceptible, as something that develops its content merely out of inner necessity. He still regarded the plant as an external, mechanical complex of individual details.

Goethe's exchanges with his many scientist friends, as well as the joy of having found recognition and imitation of his endeavors among many kindred spirits, led Goethe to the thought, in 1807, of publishing the fragments of his natural-scientific studies that he had held back until then. He gradually abandoned his intention of writing a more comprehensive natural-scientific work. But the individual essays did not yet reach publication in 1807. His interest in the color theory pushed morphology into the background again for a time. The first booklet of these essays first appeared in 1817. By 1824, two volumes of these essays had appeared, the first in four booklets, the second in two. Besides the essays on Goethe's own views, we also find here discussions of significant literary publications in the realm of morphology, and also treatises of other scholars, whose presentations, however, are always complementary to Goethe's interpretation of nature.

On yet two further occasions, Goethe was challenged to occupy himself more intensively with natural-scientific matters. Both of these involved significant literary publications – in the realm of science – that related most deeply to his own strivings. On the first occasion, the stimulus was given by the studies of the botanist Martius on the spiral tendency in plants, on the second occasion, by a natural-scientific dispute in the French Academy of Sciences.

Martius saw plant form, in its development, as comprised of a spiral and a vertical tendency. The vertical tendency brings about growth in the direction of the root and stem; the spiral tendency brings about the spreading out of leaves, blossoms, etc. Goethe saw in this thought only an elaboration of ideas he had already set down in 1790 in his book on metamorphosis, but here focusing more on spatial elements (vertical, spiral). For proof of this assertion, we refer you to our comments on Goethe's essay, *On the Spiral Tendency of Vegetation*,[44] from which the fact emerges that Goethe, in this essay, does not bring forward anything essentially new with respect to his earlier ideas. We want to direct this statement particularly to those who assert that there is evident here, in fact, a retrogression of Goethe from his earlier clear views back into the "deepest depths of mysticism."

Even at a most advanced age (1830-32), Goethe still wrote two essays on the dispute between the two French natural scientists, Cuvier and Geoffroy Saint-Hilaire. In these essays we find yet once more, in striking conciseness, a synthesis of the principles of Goethe's view of nature.

Cuvier was altogether an empiricist of the old school of natural science. For each species of animal he sought a particular corresponding concept. He believed he had to take up into the conceptual edifice of his system of organic nature as many individual types as there are animal species present in nature. But for him, the individual types stood there side by side without any mediation. What he did not take into consideration is this. Our need for knowledge is not satisfied with the particular as such in the way it approaches us directly as phenomenon. But since we approach an entity of the sense world with no other intention, in fact, than of knowing it, we should not assume that the reason we declare ourselves unsatisfied with the particular as such is to be found in the nature of our ability to know. On the contrary, the reason must lie within the object itself. The essential being of the particular itself, in fact, by no means consists only in this, its particularness; it presses, in order to be understood, toward a kind of being that is not particular, but rather, general (*ein Allgemeines*). This ideal-general is the actual being – the essence – of every particular entity. Only one side of the existence of a particular entity lies in its particularness; the other side is the general – the *typus* (see Goethe's *Aphorisms in Prose*). This is how it is to be understood when the particular is spoken of as a form of the general. Since the ideal-general is therefore the actual being, the content, of the particular, it is impossible for the ideal-general to be derived, abstracted, from the particular. Since it has nowhere from which to borrow its content, it must give this content to itself. The typical-general is therefore of such a nature that, in it, content and form are identical. But it can therefore also be grasped only as a whole, independent of what is individual. Science has the task with every particular entity of showing how, according to the entity's essential being, the entity subordinates itself to the ideal-general. Through this the particular *kinds* of existence enter the stage of mutually determining and depending upon each other. What otherwise can be perceived only as spatial-temporal juxtaposition and succession is now seen in *necessary* interconnection. But Cuvier wouldn't hear of any such view. This view, on the other hand, was the one held by Geoffroy Saint-Hilaire. This is actually the aspect that aroused Goethe's interest in this dispute. The matter has often been misrepresented because one saw the facts, through the glasses of most modern views, in a completely different light than that in which they appear if one approaches them without preconceptions. Geoffroy referred not only to his own research, but also to a number of German scientists of like mind, among whom Goethe is also named.

Goethe's interest in this matter was extraordinary. He was extremely happy to find a colleague in Geoffroy Saint-Hilaire: "Now Geoffroy Saint-Hilaire is also definitely on our side and with him all his significant students and adherents in France. This event is of inconceivably great value to me, and I am right to jubilate about the final victory of something to which I have dedicated my life and which is pre-eminently also my own," he says to Eckermann on August 2, 1830. It is altogether a strange phenomenon that in Germany Goethe's research found a response only among philosophers and but little among natural scientists, whereas the response in France was more significant among the latter. De Candolle gave Goethe's theory of metamorphosis his closest attention and treated botany generally in a way that was not far from Goethean views. Also, Goethe's *Metamorphosis* had already been translated into French by F. de Gingins-Lassaraz. Under such conditions, Goethe could definitely hope that a translation of his botanical writings into French, carried out with his collaboration, would not fall on barren ground. Such a translation was then provided in 1831, with Goethe's continuous assistance, by Friedrich Jakob Soret. It contained that first *Attempt* of 1790, the history of Goethe's botanical studies, and the effect of his theories upon his contemporaries, as well as something about de Candolle, – in French, with German on the opposite page.

V

Concluding Remarks on Goethe's Morphological Views

When, at the end of this consideration of Goethe's thoughts on metamorphosis, I look back over the views that I felt compelled to express, I cannot conceal from myself the fact that a very great number of outstanding adherents of the various tendencies in scientific thought are of a different view than I. Their position with respect to Goethe is completely clear to me; and the judgment they will pronounce on my attempt to present the standpoint of our great thinker and poet is quite predictable.

The views about Goethe's strivings in the realm of natural science are separated into two opposing camps.

The adherents of modern monism, with Professor Haeckel at their head, recognize in Goethe the prophet of Darwinism who conceives of the organic completely in the Darwinian sense: as governed by the laws that are also at work in inorganic nature. The only thing Goethe lacked, they believe, was the theory of natural selection by which Darwin first *founded* the monistic worldview and which raised the theory of evolution into a scientific conviction.

Opposing this standpoint there stands another, which assumes that Goethe's idea of the *typus* is nothing more than a general concept, an idea in the sense of Platonic philosophy. According to this view, Goethe did indeed make individual statements that remind one of the theory of evolution at which he arrived through the pantheism inherent in his nature; however, he did not feel any need to go all the way to the ultimate *mechanical foundations*. Thus there can be no question of finding the theory of evolution in the modern sense in Goethe.

As I was attempting to explain Goethe's views, *without taking any definite standpoint beforehand,* purely out of Goethe's nature, out of the whole of his spirit, it became clear to me that neither the one nor the other of these two camps – extraordinarily significant as their contributions have been toward an assessment of Goethe – has interpreted his view of nature altogether correctly.

The first of the two views characterized above is entirely right in asserting that Goethe, in striving to explain organic nature, combats the dualism that assumes insuperable barriers to exist between organic nature and the inorganic world. But Goethe asserted the possibility of this explanation not because he conceived of the forms and phenomena of organic nature in a mechanistic context, but rather because he saw that the *higher* context in which they do stand is in no way closed to our knowledge. He did indeed conceive of the universe in a monistic way as an undivided unity – from which he by no means excluded the human being – but he also therefore recognized that *within* this unity levels are to be discerned that have their own laws. Already from his youth up, he reacted negatively to efforts to picture unity as uniformity and to conceive of the organic world, as well as everything that appears as higher nature in nature, as being governed by the laws at work in the inorganic world (see *History of my Botanical Studies*). It was also this rejection that later compelled him to assume the existence of a power to judge in beholding, by which we grasp organic nature, in contrast to the discursive intellect, by which we know inorganic nature. Goethe conceives of the world as a circle of circles, each of which has its own principle of explanation. Modern monists know only one single circle: that of inorganic natural laws.

The second of the two opinions about Goethe described above recognizes that with him it is a matter of something different than with modern monism. But since the adherents of this second view consider it a postulate of science that organic nature is explained in the same way as inorganic nature, and since from the very start they reject with abhorrence a view like Goethe's, they regard it as altogether useless to go more deeply into his strivings.

Thus Goethe's high principles could gain *full* validity in neither camp. And it is precisely these principles that are so outstanding in his work, which, for someone who has recognized them in all their depth, do not lose in significance even when he sees that many a *detail* of Goethean research needs to be corrected.

This fact now requires of a person who is attempting to present Goethe's views that he direct his attention away from the critical assessment of each individual thing Goethe discovered in one or another chapter of natural science, and toward what is *central* to the Goethean view of nature.

By seeking to meet this requirement, one comes close to possibly being misunderstood by precisely those by whom it would be most painful for me to be misunderstood: by the pure empiricists. I mean those who pursue in every direction the factually demonstrable relationships of organisms, the empirically given materials, and who regard the question as to the primal principles of the organic realm as one that is still open today. What I bring cannot be directed against them, because it does not touch on them. On the contrary: I build a part of my hopes precisely on them, because their hands are still free in every respect. They are also the ones who will still have to correct many an assertion of Goethe, for he did sometimes err in the factual realm; here, of course, even the genius cannot overcome the limitations of his time.

In the realm of principles, however, he arrived at fundamental views that have the same significance for organic science that Galileo's basic laws have for mechanics.

To establish this fact was the task I set myself.

I hope that those whom my words cannot convince will at least see the good will with which I strove, without respect to persons, attentive only to the subject at hand, to solve the problem I have indicated – explaining Goethe's scientific writings out of the whole of his nature – and to express a conviction that for me is uplifting.

Since one has made a fortunate and successful beginning at explaining Goethe's literary works in that way, there already lies in that the challenge to bring all the works of his spirit under this kind of study. This cannot remain unaccomplished forever, and I will not be the last among those who will heartily rejoice if my successor succeeds better than I. May youthful and striving thinkers and researchers – especially those who are not merely interested in breadth of vision, but who rather look directly at what is *central* to our knowing activity – grant my reflections some attention, and follow in great numbers to set forth more perfectly what I was striving to present.

VI

Goethe's Way of Knowledge

In June 1794, Johann Gottlieb Fichte sent the first sections of his *Theory of Science*[45] to Goethe. The latter wrote back to the philosopher on June 24: "As far as I am concerned, I will owe you the greatest thanks if you finally reconcile me with the philosophers, with whom I can never do without and with whom I have never been able to unite myself." What the poet is here seeking from Fichte is what he sought earlier from Spinoza and later from Schelling and Hegel: a philosophical worldview that would be in accordance with his way of thinking. None of the philosophical directions with which he became acquainted, however, brought the poet complete satisfaction.

This fact makes our task considerably more difficult. We want to draw nearer to Goethe from the philosophical side. If he himself had designated one standpoint of knowledge as his own, then we could refer to it. But this is not the case. And so the task devolves on us to recognize the philosophical core of all we have from the poet and to sketch a picture of it. We consider the right way to accomplish this task to be a direction in thinking that is gained upon the foundations of German idealistic philosophy. This philosophy sought, in fact, in its own way to satisfy the same *highest* human needs to which Goethe and Schiller devoted their lives. It came forth from the same contemporary stream. It therefore also stands much nearer to Goethe than do those views that to a large degree govern the sciences today. What Goethe expressed in poetic form and what he presented scientifically can be regarded as the consequence of a view that can be formed out of that philosophy. They could definitely never be the consequence of such scientific directions as our present-day ones. We are very far removed today from that way of thinking that lay in Goethe's nature.

It is indeed true that we must acknowledge progress in all areas of culture. But that this progress is one *into the depths* of things can hardly be asserted. For the content of an epoch, however, only progress into the *depths* of things is decisive, after all.

But our epoch might best be characterized by the statement: It rejects, as unattainable for man, any progress at all into the depths of things. We have become faint-hearted in all areas, especially in that of thinking and willing. With respect to thinking: one observes endlessly, stores up the observations, and lacks the courage to develop them into a scientific, whole view of reality. One accuses German idealistic philosophy of being unscientific, however, because it did have this courage. Today one wants only to *look* with one's senses, not *think*. One has lost all trust in thinking. One does not consider it able to penetrate into the mysteries of the world and of life; one altogether renounces any solution to the great riddle questions of existence. The only thing one considers possible is: *to bring what experience tells us, into a system.* But in doing so one forgets that with this view one is approaching a standpoint considered to have been overcome long ago. The rejection of all thinking and the insistence upon sense experience is, grasped more deeply, nothing more, after all, than the blind faith in revelation of the religions. The latter rests, after all, only upon the fact that the church provides finished truths that one has to believe. Thinking may struggle to penetrate into the deeper meaning of these truths; but thinking is deprived of the ability *to test the truth itself*, to penetrate by its own power into the depths of the world. And the science of experience, what does it ask of thinking? That it listen to what the facts say, and interpret, order, etc., what is heard. It also denies to thinking the ability to penetrate independently into the core of the world.

On the one hand, theology demands the blind subjection of thinking to the statements of the church; on the other, science demands blind subjection to the statements of sense observation. Here as there, independent thinking that penetrates into the depths counts as nothing. The science of experience forgets only one thing. Thousands and thousands of people have looked at a sense-perceptible fact and passed it by without noting anything striking about it. Then someone came along who looked at it and became aware of an important law about it. How? This can only stem from the fact that the discoverer knew how to look differently than his predecessors. He saw the fact with different eyes than his fellow men. In looking, he had a definite thought as to how one must bring the fact into relationship with other facts, what is significant for it and what is not. And so, *thinking*, he set the matter in order and saw more than the others. *He saw with the eyes of the spirit.* All scientific discoveries rest on the fact that the observer knows how to observe in a way governed by the right thought. *Thinking* must naturally guide observation. It cannot do so if the researcher has lost his belief in thinking, if he does not know what to make of thinking's significance. The science of experience wanders helplessly about in the world of phenomena; the sense world becomes a confusing manifoldness for it, because it does not have enough energy in thinking to penetrate into the center.

One speaks today of limits to knowledge because one does not know where the goal of thinking lies. One has no clear view of *what* one wants to attain and doubts *that* one will attain it. If someone came today and pointed out clearly to us the solution to the riddle of the world, we would gain nothing from it, because we would not know what to make of this solution.

And it is exactly the same with willing and acting. One cannot set oneself any definite task in life of which one would be capable. One dreams oneself into indefinite unclear ideals and then complains about the fact that one does not achieve something of which one hardly has a dim, let alone a clear, picture. Just ask one of the pessimists of our day what he actually wants and what it is he despairs of attaining. He does not know. Problematical natures are they all, incapable of meeting any situation and yet satisfied with none. Do not misunderstand me. I do not wish to extol that superficial optimism which, satisfied with the trivial enjoyments of life, demands nothing higher and therefore never suffers want. I do not wish to condemn individuals who painfully feel the deep tragedy that lies in the fact that we are dependent on conditions that have a laming effect on everything we do and that we strive in vain to change. But we should not forget that pain is the woof and happiness the warp. Think of the mother, how her joy in the well-being of her children is increased if it has been achieved by earlier cares, suffering, and effort. Every right-minded person would in fact have to refuse a happiness that some external power might offer him, because he cannot after all experience something as happiness that is just handed him as an unearned gift. If some creator or other had undertaken the creation of man with the thought in mind of bestowing happiness upon his likeness at the same time, as an inheritance, then he would have done better to leave him uncreated. The fact that what man creates is always ruthlessly destroyed again raises his stature; for he must always build and create anew; and it is in activity that our happiness lies; it lies in what we ourselves accomplish. It is the same with bestowed happiness as with revealed truth. Only this is worthy of man: that he seek truth himself, that neither experience nor revelation lead him. When that has been thoroughly recognized once and for all, then the religions based on revelation will be finished. The human being will then no longer want God to reveal Himself or bestow blessings upon him. He will want to know through his own thinking and to establish his happiness through his own strength. Whether some higher power or other guides our fate to the good or to the bad, this does not concern us at all; we ourselves must determine the path we have to travel. The loftiest idea of God is still the one that assumes that God, after His creation of the human being, withdrew completely from the world and gave man completely over to himself.

Whoever acknowledges to thinking its ability to perceive beyond the grasp of the senses must necessarily acknowledge that it also has objects that lie beyond merely sense-perceptible reality. The objects of thinking, however, are *ideas*. Inasmuch as thinking takes possession of the idea, thinking fuses with the primal ground of world existence; what is at work outside enters into the spirit of man: he becomes *one* with objective reality in its highest potency. *Becoming aware of the idea within reality is the true communion of man.*

Thinking has the same significance with respect to ideas as the eye has with respect to light, the ear to tone. *It is an organ of apprehension.*

This view is in a position to unite two things that are regarded today as completely incompatible: the empirical method, and idealism as a scientific worldview. It is believed that to accept the former means necessarily to reject the latter. This is absolutely not true. To be sure, if one considers the senses to be the only organs of apprehension for objective reality, then one must arrive at the above view. For, the senses offer us only such relationships of things as can be traced back to mechanical laws. And the mechanistic worldview would thus be given as the only true form of any such worldview. In this, one is making the mistake of simply overlooking the other component parts of reality that are just as objective but that *cannot* be traced back to mechanical laws. What is *objectively* given by no means coincides with what is *sense-perceptibly* given, as the mechanistic world conception believes. What is sense-perceptibly given is only half of the given. The other half of the given is ideas, which are also objects of experience – of a higher experience, to be sure, whose organ is thinking. Ideas are also accessible to the inductive method.

Today's science of sense experience follows the altogether correct method of holding fast to the given; but it adds the inadmissible assertion that this method can provide only facts of a sense-perceptible nature. Instead of limiting itself to the question of *how* we arrive at our views, this science determines from the start *what* we can see. The only satisfactory way to grasp reality is the empirical method with idealistic results. That is idealism, but not of the kind that pursues some nebulous, dreamed-up *unity of things*, but rather of a kind that seeks the concrete ideal content of reality in a way that is just as much in accordance with experience as is the search of modern hyper-exact science for the factual content.

By approaching Goethe with these views, we believe we are entering into his essential nature. We hold fast to idealism and develop it, not on the basis of Hegel's dialectic method, but rather upon a clarified higher empiricism.

This kind of empiricism also underlies the philosophy of Eduard v. Hartmann. Eduard v. Hartmann seeks the ideal unity in nature, as this does positively yield itself to a thinking that has *real content*. He rejects the merely mechanistic view of nature and the hyper-Darwinism that is stuck on externals. In science, he is the founder of a concrete monism. In history and aesthetics, he seeks concrete ideas, and does all this according to empirical inductive methods.

Hartmann's philosophy differs from mine only on the question of pessimism and through the metaphysical orientation of his system toward the "unconscious." We will consider the latter point further on in the book. But with respect to pessimism, let the following be said: What Hartmann cites as grounds *for* pessimism – i.e., for the view that nothing in the world can fully satisfy us, that pain always outweighs pleasure – that is precisely what I would designate as the *good fortune of mankind*. What he brings forward is for me only proof that it is futile to strive for happiness. We must, in fact, entirely give up any such striving and seek our destiny purely in selflessly fulfilling those ideal tasks that our reason prescribes for us. What else does this mean other than that we should seek our happiness only in *doing,* in unflagging activity?

Only the active person, indeed only the selflessly active person who seeks no recompense for his activity, fulfills his destiny. It is foolish to want to be recompensed for one's activity; there is no true recompense. Here Hartmann ought to build further. He ought to show what, with such presuppositions, can be the only mainspring of all our actions. This can, when the prospect of a goal one is striving for falls away, only be the selfless devotion to the object to which one is dedicating one's activity; *this can only be love*. Only an action out of love can be a moral one. In science, the *idea*, and in our action, *love*, must be our guiding star. And this brings us back to Goethe. "The main thing for the active person is that he do what is right; he should not worry about whether the right occurs." "Our whole feat consists in giving up our existence in order to exist" (*Aphorisms in Prose*).

I have not arrived at my worldview only through the study of Goethe or even of Hegelianism, for example. I took my start from the mechanistic-naturalistic conception of the world, but recognized that, with intensive thinking, one cannot remain there. Proceeding strictly according to natural-scientific methods, I found in objective idealism the only satisfying worldview. My *epistemology*[46] shows the way by which a kind of thinking that understands itself and is not self-contradictory arrives at this worldview. I then found that this objective idealism, in its basic features, permeates the Goethean worldview. Thus the elaborating of my views does, to be sure, for years now run parallel with my study of Goethe; and I have never found any conflict *in principle* between my basic views and the Goethean scientific activity. I consider my task fulfilled if I have been at least partially successful in, firstly, developing my standpoint in such a way that it can also become alive in other people, and secondly, bringing about the conviction that this standpoint really is the Goethean one.

VII

The Arrangement of Goethe's Natural-Scientific Writings

In the editing of Goethe's natural-scientific writings, for which I was responsible, I was guided by the thought of enlivening the study of the particulars in these writings by presenting the magnificent world of ideas that underlies them. It is my conviction that every single assertion of Goethe's acquires an entirely new sense – its *rightful sense*, in fact – if one approaches it with a full understanding for his profound and comprehensive worldview. There is no denying the fact that many of Goethe's statements on natural-scientific matters seem entirely insignificant when one considers them from the standpoint of modern science, which has progressed so far in the meantime. But this is not a matter for any further consideration at all. The point is *what a given statement of Goethe's signifies within his worldview*. Upon the spiritual heights on which the poet stands, his scientific needs are also more intense. Without scientific needs, however, there is no science. *What questions did Goethe address to nature?* That is what is important. Whether and how he answered them are matters of only secondary consideration. If today we have more adequate means, a richer experience – well, then we will succeed in finding more comprehensive solutions to the questions he posed. But my expositions are meant to show that we can do no more than just this: to proceed with our greater means upon the paths he marked out for us. What we should learn from him, therefore, above all else, is *how one should address questions to nature*.

One overlooks the main point if one does not credit Goethe with anything more than having given us many an observation that was rediscovered by later research, and that constitutes today an important part of our worldview. The important thing for him was not at all the communicated finding, but rather the way in which he arrived at it. He himself declares appropriately: "With the opinions that one risks, it is like pieces that one pushes forward on the board; they can be taken, but they have initiated a game that will be won." He arrived at a method thoroughly in accord with nature. He sought, with the help of those means available, to introduce this method into science. It may be the case that the individual results he attained by this have been transformed by the progress of science; but the scientific process that he introduced is a lasting gain for science.

These points of view could not be without influence upon the arrangement of the materials to be published. One can, with some seeming justification, ask: Why, since I have already departed from the order of the writings that has been usual until now, did I not right away take the route that seems recommended over all the others: to bring the general scientific writings in the first volume, the organic, mineralogical, and meteorological ones in the second volume, and those on physics in the third. The first volume would then contain the general points of view, and the following volumes the particular elaborations of the basic thoughts. As tempting as this might be, it could never have occurred to me to use this arrangement. In doing so, I would not have been able – coming back to Goethe's comparison once more – to achieve what I wanted: *by the pieces that are risked first, to make the plan of the game recognizable.*

Nothing was farther from Goethe's nature than taking one's start in a conscious way from general concepts. He always takes his start from *concrete facts*, compares and orders them. During this activity, the ideas underlying the facts occur to him. It is a great mistake to assert that, because of that familiar enough remark he made about the idea of *Faust*, it is not ideas that are the driving principle in Goethe's creative work. In his contemplation of things, after he has stripped away everything incidental, everything unessential, there remains something for him that is *idea* in his sense. The *method* Goethe employs remains – even there where he lifts himself to the *idea* – one that is founded upon pure experience. For, nowhere does he allow a subjective ingredient to slip into his research. He only frees the phenomena from what is incidental in order to penetrate into their deeper foundations. His subject has no other task than that of arranging the object in such a way that it discloses its innermost nature. "The true is Godlike; it does not appear directly; we must divine it from its manifestations." The point is to bring these manifestations into such a relationship that the "true" appears. The *true,* the idea, already lies within the fact that we confront in observation; we must only remove the covering that conceals it from us. The true scientific method consists in the removing of this covering. Goethe took this path. And we must follow him upon it if we wish to penetrate completely into his nature. In other words: we must begin with Goethe's studies on organic nature, *because he began with them.* Here there first revealed itself to him a rich content of ideas that we then find again as components in his general and methodological essays. If we want to understand these last, we must already have filled ourselves with that content. The essays on method are mere networks of thought for someone who is not intent upon following the path Goethe followed. As to the studies on physical phenomena: they first arose for Goethe as a consequence of his view of nature.

VIII

From Art to Science

Someone who sets himself the task of presenting the spiritual development of a thinker has to explain that thinker's particular direction in a psychological way from the facts given in his biography. But in presenting Goethe the *thinker* the task does not end there. What is asked for here is not only a justification and explanation of his specific scientific direction, but rather, and primarily, how this genius came at all to be active in the scientific realm. Goethe had to suffer much through the incorrect views of his contemporaries who could not believe it possible that poetic creativity and scientific study could be united in one soul. The important point here is above all to answer the question: What are the motives that drive the great poet to science? Did the transition from art to science lie purely in his subjective inclinations, in personal arbitrariness? Or was Goethe's artistic direction of such a kind that it had to drive him *necessarily* to science?

If the first were the case, then his simultaneous devotion to art and science would merely signify a *chance* personal enthusiasm for both these directions of human striving; we would have to do with a poet who also happened to be a thinker, and it might very well have been the case that, if his course in life had been somewhat different, he would have taken the same path in his poetry, without concerning himself with science at all. Both sides of this man would then have interested us separately, each in its own right; each on its own would perhaps have helped the progress of mankind a good deal. All this would still be the case if the two directions in spirit had also been divided between two personalities. Goethe the *poet* would then have had nothing to do with Goethe the *thinker*.

If the second were the case, then Goethe's artistic direction was of such a kind that, from within outward, it necessarily felt the urge to be supplemented by scientific thinking. Then it is utterly inconceivable that the two directions could have been divided between two personalities. Then each of the two directions interests us *not only* for its own sake but also because of its relationship to the other. Then there is an *objective* transition from art to science; there is a point at which the two meet in such a way that perfection in the one realm demands perfection in the other. Then Goethe was not following a personal inclination, but rather the direction in art to which he devoted himself awakened needs in him that could be satisfied only by scientific activity.

Our age believes itself correct in keeping art and science as far apart as possible. They are supposed to be two completely opposing poles in the cultural evolution of mankind. Science, one thinks, is supposed to sketch for us the most objective picture of the world possible; it is supposed to show us reality in a mirror; or, in other words, it is supposed to hold fast purely to the given, renouncing all subjective arbitrariness. The objective world determines the laws of science; science must subject itself to this world. Science should take the yardstick for what is true and false entirely from the objects of experience.

The situation is supposedly quite different in the case of artistic creations. Their law is given them by the self-creative power of the human spirit. For science, any interference of human subjectivity would be a falsifying of reality, a going beyond experience; art, on the other hand, grows upon the field of the subjectivity of a genius. Its creations are the productions of human imagination, not mirror images of the outer world. Outside of us, in objective existence, lies the source of scientific laws; within us, in our individuality, lies the source of aesthetic laws. The latter, therefore, have not the slightest value for knowledge; they create illusions without the slightest element of reality.

Whoever grasps the matter in this way will never become clear about the relationship of Goethean poetry to Goethean science. He will only misunderstand both. Goethe's world-historic significance lies, indeed, precisely in the fact that his art flows directly from the *primal source of all existence*, that there is nothing illusory or subjective about it, that, on the contrary, his art appears as the herald of that lawfulness that the poet has grasped by listening to the world spirit within the depths of nature's working. At this level, art becomes the interpreter of the mysteries of the world just as science is also, in a different sense.

And Goethe always conceived of art in this way. It was for him *one* of the revelations of the primal law of the world; science was for him the *other* one. For him art and science sprang from *one* source. Whereas the researcher delves down into the depths of reality in order then to express their driving powers in the form of thoughts, the artist seeks to imbue his medium with these same driving powers. "I think that one could call science the knowledge of the general, abstracted knowing; art, on the other hand, would be science turned into action; science would be reason, and art its mechanism; therefore one could also call art practical science. And finally then science could be called the theorem and art the problem." What science states as idea (theorem) is what art has to imprint into matter, becomes art's problem. "In the works of man, as in those of nature, it is the intentions that are primarily worthy of note," says Goethe. He everywhere seeks not only what is given to the senses in the outer world, but also the tendency through which it has come into being. To grasp *this* scientifically and to give it artistic form is his mission. In its own formations, nature gets itself, "in its specific forms, into a cul-de-sac"; one must go back to what ought to have come about if the tendency could have unfolded unhindered, just as the mathematician always keeps his eye, not upon this or that particular triangle, but always upon that lawfulness which underlies every possible triangle. The point is not *what* nature has created but rather the principle by which nature has created it. Then this principle is to be developed in the way that accords with its own nature, and not in the way this has occurred in each particular entity of nature in accordance with thousands of chance factors. The artist has "to evolve the noble out of the common and the beautiful out of the unformed."

Goethe and Schiller take art in all its full profundity. The beautiful is "a manifestation of secret laws of nature, that, except for the phenomenon of the beautiful, would have remained forever hidden to us." A look into the poet's *Italian Journey* suffices for us to know that this is not an empty phrase, but rather deep inner conviction. When he says the following, one can see that for him nature and art are of the same origin: "The great works of art have at the same time been brought forth by human beings according to *true and natural laws*, just as the greatest works of nature are. Everything that is arbitrary, thought-up, falls away; there is necessity, there is God." Relative to the art of the Greeks, he says in this direction: "I have the impression that they proceeded according to the same laws by which nature itself proceeds and whose tracks I am following." And about Shakespeare: "Shakespeare allies himself with the world spirit; he penetrates the world like it does; nothing is hidden to either; however, if it is the world spirit's business to preserve mysteries before, and often after, the fact, so the poet is of a mind to give the secret away."

Here we should also recall the statement about the "joyful epoch in life" that the poet owed to Kant's *Critique of the Power of Judgment*[47] and for which he actually has only the fact to thank that he here "saw creations of art and of nature each treated like the other, and that aesthetic and teleological powers of judgment illuminated each other reciprocally." "I was happy," says the poet, "that the art of poetry and comparative natural science are so closely related, through the fact that both of them are subject to the same power of judgment." In his essay, *The Significant Benefits of a Single Intelligent Word*[48] Goethe juxtaposes, with exactly the same thought in mind, his objective *poetizing* and his objective *thinking*.

Thus, to Goethe, art seems to be just as objective as science. Only the form of each is different. Each appears to flow forth from *one* being, to be the necessary stages of *one* evolution. Any view was antithetical to him that relegates art or what is beautiful to an isolated position *outside* of the total picture of human evolution. Thus he says: "In the aesthetic realm, it is not good to speak of the idea of the beautiful; in doing so, one isolates the beautiful, which after all cannot be thought of as separate." Or: "Style rests upon the deepest foundations of *knowledge*, upon the being of things, insofar as we are allowed to *know* this being in visible and tangible forms." *Art rests therefore upon our activity of knowing*. The latter has the task of recreating in thought the order according to which the world is put together; art has the task of developing in detail the idea of this order that the world-all has. The artist incorporates into his work everything about the lawfulness of the world that is attainable to him. His work thus appears as a world in miniature. Herein lies the reason why the Goethean direction in art must supplement itself with science. As art, it is already an activity of knowing. Goethe, in fact, wanted neither science nor art: *he wanted the idea.* And he expresses or represents the idea in the direction from which the idea happens to present itself to him. Goethe sought to ally himself with the world spirit, and to reveal to us how it holds sway; he did this through the medium of art or of science as required. What lay in Goethe was not any one-sided artistic or scientific striving, but rather the indefatigable urge to behold "all working forces and seeds."

In this, Goethe is still not a philosophical poet, for his literary works do not take any roundabout path through thought in arriving at a sense-perceptible form; rather they stream directly from the source of all becoming, just as his scientific research is not imbued with poetic imagination, but rather rests directly upon his becoming aware of ideas. Without Goethe's being a philosophical poet, his basic direction seems, for the philosophical observer, to be a philosophical one.

With this, the question as to whether Goethe's scientific work has any philosophical value or not takes on an entirely new form. It is a question of inferring, from what we have of Goethe's work, the underlying principles. What must we postulate in order for Goethe's scientific assertions to appear as the results of these postulates? We must express what Goethe left unexpressed, but which alone makes his views comprehensible.

IX

Goethe's Epistemology

We have already indicated in the previous chapter that Goethe's scientific worldview does not exist for us as a complete whole, developed out of one principle. We have to do only with individual manifestations from which we see how one thought or another looks in the light of his way of thinking. This is the case with his scientific works, with the brief indications he gives about one concept or another in his *Aphorisms in Prose*, and with his letters to his friends. And the artistic development of his worldview, finally, which does also offer us the most manifold clues to his basic ideas, is there for us in his literary works. By unreservedly acknowledging that Goethe never expressed his basic principles as a coherent whole, however, we are by no means accepting at the same time the validity of any assertion to the effect that Goethe's worldview does not spring from an ideal center that can be brought into a strictly scientific formulation.

We must above all be clear about what the real question here is. What it was in Goethe's spirit that worked as the inner driving principle in all his creations, that imbued and enlivened them, could not come to the fore *as such*, in its own particular nature. Just because it imbues *everything* about Goethe, it could not at the same time appear before his consciousness as *something separate*. If the latter had been the case, then it would have had to appear before his spirit as something complete and at rest instead of being, as was actually the case, continuously active and at work. The interpreter of Goethe is obliged to follow the manifold activities and manifestations of this principle, to follow its constant flow, in order then to sketch it in its ideal outlines, and as a complete whole. If we are successful in expressing, clearly and definitely, the scientific content of this principle and in developing it on all sides with scientific consistency, only then will Goethe's exoteric expositions appear in their true light, because we will see them in their evolution, from a common center.

In this chapter we will concern ourselves with Goethe's epistemology. With respect to the task of this science, a certain confusion has unfortunately arisen since Kant that we must briefly touch upon before proceeding to Goethe's relationship to this science.

Kant believed that philosophy before him had taken wrong paths because it strove for knowledge of the being of things without first asking itself how such a knowledge might be possible. He saw what was fundamentally wrong with all philosophizing before him to lie in the fact that one reflected upon the nature of the object to be known before one had examined the activity of knowing itself, with regard to what it could do. He therefore took this latter examination as his basic philosophical problem and inaugurated thereby a new direction in thought. Since then the philosophy that has based itself on Kant has expended untold scientific force in answering this question; and today more than ever, one is seeking in philosophical circles to come closer to accomplishing this task. But epistemology, which at the present time has become nothing less than the question of the day, is supposedly nothing other than the detailed answer to the question: How is knowledge possible? Applied to Goethe the question would read: How did Goethe conceive of the possibility of knowledge?

Upon closer examination, however, the fact emerges that the answering of this question may absolutely not be placed at the forefront of epistemology. If I ask about the possibility of a thing, then I must first have examined this thing beforehand. But what if the concept of knowledge that Kant and his followers have, and about which they ask if it is possible or not, proved to be totally untenable; what if this concept could not stand up to a penetrating critique? What if our cognitive process were something entirely different from that defined by Kant? Then all that work would have been for nothing. Kant accepted the customary concept of what knowing is and asked if it were possible. According to this concept, knowing is supposed to consist in making a copy of the real conditions that stand outside our consciousness and exist *in-themselves*. But one will be able to make nothing out of the possibility of knowledge until one has answered the question as to the *what* of knowing itself. The question: *What is knowing?* thereby becomes the primary one for epistemology. With respect to Goethe, therefore, it will be our task to show what Goethe pictured *knowing* to be.

The forming of a particular judgment, the establishing of a fact or a series of facts – which according to Kant one could already call knowledge – is not yet by any means knowing in Goethe's sense. Otherwise he would not have said about style that it rests upon the deepest foundations of *knowledge* and through this fact stands in contrast to simple imitation of nature in which the artist turns to the objects of nature, imitates its forms and colors faithfully, diligently, and most exactly, and is conscientious about never *distancing* himself from nature. This *distancing* of oneself from the sense world in all its directness is indicative of Goethe's view of real knowing. The directly given is *experience*. In our knowing, however, we create a picture of the directly given that contains considerably *more* than what the senses – which are after all the mediators of all experience – can provide. In order to know nature in the Goethean sense, we must not hold onto it in its factuality; rather, nature, in the process of our knowing, must reveal itself as something essentially higher than what it appears to be when it first confronts us. The school of Mill assumes that all we can do with experience is merely bring particular things together into groups that we then hold fast as abstract concepts. This is no true knowing. For, those abstract concepts of Mill have no other task than that of bringing together what is presented to the senses with all the qualities of direct experience. A true knowing must acknowledge that the direct form of the world given to sense perception is not yet its essential one, but rather that this essential form first reveals itself to us in the process of knowing. Knowing must provide us with that which sense experience withholds from us, but which is still real. Mill's knowing is therefore no true knowing, because it is only an elaborated sense experience. He leaves the things in the form our eyes and ears convey them. It is not that we should leave the realm of the experienceable and lose ourselves in a construct of fantasy, as the metaphysicians of earlier and more recent times loved to do, but rather, we should advance from the form of the experienceable as it presents itself to us in what is given to the senses, to a form of it that satisfies our reason.

The question now confronts us: How does what is directly experienced relate to the picture of experience that arises in the process of knowing? We want first to answer this question quite independently and then show that the answer we give follows from the Goethean worldview.

At first, the world presents itself to us as a manifoldness in space and time. We perceive particulars separated in space and time: this color here, that shape there; this tone now, that sound then, etc. Let us first take an example from the inorganic world and separate quite exactly what we perceive with the senses from what the cognitive process provides. We see a stone flying toward a windowpane, breaking through it, and falling to the ground after a certain time. We ask what is given here in direct experience. A series of sequential visual perceptions, originating from the places successively occupied by the stone, a series of sound perceptions as the glass shatters, the pieces of glass flying, etc. Unless someone wishes to deceive himself he must say: Nothing more is given to *direct* experience than this unrelated aggregate of acts of perception.

One also finds the same strict delimitation of what is directly perceived (sense experience) in Volkelt's excellent book *Kant's Epistemology Analysed for its Basic Principles*,[49] which belongs to the best that modern philosophy has produced. But it is absolutely impossible to see why Volkelt regards the unrelated pictures of perception as mental pictures and thereby at the very start blocks the path to any possible objective knowledge. To regard direct experience from the very start as a complex of mental pictures is, after all, a definite preconception. When I have some object or other before me, I see, with respect to it, form and color; I perceive a certain degree of hardness, etc. Whether this aggregate of pictures given to my senses is something lying outside myself, or whether it is a mere complex of mental pictures: this I cannot know from the very start. Just as little as I know from the very start – without thinking reflection – that the warmth of a stone is a result of the enwarming rays of the sun, so just as little do I know in what relationship the world given to me stands with respect to my ability to make mental pictures. Volkelt places at the forefront of epistemology the proposition "that we have a manifoldness of mental pictures of such and such kinds." That we are given a manifoldness is correct; but how do we know that this manifoldness consists of mental pictures? Volkelt, in fact, does something quite inadmissible when first he asserts that we must hold fast to what is given us in direct experience, and then makes the presupposition, which cannot be given to direct experience, that the world of experience is a world of mental pictures. When we make a presupposition like that of Volkelt, then we are forced at once into stating our epistemological question wrongly as described above. If our perceptions are mental pictures, then our whole science is a science of mental pictures and the question arises: How is it possible for our mental picture to coincide with the object of which we make a mental picture?

But where does any real science ever have anything to do with this question? Look at mathematics! It has a figure before it

arising from the intersection of three straight lines: a triangle. The three angles a, b, c remain in a fixed relationship; their sum is one straight angle or two right angles (180°). That is a mathematical judgment. The angles a, b, and c are perceived. The cognitive judgment occurs on the basis of thinking reflection. It establishes a relationship between three perceptual pictures. There is no question here of any reflecting upon some object or other standing behind the picture of the triangle. And all the sciences do it this way. They spin threads from picture to picture, create order in what, for direct perception, is a chaos; nowhere, however, does anything else come into consideration besides the given. Truth is not the coinciding of a mental picture with its object, but rather the expression of a relationship between two perceived facts.

Let us return to our example of the thrown stone. We connect the sight perceptions that originate from the individual locations in which the stone finds itself. This connection gives us a curved line (the trajectory), and we obtain the laws of trajectory; when furthermore we take into account the material composition of the glass, and then understand the flying stone as *cause*, the shattering of the glass as *effect*, and so on, we then have permeated the given with concepts in such a way that it becomes comprehensible to us. This entire operation, which draws together the manifoldness of perception into a conceptual *unity,* occurs *within* our consciousness. The ideal interrelationship of the perceptual pictures is not given by the senses, but rather is grasped absolutely on its own by our spirit. For a being endowed only with the ability to perceive with the senses, this whole operation would simply not be there. For such a being the outer world would simply remain that disconnected chaos of perceptions we characterized as what first (directly) confronts us.

So the place, therefore, where the perceptual pictures appear in their ideal relationship, where this relationship is held out to the perceptual pictures as their conceptual *counter-image*, this place is human consciousness. Now even though this conceptual (lawful) relationship, in its substantial make-up, is produced within human consciousness, it by no means follows from this that it is also only subjective in its significance. It springs, rather, in its *content* just as much from the objective world as, in its conceptual *form*, it springs from human consciousness. It is the necessary objective complement to the perceptual picture. Precisely because the perceptual picture is something incomplete, something unfinished in itself, we are compelled to add to this picture, in its manifestation as sense experience, its necessary complement. If the directly given itself were far enough along that at every point of it a problem did not arise for us, then we would never have to go beyond it. But the perceptual pictures absolutely do not follow each other and from each other in such a way that we can regard them, themselves, as reciprocally resulting from each other; they result, rather, from something else that is closed to apprehension by the senses. Conceptual apprehension approaches them and grasps also that part of reality that remains closed to the senses. Knowing would be an absolutely useless process if something complete were conveyed to us in sense experience. All drawing together, ordering, and grouping of sense-perceptible facts would have no objective value. Knowing has meaning only if we do not regard the configuration given to the senses as a finished one, if this configuration is for us a half of something that bears within itself something still higher that, however, is no longer sense-perceptible. There the human spirit steps in. It perceives that higher element. Therefore thinking must also not be regarded as bringing something to the content of reality. It is no more and no less an organ of perception than the eye or ear. Just as the eye perceives colors and the ear sounds, so thinking perceives ideas. Idealism is therefore quite compatible with the principle of empirical research. The idea is not the content of subjective thinking, but rather the result of research. *Reality, insofar as we meet it with open senses, confronts us. It confronts us in a form that we cannot regard as its true one; we first attain its true form when we bring our thinking into flux.* Knowing means: to add the perception of thinking to the half reality of sense experience so that this picture of half reality becomes complete.

Everything depends on what one conceives the relationship between idea and sense-perceptible reality to be. By sense-perceptible reality I mean here the totality of perceptions communicated to the human being by the senses. Now the most widely held view is that the concept is a means, belonging solely to human consciousness, by which consciousness takes possession for itself of the data of reality. The essential being of reality, according to this view, lies in the "in-itselfness" of the things themselves, so that, if we were really able to arrive at the primal ground of things, we would still be able to take possession only of our conceptual copy of this primal ground and by no means of the primal ground itself. This view, therefore, assumes the existence of two completely separate worlds. The objective outer world, which bears its essential being, the ground of its existence, within itself, and the subjective-ideal inner world, which is supposedly a conceptual copy of the outer world. The inner world is a matter of no concern to the objective world, is not required by it; the inner world is present only for the knowing human being. To bring about a congruence of these two worlds would be the epistemological ideal of this basic view. I consider the adherents of this view to be not only the natural-scientific direction of our time, but also the philosophy of Kant, Schopenhauer, and the Neo-Kantians, and no less so the last phase of

Schelling's philosophy. All these directions of thought are in agreement about seeking the essence of the world in something transsubjective, and about having to admit, from their standpoint, that the subjective ideal world – which is therefore for them also merely a world of mental pictures – has no significance for reality itself, but purely and simply for human consciousness alone.

I have already indicated that this view leads to the assumption of a perfect congruency between concept (idea) and perception. What is present in the latter would also have to be contained in its conceptual counterpart, only in an ideal form. With respect to content, both worlds would have to match each other completely. The conditions of spatial-temporal reality would have to repeat themselves exactly in the idea; only, instead of perceived extension, shape, color, etc., the corresponding mental pictures would have to be present. If I were looking at a triangle, for example, I would have to follow in thought its outline, size, directions of its sides, etc., and then produce a conceptual photograph of it for myself. In the case of a second triangle, I would have to do exactly the same thing, and so on with every object of the external and internal sense world. Thus every single thing is to be found again exactly, with respect to its location and characteristics, within my ideal world picture.

We must now ask ourselves: Does the above assumption correspond to the facts? Not in the least. My concept of the triangle is a single one, comprising every single perceived triangle; and no matter how often I picture it, this concept always remains the same. My various pictures of the triangle are all identical to one another. I have absolutely only one concept of the triangle.

Within reality, every single thing presents itself as a particular, quite definite "this," surrounded by equally definite, actual, and reality-imbued "those." The concept, as a strict unity, confronts this manifoldness. In the concept there is no separation, no parts; it does not multiply itself; it is, no matter how often it is pictured, always the same.

The question now arises: What is then actually the bearer of this identity that the concept has? Its form of manifestation as a picture cannot in fact be this bearer, for Berkeley was completely right in maintaining that my present picture of a tree has absolutely nothing to do with my picture of the same tree a minute later, if I closed my eyes in between; and the various pictures that several people have of *one* object have just as little to do with each other. The identity can therefore lie only within the content of the picture, within its *what*. The significance, the content, must insure the identity for me.

But since this is so, that view collapses which denies to the concept or idea any independent content. This view believes, namely, that the conceptual unity as such is altogether without any content; that this unity arises solely through the fact that certain characteristics of the objects of experience are left aside and that what they have in common, on the other hand, is lifted out and incorporated into our intellect so that we may comfortably bring together the manifoldness of objective reality according to the principle of grasping all of experience with the mind in the fewest possible general unities – i.e., according to the principle of the smallest measure of force (*Kraftmasses*). Along with modern natural philosophy Schopenhauer takes this standpoint. But this standpoint is presented with the harshest, and therefore most one-sided consistency in the little book of Richard Avenarius, *Philosophy as Thinking about the World According to the Principle of the Smallest Measure of Force. Prolegomena of a Critique of Pure Experience.*[50]

But this view rests solely upon a total misconstruing not only of the content of the concept but also of the perception.

In order to gain some clarity here, one must go back to the reason for contrasting the perception, as something particular, with the concept, as something general.

One must ask oneself the question: Wherein do the characteristic features of the particular actually lie? Can these be determined conceptually? Can we say: *This* conceptual unity must break up into this or that particular, visible manifoldness? "No," is the very definite answer. The concept itself does not know particularity at all. The latter must therefore lie in elements that are altogether inaccessible to the concept as such. But since we do not know any in-between entity between the perception and the concept – unless one wishes to introduce something like Kant's fantastic-mystical schemata, which today, however, cannot be taken seriously after all – these elements must belong to the perception itself. The basis for particularization cannot be derived from the concept, but rather must be sought within the perception itself. What constitutes the particularity of an object cannot be *grasped conceptually*, but only *perceived*. Therein lies the reason why every philosophy must founder that wants to derive (deduce) from the concept itself the entire visible reality in all its particularization. Therein lies also the classic error of Fichte, who wanted to derive the whole world from consciousness.

But someone who wants to reproach and dismiss idealistic philosophy because he sees this impossibility of deriving the world from the concept as a defect in it – such a person is acting no more intelligently than the philosopher Krug, a follower of Kant, who demanded of the philosophy of identity that it deduce for him a pen with which to write.

What really distinguishes the perception essentially from the idea is, in fact, just this element that cannot be brought into the concept and that must, in fact, be experienced. Through this, concept and perception confront each other, to be sure, as kindred yet different sides of the world. And since the perception requires the concept, as we have shown, the perception proves that it does not have its essence in its particularity but rather in its conceptual generality. But this generality, in its manifestation, can first be found only within the subject; for, this generality can indeed be gained *in connection with* the object, but not *out of* the object.

The concept cannot derive its content from experience, for it does not take up into itself precisely that which is characteristic of experience: its particularity. Everything that constitutes this particularity is foreign to the concept. The concept must therefore give itself its own content.

It is usually said that an object of experience is individual, is a lively perception, and that the concept, on the other hand, is abstract, is poor, sorry, and empty when compared to the perception with its rich content. But wherein is the wealth of differentiations sought? In their number, which because of the infinitude of space can be infinitely great. For all this, however, the concept is no less richly defined. The number there is replaced by qualities here. But just as in the concept the numbers are not to be found, so in the perception the dynamic-qualitative character is lacking. The concept is just as individual, just as rich in content, as the perception. The difference is only that for grasping the content of perception nothing is necessary except open senses and a purely passive attitude toward the outer world, whereas the ideal core of the world must arise in man's spirit through his own spontaneous activity, if this core is to come into view at all. It is an entirely inconsequential and useless kind of talk to say that the concept is the enemy of living perception. The concept is the essential being of the perception, the actual driving and active principle in it; the concept adds its content to that of the perception, without eliminating the latter – for, the content of perception as such does not concern the concept at all – and the concept is supposed to be the enemy of perception! It is an enemy of perception only when a philosophy that does not understand itself wants to spin the whole rich content of the sense world out of the idea. For then philosophy conveys a system of empty phrases instead of living nature.

Only in the way we have indicated can a person arrive at a satisfactory explanation of what knowledge of experience actually is. The necessity of advancing to conceptual knowledge would be totally incomprehensible if the concept brought nothing new to sense perception. A knowledge purely of experience must not take one step beyond the millions of particulars that lie before us as perceptions. The science of pure experience, in order to be consistent, must negate its own content. For why create once more in concept form what is already there without it as perception? A consistent positivism, in the light of these reflections, would simply have to cease all scientific work and rely merely upon whatever happens to occur. If it does not do this, then it carries out in practice what it rejects in theory. It is altogether the case that materialism, as well as realism, implicitly admits what we are maintaining. The way they proceed is only justified from *our* standpoint and is in the most glaring contradiction to their own basic theoretical views.

From our standpoint, the necessity for scientific knowledge and the transcending of sense experience can be explained without any contradictions. The sense world confronts us as that which is first and directly given; it faces us like an immense riddle, because we can never find in the sense world itself what is driving and working in it. Reason enters then and, with the ideal world that it presents, holds out to the sense world the principle being that constitutes the solution to the riddle. These principles are just as objective as the sense world is. The fact that they do *not* come into appearance to the senses but only to reason does not affect their content. If there were no thinking beings, these principles would, indeed, never come into appearance; but they would not therefore be any less the essence of the phenomenal world.

With this we have set up a truly immanent worldview in contrast to the transcendental one of Locke, Kant, the later Schelling, Schopenhauer, Volkelt, the Neo-Kantians, and modern natural scientists.

They seek the ground of the world in something foreign to consciousness, in the beyond; immanent philosophy seeks it in what comes into appearance for reason. The transcendental worldview regards conceptual knowledge as a picture of the world; the immanent worldview regards it as the world's highest form of manifestation. The first view can therefore provide only a formal epistemology that bases itself upon the question: *What is the relationship between thinking and real being?* The second view places at the forefront of its epistemology the question: What is knowing? The first takes its start from the preconception that there is an essential difference between thinking and real being; the second begins, without preconceptions, with what alone is certain – thinking – and knows that, other than thinking, it can find no real being.

If we now summarize the results we have achieved from these epistemological reflections, we arrive at the following: We have to take our start from the completely indeterminate direct form of reality, from what is given to the senses before we bring our thinking into movement, from what is *only* seen, *only* heard, etc. The point is that we be aware what the senses convey to us and what thinking conveys. The senses do not tell us that things stand in any particular relationship to each other, such as for example that *this* is the cause and *that* is the effect. For the senses, all things are equally essential for the structure of the world. *Unthinking* observation does not know that a seed stands at a higher level of development than a grain of sand on the road. For the senses they are both of equal significance if they look the same outwardly. At this level of observation, Napoleon is no more important in world history than Jones or Smith in some remote mountain village. This is as far as present-day epistemology has advanced. That it has by no means thought these truths through exhaustively, however, is shown by the fact that almost all epistemologists make the mistake – with respect to this for the moment undefined and indeterminate configuration that we confront in the first stage of our perception – of immediately designating it as "*mental picture.*"[51] This means, in fact, a violating, in the crudest way, of its own insight that it had just achieved. If we remain at the stage of direct sense perception, we know just as little that a falling stone is a *mental picture* as we know that it is the *cause* of the depression in the ground where it hit. Just as we can arrive at the concept "cause" only by manifold reflection, so also we could arrive at the knowledge that the world given us is merely mental picture – even if this were correct – only by thinking about it. My senses reveal nothing to me as to whether what they are communicating to me is real being or whether it is merely mental picture. The sense world is there like a shot (*wie aus der Pistole geschossen*). If we want to have it in its purity, we must refrain from attaching any predicate to it that would characterize it. We can say only one thing: It confronts us; it is given us. With this, however, absolutely nothing at all is determined about it itself. Only when we proceed in this way do we not block the way for ourselves to an unbiased judgment about this given. If from the very start we attach a particular characterization to the given, then this freedom from bias ceases. If we say, for example, that the given is mental picture, then the whole investigation that follows can only be conducted under this presupposition. We would not be able in this way to provide an epistemology free of presuppositions, but rather would be answering the question "What is knowing?" *under the presupposition* that what is given to the senses is mental picture. That is the basic mistake in Volkelt's epistemology. At the beginning of it, he sets up the very strict requirement that epistemology must be *free of any presuppositions*. But he then places in the forefront the statement that what we have is a manifoldness of mental pictures. Thus his epistemology consists only in answering the question: How is knowing possible, under the presupposition that the given is a manifoldness of mental pictures? For us the matter appears quite different. We take the given as it is: as a manifoldness of – something or other that will reveal itself to us if we allow ourselves to be taken along by it. Thus we have the prospect of arriving at an objective knowledge, because we are allowing the object itself to speak. We can hope that this configuration we confront will reveal everything to us we need, if we do not make it impossible, through some hindering preconception, for it freely to approach our power of judgment with its communications. For even if reality should forever remain a riddle to us, a truth like this would be of value only if it had been attained in connection with the things of the world. It would be totally meaningless, however, to assert that our consciousness is constituted in such and such a way and that therefore we cannot gain any clarity about the things of this world. Whether our spiritual powers are adequate for grasping the essential being of things must be tested by us in connection with these things themselves. I might have the most highly developed spiritual powers; but if things reveal nothing about themselves, my gifts are of no avail. And conversely: I might know that my powers are slight; whether, in spite of this, they still might not suffice for me to know the things, this I still do not know.

What we have recognized in addition is that the directly given, in the first form of it that we have described, leaves us unsatisfied. It confronts us like a challenge, like a riddle to be solved. It says to us: I am there; but in the form in which I confront you there, I am not in my true form. As we hear this voice from outside, as we become aware that we are confronting a half of something, are confronting an entity that conceals its better side from us, then there announces itself within us the activity of that organ through which we can gain enlightenment about that other side of reality, and through which we are able to supplement that half of something and render it whole. We become aware that we must make up through thinking for what we do not see, hear, etc. Thinking is called upon to solve the riddle with which perception presents us.

We will first become clear about this relationship when we investigate why we are *unsatisfied* by perceptible reality, but are *satisfied*, on the other hand, by a thought-through reality. Perceptible reality confronts us as something finished. It is just there; we have contributed nothing to its being there in the way it is. We feel ourselves confronted, therefore, by a foreign entity that we have not produced, at whose production we were not even, in fact, present. We stand before something that has already come about. But we are able to grasp only something about which we know how it has become what it is, how it has come about; when we know where the strings are that support what appears before us. With our thinking, this is different. A thought-configuration does not come before me unless I myself participate in its coming about; it comes into the field of my perception only through the fact that I myself lift it up out of the dark abyss of imperceptibility. The thought does not arise in me as a finished entity the way a sense perception does, but rather I am conscious of the fact that, when I do hold fast to a concept in its complete form, I myself have brought it into this form. What then lies before me appears to me not as something *first*, but rather as something *last*, as the completion of a process that is so integrally merged with me that I have always stood within it. But this is what I must demand of a thing that enters the horizon of my perception, in order to understand it. Nothing may remain obscure to me; nothing may appear closed off; I myself must follow it to that stage at which it has become something finished. This is why the direct form of reality, which we usually call *experience*, moves us to work it through in knowledge. When we bring our thinking into movement, we then go back to the determining factors of the given that at first remained hidden to us; we work our way up from the product to the production; we arrive at the stage where sense perception becomes transparent to us in the same way the thought is. Our need for knowledge is thus satisfied. We can therefore come to terms with a thing in knowledge only when we have completely (thoroughly) penetrated with thinking what is directly perceived. A process of the world appears completely penetrated by us only when the process is our own activity. A thought appears as the completion of a process within which we stand. Thinking, however, is the only process into which we can completely place ourselves, into which we can merge. Therefore, to our knowing contemplation, the reality we experience must appear to emerge as though out of a thought-process, in the same way as pure thought does. To investigate the essential being of a thing means to begin at the center of the thought-world and to work from there until a thought-configuration appears before our soul that seems to us to be identical to the thing we are experiencing. When we speak of the essential being of a thing or of the world altogether, we cannot therefore mean anything else at all than the grasping of reality as *thought*, as *idea*. In the idea we recognize that from which we must derive everything else: the principle of things. What philosophers call the absolute, the eternal being, the ground of the world, what the religions call God, this we call, on the basis of our epistemological studies: the *idea*. Everything in the world that does not appear *directly* as idea will still ultimately be recognized as going forth from the idea. What seems, on superficial examination, to have no part at all in the idea is found by a deeper thinking to stem from it. No other form of existence can satisfy us except one stemming from the idea. Nothing may remain away from it; everything must become a part of the great whole that the idea encompasses. The idea, however, requires no going out beyond itself. It is self-sustained being, well founded in itself. This does not lie at all in the fact that we have the idea directly present in our consciousness. This lies in the nature of the idea itself. If the idea did not itself express its own being, then it would in fact also appear to us in the same way the rest of reality does: needing explanation. But this then seems to contradict what we said earlier, that the idea appears in a form satisfying to us because we participate actively in its coming about. But this is not due to the organization of our consciousness. If the idea were not a being founded upon itself, then we could not have any such consciousness at all. If something does not have *within* itself the center from which it springs, but rather has it *outside* itself, then, when it confronts me, I cannot declare myself satisfied with it; I must go out beyond it, to that center, in fact. Only when I meet something that does not point out beyond itself, do I then achieve the consciousness: now you are standing within the center; here you can remain. *My consciousness that I am standing within a thing is only the result of the objective nature of this thing, which is that it brings its principle along with it.* By taking possession of the idea, we arrive at the core of the world. What we grasp there is that from which everything goes forth. We become united with this principle; therefore the idea, which is most objective, appears to us at the same time as most subjective.

Sense-perceptible reality is such a riddle for us precisely because we do not find its center within itself. It ceases to be a riddle for us when we recognize that sense-perceptible reality has the *same* center as the thought-world that comes to manifestation *within us*.

This center can only be a *unified* one. It must in fact be of such a kind that everything else points to it as that which explains it. If there were several centers to the world – several principles by which the world were to be known – and if one region of reality pointed to *this* world principle and another one to *that* world principle, then, as soon as we found ourselves in one region of reality, we would be directed only toward the one center. It would not occur to us at all to ask about still other centers. One region would know nothing about the other. They would simply not be there for each other. It therefore makes no sense at all to speak of more than one world. The *idea*, therefore, in all the places of the world, in all consciousnesses, is *one and the same*. The fact that there are different consciousnesses and that each of them presents the idea to itself does not change the situation at all. The ideal content of the world is founded upon itself, is complete within itself. We do not create it, we only seek to grasp it. Thinking does not create it but rather perceives it only. Thinking is not a producer, but rather an organ of apprehension. Just as different eyes see one and the same object, so different consciousnesses think one and the same thought-content. Manifold consciousnesses think one and the same thing; only, they approach this one thing from different sides. It therefore appears to them as modified in manifold ways. This modification does not occur because the objects are different, however, but because they are apprehended from different angles of vision. The differences in people's views are just as explainable as the differences that a landscape presents to two observers standing in different places. If one is capable at all of pressing forward to the world of ideas, then one can be certain that one ultimately has a world of ideas that is common to all human beings. Then at most it can still be a question of our grasping this world in a quite one-sided way, of our taking a standpoint from which this world of ideas does not appear to us in the most suitable light, and so on.

We never do confront a sense world completely devoid of all thought-content. At most, in early childhood where there is as yet no trace of thinking, do we come close to pure sense perception. In ordinary life we have to do with an experience that is half-permeated by thinking, that already appears more or less lifted out of the darkness of perception into the bright clarity of spiritual comprehension. The sciences work toward the goal of fully overcoming this darkness and of leaving nothing in experience that has not been permeated with thought. Now what task has epistemology fulfilled with respect to the other sciences? It has made clear to us what the purpose and task of any science is. It has shown us what the significance is of the content of the individual sciences. *Our epistemology is the science that characterizes all the other sciences.* It has made clear to us that what is gained by the individual sciences is the objective ground of world existence. The sciences arrive at a series of concepts; epistemology teaches us about the actual task of these concepts. By arriving at this distinctive conclusion, our epistemology, which is in keeping with the sense of Goethe's way of thinking, diverges from all other epistemologies of the present day. Our epistemology does not merely want to establish a formal connection between thinking and real being; it does not want to solve the epistemological problem in a merely logical way; it wants to arrive at a positive result. It shows *what* the content of our thinking is; and it finds that this *what* is at the same time the objective content of the world. Thus epistemology becomes for us the most significant of the sciences for the human being. It gives man clarity about himself; it shows him his place in the world; it is thereby a source of satisfaction for him. *It* first tells him what he is called to be and to do. The human being feels himself uplifted in his possession of its truths; his scientific investigation gains a new illumination. Now he knows for the first time that he is most directly connected with the core of world existence, that *he* uncovers this core that remains hidden to all other beings, that in him the world spirit comes to manifestation, that the world spirit dwells within him. He sees himself as the one who completes the world process; he sees that he is called to accomplish what the other powers of the world are not able to do, that he has to set the crown upon creation. If religion teaches that God created man in His own image, then our epistemology teaches us that God has led His creation only to a certain point. There He let the human being arise, and the human being, by knowing himself and looking about him, sets himself the task of working on, of completing what the primal power began. The human being immerses himself in the world and recognizes how he can build further on the ground that has been laid; he grasps the indication that the primal spirit has made and carries out this indication. *Thus* epistemology is the teaching both of the significance and of the vocation (*Bestimmung*) of man; and it solves this task (of the "vocation of man") in a far more definite way than Fichte did at the turn of the eighteenth into the nineteenth century. One does not by any means achieve, through the thought-configurations of this powerful spirit, the same full satisfaction that must come to us from a genuine epistemology.

We have the task, with regard to every single entity, of working upon it in such a way that it appears as flowing from the idea, that it completely dissolves as a single thing and merges with the *idea,* into whose element we feel ourselves transferred. *Our spirit has the task of developing itself in such a way that it is capable of seeing into all the reality given it, of seeing it in the way it appears as going forth from the idea.* We must show ourselves to be continuous workers in the sense that we transform every object of experience so that it appears as part of our ideal world picture. With this we have arrived at where the Goethean way of looking at the world takes its start. We must apply what we have said in such a way that we picture to ourselves that the relation between idea and reality that we have just presented is what Goethe actually does in his investigations; Goethe grapples with things in just the way we have shown to be the valid one. He himself sees his inner working, in fact, as a living helper in learning (*Heuristik*), a helper that recognizes an unknown, dimly-sensed rule (the idea) and resolves to find it in the outer world and to introduce it into the outer world (*Aphorisms in Prose*). When Goethe demands that the human being should instruct his organs (*Aphorisms in Prose*), that also means only that the human being does not simply give himself over to what his senses convey to him, but rather directs his senses in such a way that they show him things in the right light.

X

Knowing and Human Action in the Light of the Goethean Way of Thinking

1. Methodology

We have established what the relationship is between the world of ideas – attained by scientific thinking – and directly given experience. We have learned to know the beginning and end of a process: experience devoid of ideas and idea-filled apprehension of reality. Between the two, however, there lies human activity. The human being must actively allow the end to go forth from the beginning. The way in which he does this is the method. It is of course the case, now, that our apprehension of that relationship between the beginning and end of knowledge will also require its own characteristic method. Where must we begin in developing this method? Scientific thinking must prove itself, step by step, to represent an overcoming of that dark form of reality that we have designated as the directly given, and to represent a lifting up of the directly given into the bright clarity of the idea. The method must therefore consist in our answering the question, with respect to each thing: What part does it have in the unified world of ideas; what place does it occupy in the ideal picture that I make for myself of the world? When I have understood this, when I have recognized how a thing connects itself with my ideas, then my need for knowledge is satisfied. There is only one thing that is not satisfying to my need for knowledge: when a thing confronts me that does not want to connect anywhere with the view I hold of things. The ideal discomfort must be overcome that stems from the fact that there is something or other of which I must say to myself: I see that it is there; when I approach it, it faces me like a question mark; but I find nowhere, within the harmony of my thoughts, the point at which I can incorporate it; the questions I must ask upon seeing it remain unanswered, no matter how I twist and turn my system of thoughts. From this we can see what we need when we look at anything.

When I approach it, it faces me as a single thing. Within me the thought-world presses toward that spot where the concept of the thing lies. I do not rest until that which confronted me at first as an individual thing appears as a part of my thought-world. Thus the individual thing as such dissolves and appears in a larger context. Now it is illuminated by the other thought-masses; now it is a serving member; and it is completely clear to me what it signifies within the greater harmony. This is what takes place in us when we approach an object of experience and contemplate it. All progress in science depends upon our becoming aware of the point at which some phenomenon or other can be incorporated into the harmony of the thought-world. Do not misunderstand me. This does not mean that every phenomenon must be explainable by concepts we already have, that our world of ideas is closed, nor that every new experience must coincide with some concept or other *that we already possess*. That pressing of the thought-world within us toward a concept can also go to a spot that has not yet been thought by anyone at all. And the ideal progress of the history of science rests precisely on the fact that thinking drives new configurations of ideas to the surface. Every such thought-configuration is connected by a thousand threads with all other possible thoughts – with this concept in this way, and with another in that. *And the scientific method consists in the fact that we show the concept of a certain phenomenon in its relationship with the rest of the world of ideas.* We call this process the deriving (demonstrating) of the concept. All scientific thinking, however, consists only in our finding the existing transitions from concept to concept, consists in our letting one concept go forth from another. The movement of our thinking back and forth from concept to concept: this is scientific method. One will say that this is the old story of the correspondence between the conceptual world and the world of experience. If we are to believe that the going back and forth from concept to concept leads to a picture of reality, then we would have to presuppose that the world outside ourselves (the transsubjective) would correspond to our conceptual world. But that is only a mistaken apprehension of the relationship between individual entity and concept. When I confront an entity from the world of experience, I absolutely do not know at all *what* it is. Only when I have overcome it, when its concept has lighted up for me, do I then know *what* I have before me. But this does not mean to say that this individual entity and the concept are two *different* things. No, they are the same; and what confronts me in this particular entity is nothing other than the *concept*. The reason I see that entity as a separate piece detached from the rest of reality is, in fact, that I do not yet know it in its true nature, that it does not yet confront me as *what* it is. This gives us the means of further characterizing our scientific method. Every individual entity of reality represents a definite content within our thought-system. Every such entity is founded in the wholeness of the world of ideas and can be comprehended only in connection with it. Thus each thing must necessarily call upon a twofold thought activity. First the thought corresponding to the thing has to be determined in clear contours, and after this all the threads must be determined that lead from this thought to the whole thought-world. Clarity in the details and depth in the whole are the two most significant demands of reality. The former is the intellect's concern, the latter is reason's. The intellect (*Verstand*) creates thought-configurations for the individual things of reality. It fulfills its task best the more exactly it delimits these configurations, the sharper the contours are that it draws. Reason (*Vernunft*) then has to incorporate these configurations into the harmony of the whole world of ideas. This of course presupposes the following: Within the content of the thought-configurations that the intellect creates, that unity already exists, living one and the same life; only, the intellect keeps everything artificially separated. Reason then, without blurring the clarity, merely eliminates the separation again. The intellect distances us from reality; reason brings us back to it again. Graphically this can be represented in the following way:

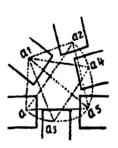

In this diagram everything is connected; the same principle lives in all the parts. The intellect causes the separation of the individual configurations – because they do indeed confront us in the given as *individual elements*[52] – and reason recognizes the unity.[53] If we have the following two perceptions: 1. the sun shining down and 2. a warm stone, the intellect keeps both things apart, because they confront us as two; it holds onto one as the cause and onto the other as the effect; then reason supervenes, tears down the wall between them, and recognizes the *unity in the duality.* All the concepts that the intellect creates – cause and effect, substance and attribute, body and soul, idea and reality, God and world, etc. – are there only in order to keep unified reality separated artificially into parts; and reason, without blurring the content thus created, without mystically obscuring the clarity of the intellect, has then to seek out the inner unity in the multiplicity. Reason thereby comes back to that from which the intellect had distanced itself: to the unified reality. If one wants an exact nomenclature, one can call the formations of the intellect "*concepts*" and the creations of reason "*ideas.*" And one sees that the path of science is to lift oneself through the concept to the idea. And here is the place where the subjective and the objective element of our knowing differentiates itself for us in the clearest way. It is plain to see that the separation has only a subjective existence, that it is only created by our intellect. It cannot hinder me from dividing one and the same objective unity into thought-configurations that are different from those of a fellow human being; this does not hinder my reason, in its connecting activity, from attaining the same objective unity again from which we both, in fact, have taken our start. Let us represent symbolically a unified configuration of reality (figure 1). I divide it intellectually thus (figure 2); another person divides it differently (figure 3). We bring it together in accordance with reason and obtain the same configuration.

Fig. 1   Fig. 2   Fig. 3

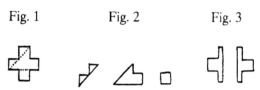

This makes it explainable to us how people can have such different concepts, such different views of reality, in spite of the fact that reality can, after all, only be one. *The difference lies in the difference between our intellectual worlds.* This sheds light for us upon the development of the different scientific standpoints. We understand where the many philosophical standpoints originate, and do not need to bestow the palm of truth exclusively upon one of them. We also know which standpoint we ourselves have to take with respect to the multiplicity of human views. We will not ask exclusively: What is true, what is false? We will always investigate how the intellectual world of a thinker goes forth from the world harmony; we will seek to understand and not to judge negatively and regard at once as error that which does not correspond with our own view. Another source of differentiation between our scientific standpoints is added to this one through the fact that every individual person has a different field of experience. Each person is indeed confronted, as it were, by one section of the whole of reality. His intellect works upon this and is his mediator on the way to the idea. But even though we all do therefore perceive the same idea, still we always do this from different places. Therefore, only the *end result* to which we come can be the *same*; our *paths*, however, can be *different*. It absolutely does not matter at all whether the individual judgments and concepts of which our knowing consists correspond to each other or not; the only thing that matters is that they ultimately lead us to the point *that we are swimming in the main channel of the idea.* And all human beings must ultimately meet each other in this channel if energetic thinking leads them out of and beyond their own particular standpoints. It can indeed be possible that a limited experience or an unproductive spirit leads us to a *one-sided*, incomplete view; but even the smallest amount of what we experience must ultimately lead us to the idea; for we do not lift ourselves to the idea through a lesser or greater experience, but rather through our abilities as a human personality alone. A limited experience can only result in the fact that we *express* the idea in a one-sided way, that we have limited means at our command for bringing to expression the light that shines in us; a limited experience, however, cannot hinder us altogether from allowing that light to shine within us. Whether our scientific or even our general *worldview* is also complete or not is an altogether different question; as is that about the spiritual depth of our views. If one now returns to Goethe, one will recognize that many of his statements, when compared with what we have presented in this chapter, simply follow from it. We consider this to be the only correct relationship between an author and his interpreter. When Goethe says: "If I know my relationship to myself and to the outer world, then I call it truth. And in this way each person can have his own truth, and it is after all always the same one" (*Aphorisms in Prose*), this can be understood only if we take into account what we have developed here.

2. Dogmatic and Immanent Methods

A scientific judgment (*Urteil*) comes about through the fact that we either join two concepts together or join a perception to a concept. The judgment that there is no effect without a cause belongs to the first kind; the judgment that a tulip is a plant belongs to the second kind. Daily life also recognizes judgments where one perception is joined to another, for example when we say that a rose is red. When we make a judgment, we do so for one reason or another. Now, there can be two different views about this reason. One view assumes that the *factual* (objective) reasons for our judgment being true lie beyond what is given us in the concepts or perceptions that enter into the judgment. *According to this view, the reason a judgment is true does not coincide with the subjective reasons out of which we make this judgment.* Our *logical* reasons, according to this view, have nothing to do with the *objective* reasons. It may be that this view proposes some way or other of arriving at the objective reasons for our insight; the means that our *knowing thinking* has are not adequate for this. For my knowing, the objective entity that determines my conclusion lies in a world unknown to me; my conclusion, along with its formal reasons (freedom from contradictions, being supported by various axioms, etc.), lies only within my world. A science based on this view is a *dogmatic* one. Both the theologizing philosophy that bases itself on a belief in revelation, and the modern science of experience are dogmatic sciences of this kind; for there is not only a *dogma of revelation*; there is also a *dogma of experience*. The dogma of revelation conveys truths to man about things that are totally removed from his field of vision. He does not know the world concerning which the ready-made assertions are prescribed for his belief. He cannot get at the grounds for these assertions. He can therefore never gain any insight as to why they are true. He can gain no *knowledge*, only *faith*. On the other hand, however, the assertions of the science of experience are also merely dogmas; it believes that one should stick merely to pure experience and only observe, describe, and systematically order its transformations, without lifting oneself to the determining factors that are *not yet* given within mere direct experience. In this case also we do not in fact gain the truth through insight into the matter, but rather it is forced upon us from outside. I see what is happening and what is there; and register it; why it is this way lies in the object. I see only the results, not the reason. The *dogma of revelation* once ruled science; today it is the *dogma of experience* that does so. It was once considered presumptuous to reflect upon the *preconditions* of revealed truths; today it is considered impossible to know anything other than what the facts express. As to why they are as they are and not something different, this is considered to be unexperienceable and therefore inaccessible.

Our considerations have shown that it is nonsensical to assume any reason for a judgment being *true* other than our reason for *recognizing* it as true. When we have pressed forward to the point where the being of something occurs to us as idea, we then behold in the idea something totally complete in itself, something self-supported and self-sustaining; it demands no further explanation from outside at all, so we can stop there. We see in the idea – if only we have the capacity for this – that it has everything that constitutes it within itself, that with it we have everything we could ask. The entire ground of existence has merged with the idea, has poured itself into it, unreservedly, in such a way that we have nowhere else to seek it except in the idea. In the idea we do not have a *picture* of what we are seeking in addition to the things; we have what we are seeking itself. When the parts of our world of ideas flow together in our judgments then it is the content of these parts itself that brings this about, not reasons lying outside them. The substantial and not merely the formal reasons for our conclusions are directly present within our thinking.

That view is thereby rejected that assumes an absolute reality – outside the ideal realm – by which all things, including thinking, are carried. For that worldview, the foundation for what exists cannot be found at all within what is accessible to us. This foundation is not innate (*eingeboren*) to the world lying before us; it is present outside this world, an entity unto itself, existing alongside this world. One can call that view *realism*. It appears in two forms. It either assumes a multiplicity of real beings underlying the world (Leibniz, Herbart), or a *uniform* real (Schopenhauer). Such an *existent real* can never be recognized as identical with the idea; it is already presupposed to be essentially different from the idea. Someone who becomes aware of the clear sense of the question as to the essential being of phenomena cannot be an adherent of this realism. What does it mean then to ask about the *essential being* of the *world*? It means nothing more than that, when I approach a thing, a voice makes itself heard in me that tells me that the thing is ultimately something quite else in addition to what I perceive with my senses. What it is in addition is already working in me, presses in me toward manifestation, while I am seeing the thing outside me. Only because the world of ideas working in me presses me to explain, out of it, the world around me, do I demand any such explanation. For a being in whom no ideas are pressing up, the urge is not there to *explain* the things any further; he is fully satisfied with the sense-perceptible phenomenon. The demand for an explanation of the world stems from the need that thinking has to unite the content accessible to thinking with manifest reality, to permeate everything conceptually, to make what we *see, hear*, etc., into something that we *understand*. Whoever takes into consideration the full implications of these statements cannot possibly be an adherent of the realism characterized above. To want to explain the world by something real that is not idea is such a self-contradiction that one absolutely cannot grasp how it could possibly find any adherents at all. To explain what is perceptibly real to us by something or other that does not take part in thinking at all, that, in fact, is supposed to be basically different from anything of a thought nature, for this we have neither the need nor any possible starting point. First of all: Where would the need originate to explain the world by something that never intrudes upon us, that conceals itself from us? And let us assume that it did approach us; then the question arises again: In what form and where? It cannot of course be in thinking. And even in outer or inner perception again? What meaning could it have to explain the sense world by a qualitative equivalent? There is only one other possibility: to assume that we had an ability to reach this most real being that lies outside thought in another way than through thinking and perception. Whoever makes this assumption has fallen into mysticism. We do not have to deal with mysticism, however; for we are concerned only with the relationship between thinking and existence, between *idea* and *reality*. A mystic must write an epistemology for mysticism. The standpoint of the later Schelling – according to which we develop only the *what (das Was)* of the world content with the help of our reason, but cannot reach the *that (das Dass)*[54] – seems to us to be the greatest nonsense. Because for us the *that* is the presupposition of the *what*, and we would not know how we are supposed to arrive at the *what* of a thing whose *that* has not already been surely established beforehand. The *that,* after all, is already inherent in the content of my reason when I grasp its *what.* This assumption of Schelling – that we can have a positive world content, without any conviction *that* it exists, and that we must first gain the *that* through *higher* experience – seems to us so incomprehensible to any thinking that understands itself, that we must assume that Schelling himself, in his later period, no longer understood the standpoint of his youth, which made such a powerful impression upon Goethe.

It will not do to assume higher forms of existence than those belonging to the world of ideas. Only because the human being is often not able to comprehend that the existence (*Sein*) of the idea is something far higher and fuller than that of perceptual reality, does he still seek a further reality. He regards ideal existence as something chimerical, as something needing to be imbued with some real element, and is not satisfied with it. He cannot, in fact, grasp the idea in its positive nature; he has it only as something abstract; he has no inkling of its fullness, of its inner perfection and genuineness. But we must demand of our education (*Bildung*) that it work its way up to that high standpoint where even an *existence* that cannot be seen with the eyes, nor grasped with the hands, but that must be apprehended by reason, is regarded as real. We have therefore actually founded an *idealism* that is *realism* at the same time. Our train of thought is: Thinking presses toward explanation of reality out of the idea. It conceals this urge in the question: *What is the real being of reality?* Only at the end of a scientific process do we ask about the content of this real being itself; we do not go about it as realism does, which presupposes something real in order then to trace reality back to it. We differ from realism in having full consciousness of the fact that only in the *idea* do we have a means of explaining the world. Even realism has *only* this means but does not realize it. It derives the world from ideas, but believes it derives it from some other reality. Leibniz's world of monads is nothing other than a world of ideas; but Leibniz believes that in it he possesses a higher reality than the ideal one. All the realists make the same mistake: they think up beings, without becoming aware that they are not getting outside of the idea. We have rejected this realism, because it deceives itself about the actual ideal nature of its world foundation; but we also have to reject that false idealism that believes that because we do not get outside of the idea, we also do not get outside of our consciousness, and that all the mental pictures given us and the whole world are only subjective illusion, only a dream that our consciousness dreams (Fichte). These idealists also do not comprehend that although we do not get outside of the idea, we do nevertheless have *in* the idea something objective, something that has its basis in itself and not in the subject. They do not consider the fact that even though we do not get outside of the unity of thinking, we do enter with the thinking of our reason into the midst of full objectivity. *The realists do not comprehend that what is objective is idea, and the idealists do not comprehend that the idea is objective.*

We still have to occupy ourselves with the empiricists of the sense-perceptible, who regard any explaining of the real by the idea as inadmissible philosophical deduction and who demand that we stick to what is graspable by the senses. Against this standpoint we can only say, simply, that its demand can, after all, only be a *methodological* one. To say that we should stick to what is given only means, after all, that we should acquire for ourselves what confronts us. *This* standpoint is the least able to determine anything about the *what* of the given; for, this *what* must in fact come, for this standpoint, from the given itself. It is totally incomprehensible to us how, along with the demand for pure experience, someone can demand at the same time that we not go outside the sense world, seeing that in fact the idea can just as well fulfill the demand that it be given. The positivistic principle of experience must leave the question entirely open as to what is given, and unites itself quite well then with the results of idealistic research. But then this demand coincides with ours as well. And we do unite in our view all standpoints, *insofar as they are valid ones*. Our standpoint is idealism, because it sees in the idea the ground of the world; it is realism because it addresses the idea as the real; and it is positivism or empiricism because it wants to arrive at the content of the idea, not through *a priori* constructions, but rather as something given. We have an empirical method that penetrates into the real and that is ultimately satisfied by the results of idealistic research. We do not recognize as valid any inferring, from something given and known to us, of an underlying, non-given, determinative element. We reject any inference in which any part of the inference is not given. Inferring is only a going from given elements over to other equally given elements. In an inference we join *a* to *b* by means of *c*; but all these must be *given*. When Volkelt says that our thinking moves us to presuppose something in addition to the given and to transcend the given, then we say: Within our thinking, something is already moving us that we want to add to the directly given. *We must therefore reject all metaphysics*. Metaphysics wants, in fact, to explain the given by something *non-given*, inferred (Wolff, Herbart). We see in inferences only a formal activity that does not lead to anything new, but only brings about transitions between elements actually present.

3. The System of Science

What form does a fully developed science (*Wissenschaft*) have in the light of the Goethean way of thinking? Above all we must hold fast to the fact that the total *content* of science is a given one; given partly as the sense world from outside, partly as the world of ideas from within. All our scientific activity will therefore consist in overcoming the form in which this total content of the given confronts us, and in making it over into a form that satisfies us. This is necessary because the inner unity of the given remains hidden in its first form of manifestation, in which only the outer surface appears to us. Now the methodological activity that establishes a relation between these two forms turns out to vary according to the realm of phenomena with which we are working. The first realm is one in which we have a manifoldness of elements given to sense perception. These interact with each other. This interaction becomes clear to us when we immerse ourselves into the matter through ideas. Then one or another element appears as more or less determined by the others, in one way or another. The existential conditions of one become comprehensible to us through those of the others. We trace one phenomenon back to the others. We trace the phenomenon of a warm stone, as effect, back to the warming rays of the sun, as cause. We have explained what we perceive about one thing, when we trace it back to some other perceptible thing. We see in what way the ideal law arises in this realm. It encompasses the things of the sense world, stands over them. It determines the lawful way of working of one thing by letting it be conditional upon another. Our task here is to bring together the series of phenomena in such a way that one necessarily goes forth out of the others, that they all constitute one whole and are lawful through and through. The realm that is to be explained in this way is *inorganic nature*. Now the individual phenomena of experience by no means confront us in such a way that what is closest in space and time is also the closest according to its inner nature. We must first pass from what is closest in space and time over into what is conceptually closest. For a certain phenomenon we must seek the phenomena that are directly connected to it in accordance with their nature. Our goal must be to bring together a series of facts that complement each other, that carry and mutually support each other. We achieve thereby a group of sense-perceptible, interacting elements of reality; and the phenomenon that unfolds before us follows directly out of the pertinent factors in a transparent, clear way. Following Goethe's example, we call such a phenomenon an "archetypal phenomenon" (*Urphänomen*) or a basic fact. *This archetypal phenomenon is identical with the objective natural law.* The bringing together discussed here can either occur merely in thoughts – as when I think about the three determining factors that come into consideration when a stone is thrown horizontally: 1. the force of the throw, 2. the force of gravity, and 3. the air's resistance, and then derive the path of the flying stone from these factors; or, on the other hand, I can actually bring the individual factors together and then await the phenomenon that follows from their interaction. This is what we do in an *experiment*. Whereas a phenomenon of the outer world is unclear to us because we know only what has been determined (the phenomenon) and not what is determining, the phenomenon that an experiment presents is clear, because we ourselves have brought together the determining factors. *This is the path of research of nature: It takes its start from experience, in order to see what is real; advances to observation, in order to see why it is real; and then intensifies into the experiment, in order to see what can be real.*

Unfortunately, precisely that essay of Goethe's seems to have been lost that could best have supported these views. It is a continuation of the essay *The Experiment as Mediator between Subject and Object.*[55] Starting from the latter, let us try to reconstruct the possible content of the lost essay from the only source available to us, the correspondence between Goethe and Schiller. The essay on *The Experiment* came out of those studies of Goethe that he undertook in order to show the validity of his work in optics. It was then put aside until the poet took up these studies again in 1798 with new energy and, with Schiller, submitted the basic principles of the natural-scientific method to a thorough and scientifically serious investigation. On January 10, 1798 (see Goethe's correspondence with Schiller) he then sent the essay on *The Experiment* to Schiller for his consideration and on January 13 informed his friend that he wanted, in a new essay, to develop further the views expressed there. And he did undertake this work; on January 17 already he sent a little essay to Schiller that contained a characterization of the methods of natural science. This is not to be found among his works. It would indisputably have been the one to provide the best points of reference for an appreciation of Goethe's basic views on the natural-scientific method. We can, however, know what thoughts were expressed there from Schiller's detailed letter of January 19, 1798; along with this, the fact comes into consideration that we find many confirmations and supplementations to the indications in Schiller's letter in Goethe's *Aphorisms in Prose*.[56]

Goethe distinguishes three methods of natural-scientific research. These rest upon three different conceptions of phenomena. The first method is *ordinary empiricism*, which does not go beyond the *empirical phenomenon*, beyond the immediate facts. It remains with *individual* phenomena. If ordinary empiricism wants to be consistent, it must limit its entire activity to exactly describing in every detail each phenomenon that meets it, i.e., to recording the empirical facts. For it, science would merely be the sum total of all these individual descriptions of recorded facts. Compared to ordinary empiricism, *rationalism* then represents the next higher level; it deals with the *scientific phenomenon*. This view no longer limits itself to the mere describing of phenomena, but rather seeks to *explain* these by discovering causes, by setting up hypotheses, etc. It is the level at which the intellect infers from the phenomena their causes and inter-relationships. Goethe declares both these methods to be one-sided. Ordinary empiricism is raw nonscience, because it never gets beyond the mere grasping of incidentals; rationalism, on the other hand, interprets into the phenomenal world causes and interrelationships that are not in it. The former cannot lift itself out of the abundance of phenomena up to free thinking; the latter loses this abundance as the sure ground under its feet and falls prey to the arbitrariness of imagination and of subjective inspiration. Goethe censures in the sharpest way the passion people have for immediately attaching to the phenomena deductions arrived at subjectively, as, for example, in *Aphorisms in Prose*: "It is bad business – but one that happens to many an observer – where a person immediately connects a deduction to a perception and considers them both as equally valid," and "Theories are usually the overly hasty conclusions of an impatient intellect that would like to be rid of the phenomenon and therefore sets in its place pictures, concepts, indeed often only words. One senses, one even sees, in fact, that it is only an expedient; but have not passion and a partisan spirit always loved expedients? And rightly so, since they need them so much." Goethe particularly criticizes the misuse to which the concept of causality has given rise. Rationalism, in its unbridled fantasy, seeks causality where, if you are looking for facts, it is not to be found. In *Aphorisms in Prose* he says: "The most innate, most necessary concept – that of cause and effect – when applied, gives rise to innumerable and ever-recurring errors." Rationalism is particularly led by its passion for simple relationships to think of phenomena as parts of a chain attached to one another by *cause* and *effect* and stretching out merely lengthwise; whereas the truth is, in fact, that one or another phenomenon that, in time, is *causally* determined by an earlier one, still depends also upon many other effects at the same time. In this case only the *length* and not the *breadth* of nature is taken into account. Both paths, ordinary empiricism and rationalism, are for Goethe certainly transitional stages to the highest scientific method, but, in fact, only *transitional stages* that must be surmounted. And this occurs with *rational empiricism*, which concerns itself with the *pure phenomenon* that is identical to the objective natural laws. The *ordinary empirical element* – direct experience – offers us only *individual things*, something incoherent, an aggregate of phenomena. That means it offers us all this not as the final conclusion of scientific consideration, but rather, in fact, as a *first* experience. Our scientific needs, however, seek only what is interrelated, comprehend the individual thing only as a part in a relationship. Thus, seemingly, our need to comprehend and the facts of nature diverge from each other. In our spirit there is only relatedness, in nature only separateness; our spirit strives for the *species*, nature creates only individuals. The solution to this contradiction is provided by the reflection that the connecting power of the human spirit, on the one hand, is without content, and therefore, by and through itself alone, cannot know *anything* positive; on the other hand, the separateness of the objects of nature does not lie in their essential being itself, but rather in their spatial manifestation; in fact, when we penetrate into the essential being of the individual, of the particular, this being itself directs us to the species. Because the objects of nature are separated in their outer manifestation, our spirit's power to draw together is needed in order to show their *inner* unity. Because the unity of the intellect by itself is empty, the intellect must fill this unity with the objects of nature. Thus, at this *third* level, phenomenon and spiritual power come to meet each other and merge into *one*, and only then can the human spirit be fully satisfied.

A further realm of investigation is that in which the individual thing, in its form of existence, does not appear as the result of something else existing beside it; we therefore also do not comprehend it by seeking help from something else of the same kind. Here, a series of sense-perceptible phenomenological elements appears to us as the direct formation of a unified principle, and we must press forward to this principle if we want to comprehend the individual phenomenon. In this realm, we cannot explain the phenomenon by anything working in from outside; we must derive it from within outward. What earlier was a determining factor is now merely an inducing factor. In the first realm I have comprehended everything when I have succeeded in regarding it as the result of something else, in tracing it back to an outer determining factor; here I am compelled to ask the question differently. When I know the outer influence, I still have not gained any information as to whether the phenomenon then occurs in this, and only in this, way. I must derive this from the central principle of that thing upon which the outer influence took place. I cannot say that this outer influence has this effect; but only that, to *this* particular outer influence, the inner working principle responds in *this* particular way. What occurs is the result of an *inner* lawfulness. I must therefore know this inner lawfulness. I must investigate what it is that is taking shape from within outward. This self-shaping principle, which in this realm underlies every phenomenon, which I must seek in every one, is the *typus*. We are in the realm of organic nature. What the archetypal phenomenon is in inorganic nature, the *typus* is in organic nature. The *typus* is a *general picture of the organism*: the idea of the organism; the animalness in the animal. We had to bring the main points here again of what we already stated about the *typus* in an earlier chapter, because of the context. In the ethical and historical sciences we then have to do with the idea in a narrower sense. Ethics and history are sciences of ideas. Their reality is ideas. It is the task of each science to work on the given until it brings the given to the archetypal phenomenon, to the *typus*, and to the leading ideas in history. "If ... the physicist can arrive at knowledge of what we have called an archetypal phenomenon, then he is secure and the philosopher along with him; he is so because he has convinced himself that he has arrived at the limits of his science, that he finds himself upon the empirical heights, from which he can look back upon experience in all its levels, and can at least look forward into the realm of theory if not enter it. The philosopher is secure, for he receives from the physicist's hand something final that becomes for him now something from which to start" (*Sketch of a Color Theory*).[57] – This is in fact where the philosopher enters and begins his work. He grasps the archetypal phenomena and brings them into a satisfying ideal relationship. We see what it is, in the sense of the Goethean worldview, that is to take the place of metaphysics: the observing (in accordance with ideas), ordering, and deriving of archetypal phenomena. Goethe speaks repeatedly in this sense about the relationship between empirical science and philosophy – with special clarity in his letters to Hegel. In his *Annals* he speaks repeatedly about a schema of science. If this were to be found, we would see from it how he himself conceived the interrelations of the individual archetypal phenomena to be, how he put them together into a necessary chain. We can also gain a picture of it when we consider the table of all possible kinds of workings that he gives in the fourth section of the first volume of *On Natural Science*[58]:

Chance
Mechanical
Physical
Chemical
Organic
Psychic
Ethical

Religious

Of a Genius

It is according to this ascending sequence that one would have to guide oneself in ordering the archetypal phenomena.

4. Limits to Knowledge and the Forming of Hypotheses

One speaks a great deal today about limits to our knowing. Man's ability to explain what exists, it is said, reaches only to a certain point, and there he must stop. We believe we can rectify the situation with respect to this question if we ask the question correctly. For, it is, indeed, so often only a matter of putting the question correctly. When this is done, a whole host of errors is dispelled. When we reflect that the object that we feel the need within us to explain must be given, then it is clear that the given itself cannot set a limit for us. For, in order to lay any claim at all to being explained and comprehended, it must confront us within given reality. Something that does not appear upon the horizon of the given does not need to be explained. Any limits could therefore lie only in the fact that, in the face of a given reality, we lacked all means of explaining it. But our need for explanation comes precisely from the fact that what we want to consider a given thing to be – that by which we want to explain it – forces itself onto the horizon of what is given us in thought. Far from being unknown to us, the explanatory *essential being* of an object is itself the very thing that, by manifesting within our spirit, makes the explanation necessary. What is to be explained and that by which it is to be explained are both present. It is only a matter of joining them. Explaining something is not the seeking of an unknown, but only a coming to terms about the reciprocal connection between two knowns. It should never occur to us to explain a given by something of which we have no knowledge. Now something does come into consideration here that gives a semblance of justification to the theory of a limit to knowledge. It could be that we do in fact have an inkling of something real that is there, but that nevertheless is beyond our perception. We can perceive some traces, some effects or other of a thing, and then make the assumption that this thing does exist. And here one can perhaps speak of a limit to our knowing. What we have presupposed to be inaccessible in this case, however, is not something by which to explain anything in principle; it is something perceivable even though it is not perceived. What hinders me from perceiving it is not any limit to knowledge in principle, but only chance outer factors. These can very well be surmounted. What I merely have inklings of today can be experienced tomorrow. But with a principle, that is not so; with it, there are no outer hindrances, which after all lie mostly only in place and time; the principle is given to me inwardly. Something else does not give me an inkling of a principle when I myself do not see the principle.

Theory about the forming of hypotheses is connected with this. A hypothesis is an assumption that we make and whose truth we cannot ascertain directly but only in its effects. We see a series of phenomena. It is explainable to us only when we found it upon something that we do not perceive directly. May such an assumption be extended to include a principle? Clearly not. For, something of an inner nature that I assume without becoming aware of it is a total contradiction. A hypothesis can only assume something, indeed, that I do not perceive, but that I would perceive at once if I cleared away the outer hindrances. *A hypothesis can indeed not presuppose something perceived, but must assume something perceivable.* Thus, every hypothesis is in the situation that its content can be directly confirmed only by a future experience. *Only* hypotheses that *can* cease to be hypotheses have any justification. Hypotheses about *central scientific principles* have no value. Something that is not explained by a positively given principle known to us is not capable of explanation at all and also does not need it.

5. Ethical and Historical Sciences

The answering of the question, What is knowing?, has illuminated for us the place of the human being in the cosmos. The view we have developed in answering this question cannot fail to shed light also upon the value and significance of human action. We must in fact attach a greater or lesser significance to what we perform in the world, according to whether we attribute a higher or lower significance to our calling as human beings.

The first task to which we must now address ourselves will be to investigate the character of human activity. How does what we must regard as the effect of human action relate to other effects within the world process? Let us look at two things: a product of nature and a creation of human activity, a crystal form and a wheel, perhaps. In both cases the object before us appears as the result of laws expressible in concepts. Their difference lies only in the fact that we must regard the crystal as the *direct* product of the natural lawfulness that determines it, whereas with the wheel the human being intervenes between the concept and the object. What we think of in the natural product as underlying the real, this we introduce into reality by our action. In knowing, we experience what the ideal determining factors of our sense experience are; we bring the world of ideas, which already lies within reality, to manifestation; we therefore complete the world process in the sense that we call into appearance the producer who eternally brings forth his products, but who, without our thinking, would remain eternally hidden within them. In human actions, however, we supplement this process through the fact that we translate the world of ideas, insofar as it is not yet reality, into such reality. Now we have recognized the idea as that which underlies all reality as the determining element, as the intention of nature. Our knowing leads us to the point of finding the tendency of the world process, the intention of the creation, out of all the indications contained in the nature surrounding us. If we have achieved this, then our action is given the task of working along independently in the realizing of that intention. And thus our action appears to us as the direct continuation of that kind of activity which nature also fulfills. It appears to us as flowing directly from the world foundation. But what a difference there is, in fact, between this and that other (nature) activity! The nature product by no means has within itself the ideal lawfulness by which it appears governed. It needs to be confronted by something higher, by human thinking; there then appears to this *thinking* that by which the nature product is governed. This is different in the case of human action. Here the idea dwells directly within the acting object; and if a higher being confronted it, this being could not find in the object's activity anything other than what this object itself had put into its action. For, a perfect human action is the result of our intentions and only that. If we look at a nature product that affects another, then the matter is like this: we see an effect; this effect is determined by laws grasped in concepts. But if we want to comprehend the effect, then it is not enough for us to compare it with some law or other; we must have a second perceptible thing – which, to be sure, must also be dissolvable entirely into concepts. When we see an impression in the ground we then look for the object that made it. This leads to the concept of a kind of effect where the cause of a phenomenon also appears in the form of an outer perception, i.e., to the concept of *force*. A force can confront us only where the idea first appears in an object of perception and only in this form acts upon another object. The opposite of this is when this intermediary is not there, when the idea approaches the sense world directly. There the idea itself appears as causative. And here is where we speak of *will*. *Will, therefore, is the idea itself, apprehended as force.* It is totally inadmissible to speak of an independent will. When a person accomplishes something or other, one cannot say that will is added to the mental picture. If one does speak in that way, then one has not grasped the concepts clearly, for, what is the human personality if one disregards the world of ideas that fills it? It is, in fact, an active existence. Whoever grasps the human personality differently – as dead, inactive nature product – puts it at the level of a stone in the road. This active existence, however, is an abstraction; it is nothing real. One cannot grasp it; it is without content. If one wants to grasp it, if one wants a content for it, then one arrives, in fact, at the world of ideas that is engaged in doing. Eduard von Hartmann makes this abstraction into a second world-constituting principle beside the idea. It is, however, nothing other than the idea itself, only in one form of manifestation. Will without idea would be *nothing*. The same cannot be said of the idea, for activity is one of its elements, while the idea itself is the self-sustaining being.

So much for the characterization of human action. Let us proceed to a further essential distinguishing feature of it that necessarily results from what has already been said. The explaining of a process in nature is a going back to its determining factors: a seeking out of the producer in addition to the product that is given. When I perceive an effect and then seek its cause, these two perceptions do not by any means satisfy my need for explanation. I must go back to the laws by which *this* cause brings forth *this* effect. It is different with human action. Here the lawfulness that determines a phenomenon itself enters into action; that which makes a product itself appears upon the scene of activity. We have to do with a manifesting existence at which we can remain, for which we do not need to ask about deeper-lying determining factors. We have comprehended a work of art when we know the idea embodied in it; we do not need to ask about any further lawful relationship between idea (cause) and creation (effect). We comprehend the actions of a statesman when we know his intentions (ideas); we do not need to go any further beyond what comes to appearance. *This is therefore what distinguishes the processes of nature from the actions of human beings: with nature processes the law is to be regarded as the determining background for what comes into manifest existence, whereas with human actions the existence is itself the law and manifests as determined by nothing other than itself.* Thus every process of nature breaks down into something determining and something determined, and the latter follows *necessarily* from the former, whereas human action determines only itself. This, however, is action out of *inner freedom* (*Freiheit*). When the intentions of nature, which stand behind its manifestations and determine them, enter into the human being, they themselves become *manifestation*; but now they are, as it were, free from any attachment behind them (*rückenfrei*). If all nature processes are only manifestations of the idea, then human doing is the idea itself in action.

Since our epistemology has arrived at the conclusion that the content of our consciousness is not merely a means of making a copy of the world ground, but rather that this world ground itself, in its most primal state, comes to light within our thinking, we can do nothing other than to recognize directly in human action also the undetermined action of that primal ground. We recognize no world director outside ourselves who sets goals and directions for our actions. The world director has given up his power, has given everything over to man, abolishing his own separate existence, and set man the task: Work on. The human being finds himself in the world, sees nature, and within it, the indication of something deeper, a determining element, an intention. His thinking enables him to know this intention. It becomes his spiritual possession. He has penetrated the world; he comes forth, acting, to carry on those intentions. Therefore, the philosophy presented here is the true *philosophy of inner freedom* (*Freiheitsphilosophie*). In the realm of human actions it acknowledges neither natural necessity nor the influence of some creator or world director outside the world. In either case, the human being would be *unfree*. If natural necessity worked in him in the same way as in other entities, then he would perform his actions out of compulsion, then it would also be necessary in his case to go back to determining factors that underlie manifest existence, and then inner freedom is out of the question. It is of course not impossible that there are innumerable human functions that can only be seen in this light; but these do not come into consideration here. The human being, insofar as he is a being of nature, is also to be understood according to the laws that apply to nature's working. But neither as a knowing nor as a truly ethical being can he, in his behavior, be understood according to merely natural laws. There, in fact, he steps outside the sphere of natural realities. And it is with respect to this, his existence's highest potency, which is more an ideal than reality, that what we have established here holds good. Man's path in life consists in his developing himself from a being of nature into a being such as we have learned to know here; he should make himself free of all laws of nature and become his own law giver.

But we must also reject the influence of any director – outside the world – of human destiny. Also where such a director is assumed, there can be no question of true inner freedom. There he determines the direction of human action and man has to carry out what this director sets him to do. He experiences the impulse to his actions not as an ideal that he sets himself, but rather as the *commandment* of that director; again his actions are not *undetermined*, but rather *determined*. The human being would not then, in fact, feel himself to be free of any attachment from behind him, but would feel dependent, like a mere intermediary for the intentions of a higher power.

We have seen that dogmatism consists in seeking the basis for the truth of anything in something beyond, and inaccessible to, our consciousness (transsubjective), in contrast to our view that declares a judgment to be true only because the reason for doing so lies in the concepts that are present in our consciousness and that flow into the judgment. Someone who conceives of a world ground outside of our world of ideas thinks that our ideal reason for recognizing something as true is a different reason than that as to why it is objectively true. Thus truth is apprehended as dogma. And in the realm of ethics a *commandment* is what a *dogma* is in science. When the human being seeks the impulse for his action in commandments, he acts then according to laws whose basis is independent of him; he conceives of a norm that is prescribed for his action from outside. He acts out of *duty*. To speak of duty makes sense only when looked at this way. We must feel the impulse from outside and acknowledge the *necessity* of responding to it; then we act out of *duty*. Our epistemology cannot accept this kind of action as valid where the human being appears in his full ethical development. We know that the world of ideas is unending perfection itself; we know that with it the impulses of our action lie *within* us; and we must therefore only acknowledge an action as ethical in which the deed flows only out of the idea, lying within us, of the deed. From this point of view, man performs an action only because its reality is a need for him. He acts because an inner (his own) urge, not an outer power, drives him. The object of his action, as soon as he makes himself a concept of it, fills him in such a way that he strives to realize it. The only impulse for our action should also lie in the need to realize an idea, in the urge to carry out an intention. Everything that urges us to a deed should live its life in the idea. Then we do not act out of duty; we do not act under the influence of a drive; we act out of *love for the object* to which our action is to be directed. The object, when we picture it, calls forth in us the urge to act in a way appropriate to it. Only such action is a free one. For if, in addition to the interest we take in the object, there had yet to be a second motivation from another quarter, then we would not want this object for its own sake; we would want *something else* and would perform *that*, which we do *not* want; we would carry out an action *against* our will. That would be the case, for example, in action out of *egoism*. There we take no interest in the action itself; it is not a need for us; we do need the benefits, however, that it brings us. But then we also feel right away as compulsion the fact that we must perform the action for this reason only. The action itself is not a need for us; for we would leave it undone if no benefits followed from it. An action, however, that we do not perform for its own sake is an unfree one. *Egoism acts unfreely.* Every person acts unfreely, in fact, who performs an action out of a motivation that does not follow from the objective content of the action itself. To carry out an action for its own sake means to act out of love. *Only someone who is guided by love in doing, by devotion to objectivity, acts truly freely.* Whoever is incapable of this selfless devotion will never be able to regard his activity as a *free one*.

If man's action is to be nothing other than the realization of his own content of ideas, then naturally such a content must lie within him. His spirit must work productively. For, what is supposed to fill him with the urge to accomplish something if not an idea working its way up in his spirit? This idea will prove to be all the more fruitful the more it arises in his spirit in definite outlines and with a clear content. For only that, in fact, can move us with full force to realize something which is completely definite in its entire "what." An ideal that is only dimly pictured to oneself, that is left in an indefinite state, is unsuitable as an impulse to action. What is there about it to fire us with enthusiasm if its content does not lie clear and open to the day? The impulses for our action must therefore always arise in the form of individual intentions. Everything fruitful that the human being accomplishes owes its existence to such individual impulses. General moral laws, ethical norms, etc., that are supposed to be valid for all human beings prove to be entirely worthless. When Kant regards as ethically valid only that which is suitable as a law for all human beings, then one can say in response to this that all positive action would cease, that everything great would disappear from the world, if each person did only what was suitable for everyone. No, it is not such vague, general ethical norms but rather the most individual ideals that should guide our actions. Everything is not equally worthy of being done by everyone, but rather *this* seems worthy to him, *that* to her, according to whether one of them feels called to do a thing. J. Kreyenbühl has spoken about this in apt words is his essay *Ethical Freedom in Kant's View*[59]: "If freedom is, in fact, to be *my* freedom, if a moral deed is to be *my* deed, if the good and right is to be realized through me, through the action of this particular individual personality, then I cannot possibly be satisfied by a general law that disregards all individuality and all the peculiarities of the concurrent circumstances of the action, and that commands me to examine every action as to whether its underlying motive corresponds to the abstract norm of general human nature and as to whether, in the way it lives and works in me, it could become a generally valid maxim." ... "An adaptation of this kind to what is generally usual and customary would render impossible any individual freedom, any progress beyond the ordinary and humdrum, any significant, outstanding ethical achievement."

These considerations shed light upon the questions a general ethics has to answer. One often treats this last, in fact, as though it were a sum total of norms according to which human action ought to direct itself. From this point of view, one compares ethics to natural science and in general to the science of what exists. Whereas science is to communicate to us the laws of that which exists, of what *is*, ethics supposedly has to teach us the laws of what ought to exist. Ethics is supposedly a codex of all the ideals of man, a detailed answer to the question: What is good? Such a science, however, is impossible. There can be no general answer to this question. Ethical action is, in fact, a product of what manifests within the individual; it is always present as an individual case, never in a general way. There are no general laws as to what one ought or ought not to do. But do not regard the individual legal statutes of the different peoples as such general laws. They are also nothing more than the outgrowth of individual intentions. What one or another personality has experienced as a moral motive has communicated itself to a whole people, has become the "*code of this people*." A general natural code that should apply to all people for all time is nonsense. Views as to what is right and wrong and concepts of morality come and go with the different peoples, indeed even with individuals. The individuality is always the decisive factor. It is therefore inadmissible to speak of an ethics in the above sense. But there are other questions to be answered in this science, questions that have in part been touched upon briefly in these discussions. Let me mention only: establishing the difference between human action and nature's working, the question as to the nature of the will and of inner freedom, etc. All these individual tasks can be summed up in one: To what extent is man an ethical being? But this aims at nothing other than knowledge of the moral nature of man. The question asked is not: What ought man to do? but rather: What is it that he is doing, in its inner nature? And thereby that partition falls that divides all science into two spheres: into a study of what exists and into one of what ought to exist. *Ethics is just as much a study of what exists as all the other sciences.* In this respect, a unified impulse runs through all the sciences in that they take their start from something given and proceed to its determining factors. But there can be no science of human action itself; for, it is undetermined, productive, creative. Jurisprudence is not a science, but only a *collection of notes* on the customs and codes characteristic of an individual people.

Now the human being does not belong only to himself; he belongs, as a part, to two higher totalities. First of all, he is part of a people with which he is united by common customs, by a common cultural life, by language, and by a common view. But then he is also a citizen of history, an individual member in the great historical process of human development. Through his belonging to these two wholes, his free action seems to be restricted. What he does does not seem to flow only from his own individual 'I'; he appears *determined* by what he has in common with his people; his individuality seems to be abolished by the character of his people. Am I still free then if one can find my actions explainable not only out of my own nature but to a considerable extent also out of the nature of my people? Do I not act, therefore, the way I do because nature has made me a member of *this* particular community of people? And it is no different with the second whole to which I belong. History assigns me the place of my working. I am dependent upon the cultural epoch into which I am born; I am a child of my age. But if one apprehends the human being at the same time as a knowing *and* as an acting entity, then this contradiction resolves itself. Through his capacity for knowledge, man penetrates into the particular character of his people; it becomes clear to him whither his fellow citizens are steering. He overcomes that by which he appears determined in this way and takes it up into himself as a picture that he has fully known; it becomes individual within him and takes on entirely the personal character that working from inner freedom has. The situation is the same with respect to the historical development within which the human being appears. He lifts himself to a knowledge of the leading ideas, of the moral forces holding sway there; and then they no longer work upon him as determining factors, but rather become individual driving powers within him. The human being must in fact work his way upward so that he is no longer led, but rather leads himself. He must not allow himself to be carried along blindly by the character of his people, but rather must lift himself to a knowledge of this character so that he acts consciously in accordance with his people. He must not allow himself to be carried by the progress of culture, but must rather make the ideas of his time into his own. In order for him to do so, it is necessary above all that he understand his time. Then, in inner freedom, he will fulfill its tasks; then he will set to at the right place with his own work. Here the humanities[60] (history, cultural and literary history, etc.) must enter as intermediaries. In the humanities the human being has to do with his own accomplishments, with the creations of culture, of literature, with art, etc. Something spiritual is grasped by the human spirit. And the purpose of the humanities should not be anything other than that man recognize where chance has placed him; he should recognize what has already been accomplished, what falls to him to do. Through the humanities he must find the right point at which to participate with his personality in the happenings of the world. The human being must know the spiritual world and determine his part in it according to this knowledge.

In the preface to the first volume of his *Pictures from the German Past*,[61] Gustav Freytag says: "All the great creations of the power of a people, inherited religion, custom, law, state configurations, are for us no longer the results of individual men; they are the organic creations of a lofty life that in every age comes to manifestation only through the individual, and in every age draws together into itself the spiritual content of the individual into a mighty whole ... Thus, without saying anything mystical, one might well speak of a folk-soul ... But the life of a people no longer works consciously, like the will forces of a man. Man represents what is free and intelligent in history; the power of a people works ceaselessly, with the *dark compulsion of a primal force*." If Freytag had investigated this life of a people, he would have found, indeed, that it breaks down into the working of a sum of single individuals who overcome that dark compulsion and lift what is unconscious up into consciousness; and he would have seen how that which he addresses as *folk-soul*, as *dark compulsion*, goes forth from the individual will impulses, from the free action of the human being.

But something else comes into consideration with respect to the working of the human being within his people. Every personality represents a spiritual potency, a sum of powers that seek to work according to the possibilities. Every person must therefore find the place where his working can incorporate itself in the most suitable way into the organism of his people. It must not be left to chance whether he finds this place. The constitution of a state has no other purpose than to take care that everyone find his appropriate sphere of work. The state is the form in which the organism of a people expresses itself.

Sociology and political science have to investigate the way the individual personality can come to play a part appropriate to it within a state. The constitution must go forth from the innermost being of a people. The character of a people, expressed in individual statements, is the best constitution for a state. A statesman cannot impose a constitution upon a people. The leader of a state must investigate the deep characteristics of his people and, through a constitution, give the tendencies slumbering in the people a direction corresponding to them. It can happen that the majority of a people wants to steer onto paths that go against its own nature. Goethe believes that in this case the statesman must let himself be guided by the people's own nature and not by the momentary demands of the majority; that he must in this case advocate the *character of his people* against the actual people (*Aphorisms in Prose*).

We must still add a word here about the *method of history*. History must always bear in mind that the causes of historical events are to be sought in the individual intentions, plans, etc., of the human being. All tracing back of historical facts to plans that underlie history is an error. It is always only a question of which goals one or another personality has set himself, which ways they have taken, and so on. History is absolutely to be based on human nature. *Its* willing, its tendencies are to be fathomed.

By statements of Goethe we can now substantiate again what has been said here about the science of ethics. The following statement is to be understood only out of the relationship in which we have seen the human being to stand with respect to historical development: "The world of reason is to be regarded as a great immortal individual, which ceaselessly brings about the necessary and thereby makes itself master, in fact, of chance happening."[62] – A reference to a positive, individual substratum of action lies in the words: "Undetermined activity, of whatever kind, leads to bankruptcy in the end." "The least of men can be complete if he moves within the limits of his abilities and skills." – The necessity for man of lifting himself up to the leading ideas of his people and of his age is expressed like this: "Each person must ask himself, after all, with which organ he can and will in any case work into his age." and: "One must know where one is standing and where the others want to go." Our view of duty is recognizable again in the words: "*Duty*: where one loves what one commands oneself to do."

We have based man, as a knowing and acting being, entirely upon himself. We have described his world of ideas as coinciding with the world ground and have recognized that everything he does is to be regarded as flowing only from his own individuality. We seek the core of existence within man himself. No one reveals a dogmatic truth to him; no one drives him in his actions. He is sufficient unto himself. He must be everything through himself, nothing through another being. He must draw forth everything from himself – even the sources of his happiness. We have already recognized, in fact, that there can be no question of any power directing man, determining the direction and content of his existence, damning him to being unfree. If happiness is to come to a person therefore, this can come about only through himself. Just as little as an outer power prescribes norms for our action, will such a power bestow upon things the ability to awaken in us a feeling of satisfaction if we do not do it ourselves. Pleasure and pain are there for man only when he himself first confers upon objects the power to call up these feelings in him. A creator who determines from outside what should cause us pleasure or pain, would simply be leading us around like children.

All optimism and pessimism are thereby refuted. Optimism assumes that the world is perfect, that it must be a source of the greatest satisfaction for man. But if this is to be the case, man would first have to develop *within himself* those needs through which to arrive at this satisfaction. He would have to gain from the objects what it is he demands. Pessimism believes that the world is constituted in such a way that it leaves man eternally dissatisfied, that he can never be happy. What a pitiful creature man would be if nature offered him satisfaction from outside! All lamentations about an existence that does not satisfy us, about this hard world, must disappear before the thought that no power in the world could satisfy us if we ourselves did not first lend it that magical power by which it uplifts and gladdens us. Satisfaction must come to us out of what we make of things, out of our own creations. Only that is worthy of free beings.

XI

Relationship of the Goethean Way of Thinking to Other Views

When one speaks of the influence of earlier or contemporary thinkers upon the development of Goethe's spirit, this cannot be done out of the assumption that he formed his views on the basis of their teachings. The way he had to think, the way he saw the world, were inherent in the whole predisposition of his nature. And it lay in his being, indeed, from his earliest youth. In this respect he then also remained the same his whole life long. It is principally two significant character traits that come into consideration here. The first is his pressing urge to find the sources, the depths of all existence. This is, ultimately, his belief in the idea. Goethe is always filled with an intimation of something higher, better. One would like to call this a deep religious impulse of his spirit. What so many people need to do – to strip things of everything holy and pull them down to their own level – is unknown to him. *But he does have the other need: to sense something higher and to work his way up to it.* He sought to gain from everything an aspect by which it becomes holy to us. K. J. Schröer has shown this in the most brilliant way with respect to Goethe's attitude toward love. Goethe divests love of everything frivolous, careless, and it becomes for him a devout state. This fundamental trait of his being is expressed most beautifully in his words:

> Within our bosom's pureness swells a striving,
>
> To give oneself, in thankful, free devotion,
>
> *To something higher, purer, as yet unknown.*
>
> We call it: *being devout!*

This side of his being, now, is inseparably connected with another one. He never seeks to approach this higher something directly; he always seeks to draw near to it through nature. "The true is like God; it does not appear directly; we must guess it from its manifestations" (*Aphorisms in Prose*). Besides his belief in the idea Goethe also has the other one: that we can gain the idea by contemplating reality; it does not occur to him to seek the divinity anywhere else than in the works of nature, but he seeks everywhere to gain from them their divine aspect. When, in his youth, he erects an altar to the great God who "*stands in direct connection with nature*" (*Poetry and Truth*), this ritual definitely springs already out of a belief that we gain the highest that we can attain by a faithful fostering of our interrelationship with nature. Thus, that way of looking at things which we have validated epistemologically is innate in Goethe. He approaches reality with the conviction that everything is only a manifestation of the idea, and that we can attain this idea only when we raise sense experience into a spiritual beholding. This conviction was inherent in him, and from his youth up, he looked at the world on the basis of this presupposition. No philosopher could give him this conviction. This is therefore not what Goethe sought from the philosophers. It was something else. Even though his way of looking at things lay deep in his nature, still he needed a language in which to express it. His nature worked in a philosophical way, i.e., in such a way that it can be expressed only in philosophical formulations and can be validated only by philosophical presuppositions. And he looked into the philosophers in order also to bring clearly to consciousness for himself what he *was*, in order also to *know* what lay in him as living *activity*. He sought in them an explanation and validation of his own being. That is his relationship to the philosophers. To this end, he studies Spinoza in his youth and entered later into scientific discourse with his philosophical contemporaries. In his early years, Spinoza and Giordano Bruno seemed to the poet to best express his own nature. It is remarkable that he first learned to know both thinkers from books hostile to them, and, in spite of this fact, recognized how their teachings relate to his nature. We see this substantiated especially in his relationship to Giordano Bruno's teachings. He becomes acquainted with him in Bayle's dictionary, where he is vehemently attacked. And Goethe receives such a deep impression from him that, in those parts of *Faust* that in their conception stem from the period around 1770 when he was reading Bayle, the language echoes sentences of Bruno. In his daily and yearly notebooks the poet relates that he again occupied himself with Giordano Bruno in 1812. This time also the impression is a powerful one, and in many of the poems written after this year we can recognize echoes of the philosopher of Nola. But all this should not be taken to mean that Goethe borrowed or learned anything from Bruno; he only found in him the formulations in which to express what had lain in his own nature for a long time. He found that he could most clearly present his own inner life if he did so in the words of that thinker. Bruno regarded universal reason as the creator and director of the universe. He calls it the *inner artist* that forms matter and shapes it from *within* outward. It is the cause of everything that exists, and there is no being in whose existence it does not take a loving interest. "However small and trifling a thing may be, it still has within it a portion of spiritual substance" (Giordano Bruno, *About the Cause*, etc.). That was also Goethe's view, that we first know how to judge a thing when we see how it has been set in its place by universal reason, how it has come to be precisely that which confronts us. Perceiving with the senses does not suffice, for the senses do not tell us how a thing relates to the general world idea, what it means for the great whole. There we must look in such a way that our reason creates an ideal basis on which there can then appear to us what the senses convey to us; we must, as Goethe expresses it, look with the *eyes of the spirit*. Even for expressing this conviction he found a formulation in Bruno: "For, just as we do not recognize colors and sounds with one and the same sense, so also we do not recognize the substratum of the arts and that of nature with one and the same eye," because we "see the first with the *physical eye* and the second with the *eye of reason*." And with Spinoza it is no different. Spinoza's teachings are indeed based on the fact that the divinity has merged with the world. Human knowing can therefore aim only to penetrate into the world in order to know God. Any other way of arriving at God must seem impossible to anyone thinking consistently according to Spinoza's way of thinking. For God has given up all existence of His own; outside the world He exists nowhere. But we must seek Him where He is. Any actual knowing must therefore be of such a kind that, in every piece of world knowledge, it conveys to us a piece of divine knowledge. *Knowing*, at its highest level, is therefore a coming together with the divinity. There we call it *knowing in beholding* (*anschauliches Wissen*). We know things "*sub specie aeternitatis,*" that is, as flowing from the divinity. The laws that our spirit recognizes in nature are therefore God in His very being; they are not only made by Him. What we recognize as logical necessity is so because the being of the divinity, i.e., the eternal lawfulness, dwells within it. That was a view which is in accordance with the Goethean spirit. His own firm belief that nature, in all its doings, reveals something divine to us lay before him in Spinoza's writings in the clearest statements. "I am holding firmly and ever more firmly to the atheist's (Spinoza) way of revering God," he writes to Jacobi when the latter wanted to put the teachings of Spinoza in another light. Therein lies the relatedness of Goethe to Spinoza. And it indicates a superficial judgment of the matter when, with respect to this deep inner harmony between Goethe's nature and Spinoza's teachings, one ever and again emphasizes something purely external by saying that Goethe was drawn to Spinoza because he, like Spinoza, would not tolerate a final cause in explaining the world. The fact that Goethe, like Spinoza, rejected final causes was only one *result* of their views. But let us put the theory of final causes clearly before us. A thing is explained, in its existence and nature, by the fact that one demonstrates its necessity for something else. One shows that this thing is of such and such a nature because that other thing is like this or that. This presupposes that a world ground exists which stands over and above both beings and arranges them in such a way that they match each other. But if the world ground is inherent in every single thing, then this kind of explanation makes no sense. For then the nature of a thing must appear to us as the result of the principle at work *within* it. We will seek, within the nature of a thing, the reason why it is *as it is* and not different than it is. If we hold the belief that something divine is inherent in each thing, then it will not in fact occur to us to seek to explain its lawfulness by any outer principle. The relationship of Goethe to Spinoza should also not be grasped in any other way than that he found in Spinoza the formulations, the scientific language, for expressing the world lying within him.

When we now pass on to Goethe's connection to contemporary philosophers, we must speak above all about Kant. Kant is generally regarded as the founder of present-day philosophy. In his time he called forth such a powerful movement that every educated person needed to come to terms with it. It was also necessary for Goethe to do so. But this did not prove to be a fruitful undertaking for him. For there is a deep antithesis between what the Kantian philosophy teaches and what we have recognized as the Goethean way of thinking. In fact, one can even say that all German thinking runs it course in two parallel streams: one permeated by the Kantian way of thinking and another that is close to Goethean thinking. But as philosophy today draws ever closer to Kant, it is distancing itself from Goethe, and through this the possibility for our age of grasping and appreciating the Goethean worldview is being lost more and more. Let us set before us the main postulates of Kant's teachings insofar as they are of interest with respect to Goethe's views. For Kant, the starting point for human thinking is experience, i.e., the world given to the senses (among which is included the inner sense that conveys to us such facts as the psychic, historical, and the like). This world is a manifoldness of things in space and of processes in time. The fact that precisely this thing confronts me or that I experience precisely that process is of no consequence; it could also be different. I can think away the whole manifoldness of things and processes altogether. What I cannot think away, however, are *space* and *time*. For me, there can be nothing that is not spatial or temporal. Even if there were some non-spatial or non-temporal thing, I can know nothing about it, for I can picture nothing to myself without space and time. I do not know whether the things themselves partake of space and time; I only know that the things must *appear* to me in these forms. Space and time are therefore the prerequisites of *my* sense perception. I know nothing of any thing-in-itself; I only know how it must appear to me if it is to be there for me. With these postulates Kant introduces a new problem. He appears in science with a new way of asking questions. Instead of asking, as earlier philosophers did: What is the nature of things?, he asks: How must things appear to us in such a way that they can become the object of our knowing? For Kant, philosophy is the science of the factors that determine the possibility of the world as a manifestation for human beings. We know nothing about the thing-in-itself. We have not yet fulfilled our task when we arrive at a sense perception of a manifoldness in time and space. We strive to draw this manifoldness together into a unity. This is a matter for the intellect. The intellect is to be understood as a sum of activities whose purpose is to draw the sense world together according to certain forms already sketched out in the intellect. It draws together two sense perceptions by, for example, designating one as the cause and the other as the effect, or the one as substance and the other as attribute, etc. Here also it is the task of the science of philosophy to show under which conditions the intellect succeeds in forming a system of the world. Thus the world, according to Kant, is actually a subjective phenomenon arising in the forms of the sense world and of the intellect. Only one thing is certain: that there is a thing-in-itself; how it appears to us depends upon our organization. It is also obvious now that it makes no sense to ascribe to that world which the intellect has formed in association with the senses any significance other than what it has for our ability to know. This becomes clearest of all where Kant speaks of the significance of the world of ideas. Ideas for him are nothing other than the higher points of view of reason from which the lower entities, which the intellect has created, are understood. The intellect brings soul phenomena, for example, into a relationship; reason, as the faculty for ideas, then grasps this relationship *as though* everything went forth from one soul. But this has no significance for the thing itself; it is only a means of orientation for our cognitive faculty. This is the content of Kant's theoretical philosophy insofar as it can be of interest to us here. One sees at once that it is the polar opposite of the Goethean philosophy. Given reality is determined, according to Kant, by us ourselves; it is as it is because we picture it that way. Kant skips over the real epistemological question. At the beginning of his *Critique of Reason* he takes two steps that he does not justify, and his whole edifice of philosophical teachings suffers from this mistake. He right away sets up a distinction between object and subject, without asking at all what significance it has then for the intellect to undertake the separation of two regions of reality (in this case the knowing subject and the object to be known). Then he seeks to establish *conceptually* the reciprocal relationship of these two regions, again without asking what it means to establish something like that. If his view of the main epistemological question had not been all askew, he would have seen that the holding apart of subject and object is only a transitional point in our knowing, that a deeper unity, which reason can grasp, underlies them both, and that what is attributed to a thing as a trait, when considered in connection with a knowing subject, by no means has only subjective validity. A thing is a unity for our reason and the separation into "thing-in-itself" and "thing-for-us" is a product of our intellect. It will not do, therefore, to say that what is attributed to a thing in one connection can be denied it in other connections. For, whether I look at the same thing one time from this point of view and another time from that: it is after all still a unified whole.

It is an error, running through Kant's entire edifice of teachings, for him to regard the sense-perceptible manifoldness as something fixed, and for him to believe that science consists in bringing this manifoldness into a system. He has no inkling at all that the manifoldness is not something *ultimate*, that one must *overcome* it if one wants to comprehend it; and therefore all theory becomes for him merely a supplement that the intellect and reason add onto experience. For him, the idea is not what appears to reason as the deeper ground of the given world when reason has overcome the manifoldness lying on the surface, but rather the idea is only a methodological principle by which reason orders the phenomena in order to have a better overview of them. According to the Kantian view, we would be going totally amiss if we were to regard things as traceable back to the idea; in his opinion, we can only order our experiences *as though* they stemmed from a unity. According to Kant, we have no inkling of the ground of things, of the "in-itself." Our knowing of things is only there in connection with us; it is valid only for our individuality. Goethe could not gain much from this view of the world. The contemplation of things in their connection to us always remained for him a quite subordinate one, having to do with the effect of objects upon our feelings of pleasure and pain; he demands more of science than a mere statement as to how things are in their connection to us. In the essay *The Experiment as Mediator between Subject and Object*, he determines what the task of the researcher is: He should take his yardstick for knowledge, the data for his judgment, not from himself, but rather from the sphere of the things he observes. This one statement characterizes the deep antithesis between the Kantian and the Goethean way of thinking. Whereas with Kant, all judgments about things are only a product of subject *and* object, and only provide a knowing about how the subject beholds the object, with Goethe, the subject merges selflessly into the object and draws the data for his judgment from the sphere of the things. Goethe himself says therefore of Kant's adherents: "They certainly heard me but had no answer for me *nor could be in any way helpful.*" The poet believed that he gained more from Kant's critique of the power of judgment.

Philosophically, Goethe benefited far more from Schiller than from Kant. Through him, namely, Goethe was really brought one stage further in the recognition of his own way of viewing things. Up to the time of that first famous conversation with Schiller, Goethe had practiced a certain way of viewing the world. He had observed plants, found that an archetypal plant underlies them, and derived the individual forms from it. This archetypal plant (and also a corresponding archetypal animal) had taken shape in his spirit, was useful to him in explaining the relevant phenomena. But he had never reflected upon *what* this archetypal plant was in its essential nature. Schiller opened his eyes by saying to him: It is an *idea.* Only from then on is Goethe aware of his idealism. Up until that conversation, he calls the archetypal plant an experience, for he believed he saw it with his eyes. But in the introduction that he later added to his essay on the metamorphosis of the plants, he says: "So from now on, I undertook to find the archetypal animal, which means, ultimately, the concept, the *idea* of the animal." But we must bear in mind here that Schiller did not provide Goethe with something foreign to him, but rather Schiller, by observing the Goethean spirit, struggled through for the first time to a knowledge of *ob-*

jective idealism. He only found the right term for the way of viewing things that he recognized and marveled at in Goethe.

Goethe experienced but little benefit from Fichte. Fichte moved in a sphere that was much too foreign to Goethean thinking to be of much possible benefit. Fichte founded the science of consciousness in the most brilliant way. In a unique and exemplary way, he traced the activity by which the 'I' transforms the world that is given, into a world that is thought. But in doing so, he made the mistake of not merely regarding this activity of the 'I' as one that brings the given content into a satisfactory form, that brings the unrelated given into the appropriate relationships; he saw this activity as a creating of everything that takes place within the 'I.' Therefore his teachings appear as a one-sided idealism that takes its whole content from consciousness. Goethe, who always devoted himself wholly to what is objective, could find very little to attract him in Fichte's philosophy of consciousness. Goethe lacked understanding for the region where that philosophy is valid; but the lengths to which Fichte carried it (he saw it as the universal science) could only appear to the poet as an error.

Goethe had many more points of contact with the young Schelling. Schelling was a student of Fichte. He did not only carry further the analysis of the activity of the 'I,' however, but also investigated this activity within the consciousness by which *nature* is grasped. What takes place in the 'I' when it is knowing nature seemed to Schelling to be at the same time that which is objective about nature, the actual principle within it. External nature was for him only a form of our nature concepts that has become fixed. What lives in us as a view of nature appears to us again outside, only spread out, spatial-temporally. What confronts us from outside as nature is a finished product, is only something already determined, the form of a living principle that has become rigid. We cannot gain this principle through experience from outside. We must first create it within our inner being. "To philosophize about nature means to *create* nature," our philosopher says therefore. "We call nature, as a mere product (*natura naturata*), 'nature as object' (all empiricism devotes itself to this alone). We call nature, as productivity (*natura naturans*), 'nature as subject' (all theory devotes itself to this alone)."

(Introduction to Schelling's *First Sketch of a System of Natural Philosophy*)[63] "The contrast between empiricism and science rests, indeed, on the fact that empiricism studies its object in existence as something finished and already brought about, whereas science, on the other hand, studies the object in its *becoming* and as something still to be brought about." (*Ibid.*) Through these teachings, with which Goethe became acquainted partly from Schelling's writings and partly from personal encounters with the philosopher, the poet was again brought a stage higher. He now developed the view that his tendency was to proceed from what is finished, the product, to what is becoming, the productive. And, with a definite echo of Schelling, he writes in his essay *The Power to Judge in Beholding* that his striving was to make himself "worthy, through beholding an ever-creating nature, of participating spiritually in its *productions*."

And through Hegel, finally, Goethe received his last help from the side of philosophy. Through him he gained clarity, namely, as to how what he called the *archetypal phenomenon* fitted into philosophy. Hegel understood the significance of the archetypal phenomenon more deeply than anyone else and characterized it aptly in a letter to Goethe on February 20, 1821 with the words: "The simple and abstract, what you quite aptly call the archetypal phenomenon, this you put first, and then show the concrete phenomena as arising through the participation of yet other influences and circumstances; and you direct the whole process in such a way that the sequence proceeds from the simple, determining factors to the composite ones, and, thus arranged, something complex appears in all its clarity through this decomposition. To seek out the archetypal phenomenon, to free it from other extraneous chance surroundings – to grasp it abstractly, as we call it – this I consider to be the task for a great spiritual sense for nature, just as I consider that procedure altogether to be what is truly scientific in gaining knowledge in this field." ... "But may I now also speak to you about the particular interest that the archetypal phenomenon, lifted out in this way, has for us philosophers; namely, that we can put something prepared in this way precisely to philosophical use! If, in spite of everything, we have finally led our initially oysterlike, gray, or completely black absolute out toward the air and light, so that it desires them, then we need windows in order to lead it out fully into the light of day; our schemata would disperse into mist if we were to transfer them directly into the colorful, confused society of a resistant world. Here is where your archetypal phenomena now stand us in excellent stead; in this twilight – spiritual and comprehensible through its simplicity, visible or graspable through its sense-perceptibility – the two worlds greet each other: our abstruse existence and the manifest one." In this way, through Hegel, the thought becomes clear to Goethe that the empirical researcher has to go as far as the archetypal phenomena and that the paths of the philosopher lead on from there. But from this it is also clear that the basic thought of Hegelian philosophy follows from the Goethean way of thinking. The overcoming of human nature, the entering deeply into it in order to ascend from the created to the creating, from the determined to the determining, is fundamental to Goethe, but also to Hegel. Hegel, indeed, wants to present nothing other in philosophy than the eternal process from which everything finite emerges. He wants to know the given as a result of that to which he can grant validity as something undetermined.

Thus for Goethe, acquainting himself with philosophers and with directions in philosophy means an ongoing clarification of what already lay in him. He gained nothing new for his views; he was only given the means of speaking about what he did, about what was going on in his soul.

Thus the Goethean worldview offers many points of reference for philosophical elaboration. But these were initially taken up only by the pupils of Hegel. The rest of philosophy took a stand of dignified rejection toward the Goethean view. Only Schopenhauer bases himself in many respects upon the poet, whom he values highly. We will speak in a later chapter about his apologetic of the color theory. Here it is a matter of describing the general relationship of Schopenhauer's teachings to Goethe.[64] In one point the Frankfurt philosopher comes close to Goethe. Schopenhauer rejects, namely, any deriving from outer causes of the phenomena given us and admits the validity only of an inner lawfulness, of a deriving of one phenomenon from another. This seems to be the same as the Goethean principle of taking the data for an explanation from the things themselves;

but only seemingly. Schopenhauer wants to remain in the realm of phenomena because he believes we cannot attain in knowledge the "in-itself" lying outside this realm, since all the phenomena given us are only mental pictures[65] and our ability to make mental pictures never takes us outside our consciousness; Goethe, on the other hand, wants to remain within the phenomena, because he in fact seeks within the phenomena themselves the data needed for their explanation.

In conclusion, let us still compare the Goethean worldview with the most significant scientific phenomenon of our time, with the views of Eduard von Hartmann. This thinker's *Philosophy of the Unconscious*[66] is a work of the greatest historical significance. Taken together with the other writings of Hartmann (which elaborate in all directions what he there sketched out and in fact bring new points of view to that main work in many respects), this book mirrors the entire spiritual content of our age. Hartmann demonstrates a remarkable profundity and an amazing mastery of the material of the individual sciences. He stands today in the vanguard of culture. One does not need to be an adherent of his to have to acknowledge this unreservedly.

His view is not so far from Goethe's as one might believe at first glance. Someone who has access only to the *Philosophy of the Unconscious* will not, to be sure, be able to see this. For, one sees the definite points of contact between these two thinkers only when one goes into the *consequences* that Hartmann drew from his principles and that he set down in his later writings.

Hartmann's philosophy is idealism. He does not want to be a *mere* idealist, it is true. But where, for the purpose of explaining the world, he needs something positive, he does after all seek help from ideas. And the most important thing is that he thinks of the idea as the underlying principle everywhere. His assumption of an unconscious means nothing other, in fact, than that what is present in our consciousness as idea is not necessarily bound to this form of manifestation within our consciousness. The idea is not only present (active), where it becomes *conscious*, but also in another form. The idea is more than a merely subjective phenomenon; it has a significance founded within itself. It is not merely present within the subject; it is the objective world principle. Even though Hartmann includes will, *in addition* to the idea, among the principles constituting the world, it is nevertheless incomprehensible that there are still philosophers who regard him as an adherent of Schopenhauer. Schopenhauer carried to extremes the view that all conceptual content is only subjective, is only a phenomenon of consciousness. With him, it is absolutely out of the question for the idea to have participated as a real principle in the constitution of the world. For him, will is the *exclusive* world ground. Therefore Schopenhauer could never find a way, with any content, of handling the specialized branches of philosophy, whereas Hartmann followed up his principles into all the particular sciences. Whereas Schopenhauer can say nothing more about the extremely rich content of history than that it is a manifestation of will, Eduard von Hartmann knows how to find the ideal core of every single historical phenomenon, and how to incorporate each phenomenon into the total historical development of mankind. The individual entity, the individual phenomenon, cannot be of interest to Schopenhauer, for he knows only *one* essential thing to say about it: that it is a manifestation of the will. Hartmann takes up each particular entity and shows how the idea is everywhere perceptible. The basic character of Schopenhauer's worldview is uniformity; that of von Hartmann is unity. Schopenhauer bases the world upon an empty uniform urge; Hartmann bases it upon the rich content of the idea. Schopenhauer sets an abstract unity as a basis; with Hartmann, we find the concrete idea as principle, whose unity – or rather unifiedness – is only one characteristic of the idea. Schopenhauer would never have been able, as Hartmann was, to create a philosophy of history or a science of religion. When Hartmann says that "reason is the logical form principle of the idea – of the idea that is inseparably united with the will – and as such altogether governs and determines the content of the world process" (*Philosophical Questions of the Present Day*[67]), then this presupposition makes it possible for him, in every phenomenon that confronts us in nature and in history, to seek out its logical core, which, although *not* graspable by the senses, is quite graspable by thinking, and in this way to explain the phenomenon. Whoever does not make this presupposition will never be able to justify his wanting to determine anything at all about the world by reflection in the medium of ideas.

In his objective idealism Eduard von Hartmann stands entirely upon the ground of the Goethean worldview. When Goethe says that "everything of which we become aware and about which we are able to speak is only a manifestation of the idea" (*Aphorisms in Prose*), and when he states that the human being must develop within himself a capacity for knowledge of such a kind that the idea becomes just as observable to him as an outer perception is to his senses, then he stands upon that ground where the idea is not merely a phenomenon of consciousness but is an objective world principle; thinking is the flashing up in consciousness of that which objectively constitutes the world. The essential thing about the idea, therefore, is not what it is for us, for our consciousness, but rather what it is in itself. For, through its own particular being it underlies the world as principle. Therefore thinking is a becoming aware of what exists in and of itself. Therefore, although the idea would not come to manifestation at all if there were no consciousness, still the idea must be grasped in such a way that its characteristic feature consists not of its being conscious but rather of what it is in itself, of what lies within the idea itself; and this is not affected by its becoming conscious. Therefore, according to Eduard von Hartmann, we must base the world upon the idea – without regard to its becoming conscious – as something working and unconscious. That is what is essential for Hartmann: that we must seek the idea in everything unconscious.

But not much is accomplished by this distinguishing between what is conscious and what is unconscious. For that is, after all, only a distinction for *my consciousness*. But one must grapple with the idea in all its objectivity, in all its fullness of content; one must consider not only *that* the idea is at work unconsciously, but also *what* this working element is. If Hartmann had stopped at the fact that the idea is unconscious and if he had explained the world out of this unconscious element – that is, out of a one-sided characteristic of the idea – then he would have added a new uniform system to the many systems that derive the world from some abstract formal principle or other. And one cannot declare his first main work to be entirely free of this uniformity. But Eduard von Hartmann's spirit works too intensively, too comprehensively and penetratingly, for him not to have recognized that the idea cannot be grasped merely as something unconscious; rather, one must in fact go deeply into what one has to address as unconscious, must go beyond this characteristic to its concrete content and derive from it the world of individual phenomena. In this way, Hartmann transformed himself from the abstract monist, which he still is in his *Philosophy of the Unconscious,* into a concrete monist. And it is the concrete idea that Goethe addresses in the three forms: archetypal phenomenon, *typus,* and "idea in the narrower sense."

What we find of Goethe's worldview in Eduard von Hartmann's philosophy is the becoming aware of something objective within our world of ideas, and the devotion, arising from this becoming aware, to this objective element. Hartmann was led by his philosophy of the unconscious to this merging with the objective idea. Since he recognized that the being of the idea does not lie in its being conscious, he had to recognize the idea also as something existing in and of itself, as something objective. The fact that he also includes the will among the principles constituting the world does make him differ again from Goethe, to be sure. Nevertheless, where Hartmann is really fruitful, the will motif does not come into consideration at all. That he assumes this motif at all comes from the fact that he regards the ideas as something static which, in order to begin working, needs the impetus of will. According to Hartmann, the will alone can never achieve the creation of the world, for it is the empty, blind urge for existence. If the will is to bring forth *something,* then the idea must enter in, because only the idea gives the will a *content* for its working. But what are we to make of this will? It slips away from us when we want to grasp it; for we cannot after all grasp an empty urging that has no content. And so it turns out after all that everything which we actually grasp of the world principle is idea, *because what is graspable must in fact have content.* We can only grasp what is full of content, not what is empty of content. If therefore we are to grasp the concept 'will,' it must after all arise in the content of the idea; it can appear only in and along with the idea, as the form in which it arises, never independently. What exists must have *content*; there can only be existence that is full; there cannot be an empty one. Therefore, Goethe pictures the idea as *active,* as something working, which needs no further impetus. For, something full of content may not and cannot first receive from something empty of content, the impetus to come into existence. The idea therefore, according to Goethe, is to be grasped as *entelechy*, i.e., as an already active existence; and one must first draw an abstraction from its form as an active existence if one then wants to bring it back again under the name 'will.' The will motif also has no value at all for positive science. Hartmann also does not need it when he confronts the concrete phenomenon.

If we have recognized in Hartmann's view of nature an echo of Goethe's worldview, we find an even more significant one in that philosopher's ethics. Eduard von Hartmann finds that all striving for happiness, all pursuing of egoism, is ethically worthless, because we can, after all, never achieve contentment on this path. Hartmann considers acting out of egoism, and trying to satisfy it, to be illusory. We should grasp the task we are set in the world, and act purely for the sake of *this task* itself, with self-renunciation. We should find our goal in our devotion to the object, without demanding that our subject profit from it in some way. But this forms the basic impulse of Goethe's ethics. Hartmann should not have suppressed the word that expresses the character of his teachings on morality: *love*.[68] Where we claim nothing personally, where we act only because something objective moves us, where we find in the act itself the motive for our action, there we are acting morally. *But there we are acting out of love*. All self-will, everything personal, must disappear there. It is characteristic of the way Hartmann's powerful and healthy spirit works, that in spite of the fact that he first grasped the idea one-sidedly as unconscious, he still pressed forward to concrete idealism; and that in spite of the fact that he took his start in ethics from pessimism, he was still led by this mistaken standpoint to the *ethical teaching of love*. Hartmann's pessimism, in fact, does not mean what those people interpret it to mean who like to lament about the fruitlessness of our activity because they hope to find themselves justified by this in folding their hands in their laps and accomplishing nothing. Hartmann does not stop at such lamenting; he raises himself above any such impulse to a pure ethics. He shows the worthlessness of the pursuit of happiness by revealing its fruitlessness. He directs us thereby to our own activity. That he is a pessimist at all is his error. That is perhaps still a remnant from earlier stages of his thinking. From where he stands now, he would have to realize that the empirical demonstration that in the world of reality what is unsatisfying outweighs what is satisfying cannot establish pessimism. For the higher human being cannot wish for anything else at all than that he must achieve his happiness for himself. He does not want it as a gift from outside. He wants his happiness to consist only in his action. Hartmann's pessimism dissolves before (Hartmann's own) higher thinking. *Because the world leaves us dissatisfied, we create for ourselves the most beautiful happiness in our own activity.*

Thus Hartmann's philosophy is yet another proof of how people starting from different points of departure arrive at the same goal; Hartmann takes his start from different presuppositions than Goethe does, but in his development of them, the Goethean train of thought confronts us at every turn. We have presented this here because we wanted to show the deep inner soundness of the Goethean worldview. It lies so deeply founded in the being of the world that we must meet its basic features wherever energetic thinking penetrates to the sources of knowledge. Within Goethe everything was so very original, so totally free from the incidental, fashionable views of the time, that even his opponent must think in his sense. The eternal riddle of the world expresses itself, in fact, in single individuals; in Goethe most significantly of all in recent time; therefore one can even say that the level of a person's view can *be measured today by the relationship in which it stands to the Goethean view.*

XII

Goethe and Mathematics

Among the main hindrances standing in the way of a just evaluation of Goethe's significance for science belongs the preconception that exists about his relationship to mathematics. This preconception is twofold. Firstly, one believes that Goethe was an enemy of this science and failed in the worst way to recognize its great significance for human knowing; and secondly, one maintains that the poet excluded any mathematical approach from the physical parts of the natural science pursued by him only because the mathematical approach was uncomfortable to him, as he had benefited from no training in mathematics.

As regards the first point, one can say in refutation of it that Goethe repeatedly gave expression to his admiration for the science of mathematics in such a decisive manner that there can be absolutely no question of his attaching little value to it. In fact, he wants to be sure that all natural science is permeated by that strictness that is characteristic of mathematics. "We must learn from the mathematicians to take care to place next to each other only the elements that are closest to each other, or rather to deduce from each the elements closest to it, and even where we use no calculations, we must always proceed as though obliged to render account to the strictest geometrician." "I heard myself accused of being an opponent, an enemy, of mathematics altogether, *which no one, after all, can value more highly than I do* ..."

As regards the second criticism: it is of such a kind that hardly anyone who has once looked into Goethe's nature could raise it seriously. How often has Goethe spoken out against the undertakings of problematical people who strive for goals without bothering about whether, in doing so, they are keeping within the bounds of their abilities! And he himself should have violated this precept, he should have set up natural-scientific views, ignoring his insufficiencies in mathematical things! Goethe knew that the paths to what is *true* are infinitely many, and that each person can travel the one most in accordance with his abilities, and will arrive at his goal. "Every human being must think in his own way: for he will always find something true along his path, or a kind of truth that will help him through life; but he must not just let himself go; he must control himself ..." (*Aphorisms in Prose*). "The least of men can be complete if he is active within the limits of his abilities and skills; but even good qualities become obscured, cancelled out, and destroyed if that absolutely essential proportion is lost." (*Ibid.*)

It would be ludicrous for someone to assert that Goethe would go into an area lying outside his field of vision in order to accomplish anything at all. Everything depends upon establishing what task mathematics has and where its application to natural science begins. Now Goethe did actually undertake the most conscientious study of this. Where it is a question of determining the limits of his productive powers, the poet develops a sharpness of understanding surpassed only by his genius' depth of understanding. We would especially like to make those people aware of this who have nothing else to say about Goethe's scientific thinking than that he lacked a logical, reflective way of thinking. The manner in which Goethe established the boundary between the natural-scientific method he employed and that of the mathematicians reveals a deep insight into the *nature* of the science of mathematics. He knew exactly what the basis is for the certainty of mathematical theorems; he had formed a clear picture for himself of the relationship in which mathematical lawfulness stands with respect to the lawfulness of the rest of nature.

If a science is to have any value at all as knowledge, it must open up for us a particular region of reality. Some aspect or other of the world content must manifest itself in it. The way in which it does this constitutes the *spirit* of a particular science. Goethe had to recognize the spirit of mathematics in order to know what can be attained in natural science without the help of computation and what cannot. This is the point that really matters. Goethe himself indicated this with great decisiveness. The way he does this reveals a deep insight into the nature of the mathematical.

Let us examine this nature more closely. Mathematics deals with magnitude, with that which allows of a more or less. Magnitude, however, is not something existing in itself. In the broad scope of human experience there is nothing that is *only* magnitude. Along with its other characteristics, each thing also has some that are determined by numbers. Since mathematics concerns itself with magnitudes, what it studies are not objects of experience complete in themselves, but rather only everything about them that can be measured or counted. It separates off from things everything that can be subjected to this latter operation. It thus acquires a whole world of abstractions within which it then works. It does not have to do with things, but only with things insofar as they are magnitudes. It must admit that here it is dealing only with *one* aspect of what is real, and that reality has yet many other aspects over which mathematics has no power. Mathematical judgments are not judgments that fully encompass real objects, but rather are valid only within the ideal world of abstractions that we ourselves have conceptually separated off from the objects as *one* aspect of reality. Mathematics abstracts magnitude and number from things, establishes the completely ideal relationships between magnitudes and numbers, and hovers in this way in a pure world of thoughts. The things of reality, insofar as they are magnitude and number, allow one then to apply mathematical truths. It is therefore definitely an error to believe that one could grasp the whole of nature with mathematical judgments. Nature, in fact, is not merely quantity; it is also quality, and mathematics has to do only with the first. The mathematical approach and the approach that deals purely with what is qualitative must work hand in hand; they will meet in the thing, of which they each grasp *one aspect*. Goethe characterizes this relationship with the words: "Mathematics, like dialectics, is an organ of the inner, higher sense; its practice is an art, like oratory. For both, nothing is of value except the form; the content is a matter of indifference to them. It is all the same to them whether mathematics is calculating in pennies or dollars or whether rhetoric is defending something true or false." (*Aphorisms in Prose*) And, from *Sketch of a Color Theory*: "Who does not acknowledge that mathematics is one of the most splendid organs of man, is *from one aspect* very useful to physics?" In this recognition, Goethe saw the possibility that a mind that does not have the benefit of a mathematical training can still occupy itself with physical problems. Such a mind must limit itself to what is qualitative.

XIII

Goethe's Basic Geological Principle

Goethe is very often sought where he is absolutely not to be found. Among the many other areas where this has happened is the way the geological research of the poet has been judged. But here more than anywhere it is necessary for everything that Goethe wrote about details to recede into the background before the wonderful intention from which he took his start. He must be judged here above all according to his own maxim: "In the works of man, as in those of nature, it is actually the intentions that are primarily worthy of attention" and "The *spirit* out of which we act is the highest thing." Not what he achieved but rather *how* he strove for it is what is exemplary for us. We are dealing, not with a doctrine, but rather with a method to be communicated. Goethe's doctrine depends upon the scientific means of the times and can be superseded; his method sprang from his great spiritual endowment and stands up even though scientific instruments are being perfected and our experience broadened.

Goethe was introduced into geology through his occupation with the Ilmenau mine, which was one of his official duties. When Karl August became ruler, he devoted himself with great earnestness to this mine, which had been neglected for a long time. First, the reasons for its decline were to be thoroughly investigated by experts and then everything possible was to be done to revive the operation. Goethe stood by Duke Karl August in his undertaking. He pressed on most energetically with this matter. This led him often into the Ilmenau mine. He wanted to familiarize himself completely with the state of affairs. He was in Ilmenau for the first time in May 1776 and often thereafter.

In the midst of this *practical* concern, there now arose in him the *scientific* need to arrive at the laws of those phenomena that he was in a position to observe there. The comprehensive view of nature that worked its way up in his spirit to ever greater clarity (see his essay *Nature*) compelled him to explain, in his sense, what was spread out there before his eyes.

Here right away a deep-lying characteristic of Goethe's nature manifests itself. He has an essentially different need than many investigators. Whereas, for the latter, the main thing is knowledge of the particulars, whereas they are usually interested in an edifice of ideas, in a system, only insofar as it is helpful in observing the particulars, for Goethe, the particulars are only intermediaries to a comprehensive, total view of existence. We read in the essay Nature: "*Nature* consists solely of children, and the *mother*, where is she?" We also find in *Faust* ("See all the working power and seeds") the same striving to know not only the immediately existing, but also its deeper foundations. In this way, what he observes upon and beneath the surface of the earth also becomes for him a means of penetrating into the riddle of how the world is formed. What he writes to the Duchess Luise on December 23, 1786, ensouls all his research: "The works of nature are always like a word that has just been spoken by God"; and what is experienceable to the senses becomes for him a writing from which he must read that word of creation. In this vein he writes to Frau v. Stein on August 22, 1784: "*The great and beautiful writing* is always legible and is indecipherable only when people want to transfer their own petty images and their own narrow-mindedness onto the infinite beings." We find the same tendency in *Wilhelm Meister*: "But if I were now to treat precisely these cracks and fissures as letters, had to decipher them, were to form them into words, and learned to read them fully, would you have anything against that?"

Thus, from the end of the 1770's on, we see the poet engaged in an unceasing effort to decipher this writing. The goal of his striving was to work his way up to a view such that what he *saw* separated would appear to him in inner, necessary relationship. His method was "one that develops and unfolds things, by no means one that compiles and orders them." It did not suffice for him to see granite here and porphyry there, etc., and then simply to arrange them according to external characteristics; he strove for a law that underlay all rock formation and that he needed only to hold before himself in spirit in order to understand how granite had to arise here and porphyry there. He went back from that which differentiates, to that which is held in common. On June 12, 1784, he writes to Frau v. Stein: "The simple thread that I have spun for myself is leading me beautifully through all these subterranean labyrinths, and is giving me an overview even in the confusion." He seeks the common principle that, according to the different conditions under which it comes to manifestation, at one time brings forth *this* kind of rock and another time brings forth that. Nothing in the realm of experience is a constant for him at which one could remain; only the *principle*, which underlies everything, is something of that kind. Goethe therefore also endeavors always to find the *transitions* from rock to rock. One can recognize much better from them, in fact, the intention, the tendency of their genesis, than from a product that has already developed in a *definite* way, where nature in fact reveals its being only in a one-sided way, indeed very often "goes astray into a blind alley by specializing."

It is an error to believe that one has refuted this method of Goethe by indicating that present-day geology does not know of any such transition of one rock into another. Goethe, in fact, never maintained that granite actually passes over into something different. What is once granite is a finished, complete product and no longer has the inner driving power to become something else out of itself. What Goethe was seeking, however, is in fact lacking in present-day geology, and that is the *idea*, the principle that constitutes granite before it has become granite, and *this* idea is the same one that also underlies all other formations. When Goethe speaks therefore of the transition of one rock into a different one he does not mean by this a *factual* transformation but rather a development of the objective idea that takes shape in the individual forms, that now holds fast to one form and becomes granite, and then again develops another possibility out of itself and becomes slate, etc. Also in this realm Goethe's view is not a barren theory of metamorphosis but rather *concrete idealism*. But that rock-forming principle can come to full expression, with all that lies in this expression, only within the whole body of the earth. Therefore the history of the formation of the earth's body becomes the main thing for Goethe, and all the particulars have to fit into it. The important thing for him is the place a given rock occupies in the totality of the earth;

the particular thing interests him only as a part of the whole. Ultimately, that mineralogical-geological system seems to him to be the correct one that recreates the processes in the earth, which shows why precisely this had to arise at this place and that had to arise in another. Geological deposits become of decisive importance for him. He therefore criticizes Werner's teachings, which he otherwise reveres so highly, for not arranging the minerals according to the way they are deposited, which informs us about how they arose, but rather according to incidental external features. *It is not the investigator who makes the perfect system, but rather nature itself that has done that.*

It should be borne in mind that Goethe saw in the whole of nature *one* great realm, a harmony. He maintains that all natural things are ensouled with one tendency. What is therefore of the same kind had to appear to him as determined by the same lawfulness. He could not grant that other forces are at work in geological phenomena – which are in fact nothing more than inorganic entities – than in the rest of inorganic nature. *The extending into geology of the laws of inorganic activity is Goethe's first geological deed.* It was this principle that guided him in his explanation of the Bohemian mountains and in his explanation of the phenomena observed at the temple of Serapis at Pozzuoli. He sought to bring principle into the dead earth crust by thinking of it as having arisen through those laws that we always see at work before our eyes in physical phenomena. The geological theories of a Hutton, an Elie de Beaumont were deeply repugnant to him. What was he supposed to do with explanations that *violate* all natural order? It is banal to repeat so often the empty remark that it was Goethe's *peaceful nature* that was repelled by the theory of rising and sinking, etc. No, this theory affronted his sense for a *unified* view of nature. He could not insert this theory into what is in accordance with nature. And he owes it to this sense that he early on (in 1782 already) arrived at a view that professional geologists attained only decades later: the view that fossilized animal and plant remains stand in a necessary relationship with the rock in which they are found. Voltaire had still spoken of them as *freaks* of nature, because he had no inkling of the consistency of natural lawfulness. Goethe could make sense of a thing in one place or other only if a simple, natural connection existed between this thing and its environment. It is also the same principle that led Goethe to the fruitful *idea of an ice age.* (see *Geological Problems and an Attempt at their Solution*)[69] He sought a simple explanation, in accordance with nature, for deposits of granite masses widely separated over large areas. He had indeed to reject the explanation that they *had been hurled* there by a tumultuous upheaval of mountains lying far behind them, because this explanation did not trace a fact of nature back to the existing working laws of nature but rather derived this fact from an exception, from an abandonment, in fact, of these laws. He assumed that northern Germany had once had, under conditions of extreme cold, a general water level of a thousand feet, that a large part was covered with a layer of ice, and that those granite blocks were left lying after the ice had melted away. With this, a view was expressed that is based upon known laws experienceable by us. Goethe's significance for geology is to be sought in his establishment of a general lawfulness of nature. *How* he explained the Kammerberg, whether or not he was correct in his opinion about the springs of Karlsbad, is unimportant. "It is a question here not of an opinion to be disseminated, but rather of a method to be communicated that anyone may make use of in his own way as a tool" (Goethe to Hegel, October 7, 1820).

XIV

Goethe's Meteorological Conceptions

Just as in geology, so in meteorology it would be an error to go into what Goethe actually achieved and consider that to be the main thing. His meteorological experiments are in fact nowhere complete. One can only look everywhere at his intention. His thinking was always directed at finding the *pregnant*[70] point from which a series of phenomena governs itself from within outward. Any explanation that takes manifestations, incidentals, from here and there in order to construct a regular series of phenomena was not in accordance with his approach. When confronted by a phenomenon, he looked for everything related to it, for all the facts belonging in the same sphere, in such a way that a whole, a totality, lay before him. Within this sphere, a principle then had to be found that made all the regularity, the whole sphere of related phenomena, in fact, appear as a necessity. It did not seem to him to be in accordance with nature to explain the phenomena in *this* sphere by introducing circumstances lying outside it. This is where we must seek the key to the principle he set up in meteorology. "More and more each day I felt the complete inadequacy of ascribing such constant phenomena to the planets, to the moon, or to some unknown ebb and flow of the atmosphere ..." "But we reject all such influences; we consider the weather phenomena on earth to be neither cosmic nor planetary, but rather, according to our premises, we must explain them as being purely *telluric*." He wanted to trace back the phenomena of the atmosphere to their causes, which lay in the being of the earth itself. The important thing, to begin with, was to find the point where the basic lawfulness that determines everything else expresses itself directly. Barometric pressure provided just such a phenomenon. Goethe then regarded this also as the archetypal phenomenon and sought to connect everything else to it. He tried to follow the rise and fall of the barometer and believed that he also perceived a regularity in it. He studied Schrön's tables and found "that the aforementioned rise and fall *follow an almost parallel course* at different points of observation, whether nearby or remote, and also in different longitudes, latitudes, and altitudes." Since this rising and falling seemed to him to be a direct manifestation of gravity, he believed that he saw in barometric changes a direct expression of the quality of the force of gravity itself. But one must not infer anything more from this Goethean explanation. Goethe rejected any setting up of hypotheses. He wanted to provide only an *expression* for an observable phenomenon, not an actual factual cause, in the sense of present-day natural science. He believed the other atmospheric phenomena should fit in quite well with *this* phenomenon. The formation of clouds interested the poet most of all. For this, he had found in Howard's teachings a means of grasping the ever-changing forms in certain basic configurations and thus of "firming up with enduring thoughts, something that exists as a changing phenomenon." He still sought in addition only some means that would help him understand the transformations of the cloud forms, just as he found in that "spiritual ladder" a means of explaining the transformation of the typical leaf shape in the plant. Just as there the spiritual ladder was for him the red thread running through the individual configurations, so here in meteorology it is for him a varying "constitution" (*Geeigenschaftetsein*) of the atmosphere at varying altitudes. In both cases, we must bear in mind that it could never occur to Goethe to regard such a red thread as a real configuration. He was perfectly aware of the fact that only the individual configuration is to be regarded as real for the senses *in space*, and that all higher principles of explanation are there only for the *eyes of the spirit*. Present-day refutations of Goethe are therefore mostly a jousting with windmills. One attributes to his principles a form of reality that he himself denied them and believes one has overcome him in this way. But present-day natural science does not know that form of reality upon which he based things: the objective, concrete idea. From this side, Goethe must therefore remain foreign to present-day science.

XV

Goethe and Natural-scientific Illusionism

The reason for writing this chapter does not lie in the fact that the *Color Theory*, accompanied by an introduction, must also be included in a Goethe edition. It stems from a deep, spiritual need of the editor of this edition. The latter took his start from the study of mathematics and physics and with inner necessity was led, by the many contradictions pervading the system of our modern view of nature, to a critical investigation of the method-ological basis of these sciences. His initial studies led him to the principle of strict knowledge through experience; his insight into those contradictions led him to a strict scientific epistemology. He was protected by his positive starting point from any rever-sion to purely Hegelian conceptual constructs. With the help of his epistemological studies, he finally found the reason for many of the errors of modern natural science to lie in the completely incorrect standing that science had assigned to the simple sense impression. Our science transfers all sense qualities (sound, col-or, warmth, etc.) into the subject and is of the opinion that "out-side" the subject there is nothing corresponding to these qualities except processes of motion of matter. These processes of mo-tion, which are supposedly all that exists within the "realm of nature," can of course no longer be perceived. They are *inferred* on the basis of subjective qualities.

But this inference must appear to consistent thinking as fragmentary. *Motion* is, to begin with, only a concept that we have borrowed from the sense world; i.e., it confronts us only in things with sense-perceptible qualities. We do not know of any motion other than that connected with sense objects. If one now transfers this attribute onto entities that are not sense-perceptible – such as the elements of discontinuous matter (atoms) are sup-posed to be – then one must after all be clear about the fact that through this transference, an attribute perceived by the senses is ascribed to a form of existence essentially different from what is conceived of as sense-perceptible. One falls into the same contradiction when one wants to arrive at a real content for the initially completely empty concept of the atom. Sense qualities, in fact, even though ever so sublimated, must be added to this concept. One person ascribes impenetrability, exertion of force, to the atom; another ascribes extension in space, and so on; in short, each one ascribes certain characteristics or other that are borrowed from the sense world. If one does not do this, one remains in a complete void.

That is why the above inference is only fragmentary. One draws a line through the middle of what is sense-perceptible and declares the one part to be objective and the other to be subjective. The only consistent statement would be: If there are atoms, then these are simple parts of matter, with the characteristics of matter, and are not perceptible only because their small size makes them inaccessible to our senses.

But with this there disappears any possibility of seeking anything in the motion of atoms that could be held up as something objective in contrast to the subjective qualities of sound, color, etc. And the possibility also ceases of seeking anything more, for example, in the connection between motion and the sensation "red" than a connection between two processes that both belong entirely to the sense world.

It was therefore clear to the editor that motion of ether, position of atoms, etc., belong in the same category as the sense impressions themselves. Declaring the latter to be subjective is only the result of unclear reflection. If one declares sense qualities to be subjective, then one must do exactly the same with the motion of ether. It is not for any principle reason that we do not perceive the latter, but only because our sense organs are not organized finely enough. But that is a purely coincidental state of affairs. It could be the case that someday mankind, by increasing refinement of our sense organs, would arrive at the point of also perceiving the motion of ether directly. If then a person of that distant future accepted our subjectivistic theory of sense impressions, then he would have to declare these motions of ether to be just as subjective as we declare color, sound, etc., to be today.

It is clear that this theory of physics leads to a contradiction that cannot be resolved.

This subjectivistic view has a second support in *physiological considerations.*

Physiology shows that a sensation appears only as the final result of a mechanical process that first communicates itself, from that part of the corporeal world lying outside the substance of our body, to the periphery of our nervous system, into our sense organs; from here, the process is transmitted to our highest center, in order to be released there for the first time as sensation. The contradictions of this physiological theory are presented in the chapter on "The Archetypal Phenomenon." One can, after all, label only the brain substance's form of motion as subjective here. No matter how far one might go in investigating the processes within the subject, one must always remain, on this path, within what is mechanical. And one will nowhere discover the sensation in the central organ.

Therefore only *philosophical* consideration remains as a way of gaining information about the subjectivity and objectivity of sensation. And this provides us with the following.

What can be designated as "subjective" about a perception? Without having an exact analysis of the concept "subjective," one cannot go forward at all. Subjectivity, of course, cannot be determined by anything other than itself. Everything that cannot be shown to be conditional upon the subject may not be designated as "subjective." Now we must ask ourselves: What can we designate as the human subject's *own*? That which it can experience about itself through outer or inner perception. Through *outer* perception we grasp our bodily constitution; through *inner* experience, we grasp our own thinking, feeling, and willing. Now what is to be designated as subjective in the first case? The constitution of the whole organism, and therefore also the sense organs and brain, which will probably appear in each human being in somewhat different modifications. But everything that can be indicated here in this way is only a particular formation in the arrangement and function of substances by which a sensation is transmitted. Only the path, therefore, is actually subjective that the sensation has to take before it can become my sensation. Our organization transmits the sensation and these paths of transmission are subjective; the sensation itself, however, is not subjective.

Now there still remains the path of inner experience for us consider. What do I experience within myself when I designate a sensation as my own? I experience that in my thinking I effect a connection to my individuality, that I extend my sphere of knowing out over this sensation; but I am not conscious of creating any *content* for the sensation. I only register its connection to myself; the quality of the sensation is a fact founded within itself.

No matter where we begin, whether within or without, we do not arrive at a place where we could say that here the subjective character of the sensation is given. The concept "subjective" is not applicable to the content of sensation.

It is these considerations that compelled me to reject as impossible any theory of nature that in a principle way goes *beyond* the realm of the perceived world, and to seek the sole object of natural science exclusively within the sense world. But then I had to seek, within the mutual interdependencies of the facts of precisely this sense world, that which we designate as the *laws of nature*.

And in this way, I was forced to that view of the natural-scientific method that underlies the Goethean color theory. Whoever finds these considerations to be correct will read this color theory with very different eyes than modern natural scientists can. Such a person will see that what we have here is not Goethe's hypothesis confronting that of Newton, but rather at issue here is the question: Is today's theoretical physics acceptable or not? If not, however, then neither is the light that this physics casts upon color theory. May the reader experience from the following chapters what our principle foundation is for physics, in order then, from this foundation, to see Goethe's undertakings in the right light.

XVI

Goethe as Thinker and Investigator

1. Goethe and Modern Natural Science

If it were not a person's duty to state the truth without reserve once he believes he has come to know it, the following exposition would certainly have remained unwritten. I have no doubts about the judgment that the specialists will pass on it, given the dominant trend in natural science today. One will regard it as someone's dilettantish attempt to speak for something upon which judgment has long since been passed by all "discerning" people. When I picture to myself the scorn of all those who consider themselves the only ones qualified today to speak on natural-scientific questions, I must admit to myself that there is nothing tempting, in any ordinary sense, about this undertaking. But I could not let myself be deterred by these anticipated objections. For I can raise all these objections myself and know therefore how poorly they stand up. It is not difficult, indeed, to think "scientifically" in the sense of modern natural science. Not too long ago, in fact, we experienced an interesting case in point. Eduard von Hartmann appeared with his *Philosophy of the Unconscious*. The gifted author of this book himself would be the last one today to deny its imperfections. But the direction of thought we encounter there is a penetrating one, which gets to the bottom of things. It therefore made a powerful impression on all those minds that had a need for deeper knowledge. But it ran counter to the paths of the natural scientists who were feeling their way along on the surface of things. They were all against the book. After various attacks from their side had proven rather ineffective, a book appeared by an anonymous author, *The Unconscious from the Standpoint of Darwinism and the Theory of Evolution*,[71] which brought forward with the greatest possible critical acuity everything against the newly founded philosophy that could be said against it from the standpoint of modern natural science. This book caused a stir. The adherents of the current trend were satisfied by it to the highest degree. They publicly acknowledged that the author was one of them and proclaimed his views as their own. What a disillusionment they had to suffer! When the author actually revealed himself, it was Eduard v. Hartmann. This proved one thing convincingly, however: Ignorance about the findings of natural science, dilettantism, is not the reason why it is impossible for certain minds, who are striving for a deeper insight, to join that school of thought which wants to establish itself today as the dominant one. The reason, however, is their knowledge that this school is not on the right path. It is not difficult for philosophy hypothetically to take the standpoint of the present-day view of nature. In what he did, Eduard v. Hartmann showed this irrefutably to anyone who wants to see. I bring this as confirmation of my above assertion that it is also not difficult for me to raise the objections myself that someone else can make against what I bring.

Indeed, anyone is considered a dilettante today who takes philosophical reflection about the essential being of things at all seriously. Having a worldview is regarded as an idealistic quirk by our contemporaries of a "mechanical," or even by those of a "positivistic," persuasion. This view becomes comprehensible, to be sure, when one sees the helpless ignorance in which these positivistic thinkers find themselves when they make themselves heard on the subject of the "being of matter," of "the limits of our knowing," of "the nature of the atom," or of other such things. In connection with these examples, one can make real studies of dilettantish treatment of decisive questions of science.

One must have the courage to admit all this to oneself with respect to the natural science of the present day, in spite of the tremendous and remarkable achievements that this same natural science has to show in the realm of technology. For, these achievements have nothing to do with our real need for knowledge of nature. We have indeed experienced – precisely in those contemporaries to whom we owe inventions whose significance for the future we cannot for a long time even begin to imagine – that they lack a deeper *scientific* need. It is something entirely different to observe the processes of nature in order to place its forces in the service of technology, than to seek, with the help of these processes, to look more deeply into the being of natural science. True science is present only where the human spirit seeks to satisfy *its* needs, without any *external* purpose.

True science, in the higher sense of the word, has to do only with ideal objects; *it can only be idealism*. For, it has its ultimate foundation in needs that stem from the human spirit. Nature awakens questions in us, problems that strive for solution. But nature cannot itself provide this solution. Through our capacity for knowledge a higher world confronts nature; and this fact creates higher demands. For a being who did not possess this higher nature, these problems would simply not arise. These questions can therefore also not receive an answer from any authority other than precisely this higher nature. Scientific questions are therefore essentially a matter that the human spirit has to settle with itself. They do not lead the human spirit out of its element. The realm, however, in which the human spirit lives and weaves as though within its primally own, is the idea, is the world of thoughts. To solve thought-questions with thought-answers is the scientific activity in the highest sense of the word. And all other scientific procedures are there, ultimately, only in order to serve this highest purpose. Take scientific observation, for example. It is supposed to lead us to knowledge of a law of nature. The law itself is purely ideal. The need to find a lawfulness holding sway behind the phenomena already stems from the human spirit. An unspiritual being would not have this need. Now let us proceed to the observation! What do we actually want to achieve by it? In response to the question created in our spirit, is something supposed to be provided from outside, by sense observation, that could be the answer to that question? Never. For why should we feel ourselves more satisfied by a second observation than by the first? If the human spirit were satisfied at all by an observed object, then it would have to be satisfied right away by the first. But the actual question is not at all one about any second observation, but rather about the ideal foundation of the observations. What does this observation admit as an ideal explanation; how must I *think* it so that it appears possible to me? Those are the questions that come to us with respect to the sense world. I must seek, out of the depths of my spirit itself, what I lack when confronted by the sense world. If I cannot create for myself the higher nature for which my spirit strives when confronted by sense-perceptible nature, then no power in the external world will create it for me. The results of science therefore can come only from the human spirit; thus they can only be *ideas*. No objections can be raised against this necessary reflection. The ideal character of all science, however, is established thereby.

Modern natural science, in accordance with its whole being, cannot believe in the ideal character of knowledge. For, it does not regard the idea as that which is primary, most original, and creative, but rather as the final *product* of material processes. But in doing so, it is not at all aware of the fact that these material processes belong only to the sense-perceptible, observable world that, however, grasped more deeply, dissolves completely into idea. The process under consideration presents itself to observation, namely, in the following way: We perceive facts with our senses, facts that run their course according to the laws of mechanics, then phenomena of warmth, of light, of magnetism, of electricity, and finally of life processes, etc. At the highest level of life, we find that life raises itself up to the forming of concepts and ideas, whose bearer, in fact, is the human brain. We find our own 'I' springing from just such a sphere of thoughts. The 'I' seems to be the highest product of a complicated process that is mediated by a long series of physical, chemical, and organic occurrences. But if we investigate the ideal world of which the content of that 'I' consists, we find in that world essentially *more* than merely the end product of that process. We find that the individual parts of that world are connected to each other in a completely different way than the parts of that merely observed process are. As one thought arises in us, which then demands a second, we find that there is an ideal connection between these two objects in an entirely different way than if I observe the color of a substance, for example, as the result of a chemical agent. It is of course entirely obvious that the successive stages of the brain process have their source in organic metabolism, even though the brain process itself is the bearer of those thought-configurations. But the reason as to why the second thought *follows* from the first: this I do *not* find within this metabolism, but do indeed find within the logical thought-connection. Thus, in the world of thoughts, there holds sway, besides *organic necessity*, a *higher ideal* necessity. But this necessity, which the human spirit finds within its world of ideas, this it also seeks in the rest of the universe. For this necessity arises for us, indeed, only through the fact that we not only *observe*, but also *think*. Or in other words, the things no longer appear in a merely factual connection, but rather as joined by an inner, ideal necessity, if we grasp them not merely through observation but rather through thoughts.

With respect to this, one cannot say: What good is it to grasp the phenomenal world in thoughts, when the things of this world perhaps do not, according to their nature, allow of any such grasp? Only someone who has not grasped the core of this whole matter can ask such a question. The world of thoughts rises up within our inner being; it confronts the objects observable to the senses; and then asks: What relationship does the world confronting me there have to myself? What is it with respect to me? I am here with all my ideal necessity, which hovers above everything transitory; I have the power within me to explain myself. But how do I explain what confronts me?

It is here that a significant question is answered for us that Friedrich Theodore Vischer, for example, has raised repeatedly and declared to be the pivotal point of all philosophical reflection: the question as to the connection between the human spirit and nature. What kind of a relationship exists between these two things, which to us always appear separated from each other? If one asks this question *correctly*, then its answer is not as difficult as it appears to be. What meaning can this question actually have then? The question is not in fact asked by some being that stands above nature and human spirit as a third entity and that investigates that connection from this standpoint, but rather it is asked by one of the two beings themselves, *by the human spirit*. The latter asks: What connection exists between me and nature? But that again means nothing other than: How can I bring myself into a relationship with the nature confronting me? How can I express this relationship in accordance with the needs living in me? I live in *ideas*; what kind of an idea corresponds to nature; how can I express, as *idea*, that which I *behold* as nature? It is as though we have often obstructed our own path to a satisfactory answer by putting the question wrongly. A correct question, however, is already half an answer.

The human spirit seeks everywhere to go beyond the succession of facts, as mere observation provides him with them, and to penetrate to the *ideas of the things*. Science, indeed, begins at the place where thinking begins. In the findings of science there lies, in the form of ideal necessity, that which appears to the senses only as a succession of facts. These findings only seem to be the final product of the process described above; the truth is that they are that which we must regard, in the whole universe, as the foundation of everything. Where these findings then appear for observation is a matter of indifference; for, as we have seen, their significance does not in fact depend upon that. They spread the net of their ideal necessity out over the whole universe.

No matter where we take our start, if we have enough spiritual power, we will finally meet up with the *idea*.

Through the fact that modern physics completely fails to recognize this, it is led into a whole series of errors. I want to point to only one such error here, as an example.

Let us take the definition of *inertia*, which in physics is usually included among the "general characteristics of bodies." This is usually defined in the following way: Without an external cause, no body can change the state of motion in which it finds itself. This definition gives rise to the picture that the concept of a body, inert in itself, is abstracted from the world of phenomena. And John Stuart Mill, who nowhere goes into the matter itself, but who, for the sake of an arbitrary theory, stands everything on its head, would not hesitate for a moment also to explain the matter in this way. But this is after all completely incorrect. The concept of an inert body arises purely through a conceptual construction. In designating as "body" what has extension in space, I can picture to myself a kind of body whose changes stem from external influences, and a kind whose changes occur out of its own impulse. If I now find something in the outer world that corresponds to the concept I have formed of a "body that cannot change itself without an outer influence," I then call this body *inert* or subject to the law of inertia. My concepts are not abstracted from the sense world, but rather are constructed freely out of the idea, and with their help I only first find my way rightly in the sense world. The above definition could only take this form: A body that out of itself cannot alter its state of motion is called an inert body. And when I have recognized a body to be of this kind, I can then apply to it everything that is connected with an inert body.

2. The "Archetypal Phenomenon"

If we could follow the whole series of processes that occur with respect to some sense perception or other from the peripheral nerve endings of the sense organs all the way into the brain, we would in fact nowhere arrive at a point where the mechanical, chemical, and organic – in short, the temporal-spatial processes – end and *that* appears which we actually call sense perception; for example, the sensation of warmth, of light, of sound, etc. One cannot find a place where the causal motion supposedly goes over into its effect, the perception. But can we then speak at all of the two things as standing in a relationship of cause and effect?

Let us just examine the facts, quite objectively. Let us assume that a particular sensation appears within our consciousness. It appears at the same time *in such a way* that it directs us to some object or other from which it stems. When I have the sensation "red," I generally associate with it, by virtue of the content of this mental picture, a particular place, i.e., a location in space, or the surface of a thing, to which I ascribe what this sensation expresses. This is not the case only where, through an external influence, the sense organ itself responds in its own characteristic way, as when I have a sensation of light from a blow to the eye. Let us disregard such cases in which, what is more, the sensations never arise with their usual definiteness. As exceptions, they cannot in fact teach us about the nature of things. If I have the sensation "red" along with a particular location, then I am at first directed to something or other in the outer world as the bearer of this sensation. I can very well ask myself now what spatial-temporal processes are taking place in this thing while it is appearing to me as though possessed of the color red. I shall then discover that mechanical, chemical, or other processes offer themselves as an answer to my question. I can go further now and investigate the processes that have occurred on the way from that thing to my sense organ to mediate the sensation of the color "red" for me. There again, in fact, nothing other than processes of motion or electrical currents or chemical changes can present themselves to me as such mediators. The result would be the same for me if I could investigate the further mediation from the sense organ to the center of the brain. *What* is mediated on this whole path is the perception "red" that we are discussing. *How* this perception manifests in a particular thing lying on the path from the stimulus to the perception depends solely upon the nature of this thing. The sensation is present at every point, from the stimulator to the brain, but not as such, not explicitly, but rather in a way corresponding to the nature of the object existing at each point.

A truth results from this, however, that is qualified to shed light upon the entire theoretical foundation of physics and physiology. What do I experience from the investigation of a thing caught up in a process that appears in my consciousness as sensation? I experience no more than the way that thing responds to the action that issues from the sensation, or, in other words the way a sensation *expresses itself* in some object or other of the spatial-temporal world. It is far from the truth to regard such a spatial-temporal process as the *cause*, as that which causes the sensation in me; something quite different is the correct view: The spatial-temporal process is the *effect* of the sensation within a thing that has extension in space and time. I could insert as many things as I wanted into the path from the stimulator to the organ of perception: only that will occur in each one of them that can occur in it by virtue of its nature. But it is still the *sensation,* therefore, that expresses itself in all these processes.

One should therefore regard the longitudinal vibrations of the air in the mediating of sound or the hypothetical oscillation of the ether in the mediating of light to be nothing other than the way the sensations in question can appear in a medium that, in accordance with its nature, is capable only of rarification and densification or of oscillating motion, as the case may be. I cannot find the sensation as such in this world, *because it simply cannot be there.* But in those processes I am absolutely not given what is objective about the processes of sensation, but rather a form of their manifestation.

And now let us ask ourselves: What is the nature of those mediating processes themselves? Do we then investigate them by any means other than with the help of our senses? Can I in fact investigate my senses? Is the peripheral nerve ending, are the convolutions of the brain given to me by anything other than by sense perception? All this is both subjective and objective at the same time, if this distinction can be considered to be justified at all. Now we can grasp the matter still more exactly. By following the perception from its stimulus to the organ of perception, we are investigating nothing other than the continuous transition from one perception to the other. The "red" is present before us as that for whose sake we are undertaking the whole investigation at all. It directs us to its stimulator. In the latter we observe other sensations as connected with this "red." These are processes of motion. The latter then appear as further processes of motion between the stimulator and the sense organ, and so on. But all of these are likewise perceived sensations. And they represent nothing more than a metamorphosis of processes that, insofar as they come into consideration at all for sense observation, break down entirely into perceptions.

The perceived world is therefore nothing other than a sum total of metamorphosed perceptions.

For the sake of convenience, we had to use an expression that cannot be brought into complete harmony with our present conclusions. We said that each *thing* which is inserted into the space between the stimulator and the organ of perception brings a sensation to expression in a way that is in accordance with the nature of that thing. But strictly speaking the thing is nothing more than the sum total of those processes as which it appears.

The objection might now be raised that this kind of conclusion eliminates any enduring element in the ongoing world process, that we, like Heraclitus, are making the flux of things, in which nothing is abiding, the one and only world principle. Behind the phenomena, there must be a "thing-in-itself"; behind the changing world there must be an "enduring matter." But let us in fact investigate more exactly what the case really is with this "enduring matter," with what "endures amidst change."

When I confront my eye with a red surface, the sensation "red" arises in my consciousness. In connection with this sensation, we must now distinguish beginning, duration, and end. Over against the transitory sensation there supposedly now stands an enduring objective process that as such is itself objectively limited in time, i.e., has beginning, duration, and end. This process, however, is supposedly occurring in connection with a matter that is without beginning or end, that is therefore indestructible, eternal. This matter is supposedly what actually endures within the changing processes. This conclusion would perhaps have some justification if the concept of time had been correctly applied to the sensation in the above manner. But must we not then distinguish strictly between the content of the sensation and the appearing of the sensation? In my perception, to be sure, they are one and the same. For, the content of the sensation must after all be present in the perception or the sensation would otherwise not come into consideration for me at all. But is it not a matter of complete indifference for this content, taken purely as such, that it enters my consciousness now at this particular moment and then, after so and so many seconds, leaves it again? That which constitutes the content of the sensation, i.e., that which alone comes objectively into consideration, does not depend at all upon that. But now *that* which is a matter of complete indifference to the content of something cannot, after all, be regarded as an essential determining factor for the existence of that something.

But our application of the time-concept is also not correct for an objective process that has a beginning and an end. When a new characteristic arises in a particular thing, maintains itself for a time in different states of development, and then disappears again, there also we must regard the content of this characteristic as what is essential. And what is essential has absolutely nothing as such to do with the concepts of beginning, duration, and end. By "essential" we mean that by which a thing actually is precisely what it presents itself to be. What matters is not the fact that something arises at a certain moment in time, but rather *what* arises. The sum total of all the traits expressed by this "what" makes up the content of the world. But this "what" exists in the most manifold traits, in the most diverse forms. All these forms are in a relationship to each other; they determine each other reciprocally. Through this, they enter into a relationship of separation according to *space* and *time*. But it is only to a completely mistaken understanding of the concept of time that the concept of *matter* owes its existence. One believes that one would rarify the world into a semblance without being, if one did not picture, as underlying the changeable sum total of occurrences, something that endures in time, something unchangeable, that abides while its traits are varying. But time is not after all a container within which the changes occur; it is not there before the things are, nor *outside* of them. *Time* is the sense-perceptible expression of the situation that the facts, in their content, are mutually dependent upon each other sequentially. Let us imagine we have to do with the perceptible complex of facts a1, b1, c1, d1, and e1. Another complex, a2, b2, c2, d2, and e2, depends with inner necessity upon the first complex; I understand the content of the second complex when I derive it ideally from the first one. Now let us imagine that both complexes make their appearance. For, what we discussed earlier is the entirely non-temporal and non-spatial essential being (*Wesen*) of these complexes. If a2, b2, c2, d2, and e2 is to come to outer manifestation, then a1, b1, c1, d1, and e1 must likewise be outer phenomena, in such a way, in fact, that a2, b2, c2, d2, and e2 also appear in their dependency upon the first complex. This means that the phenomenon a1, b1, c1, d1, and e1 must be there and make room for the phenomenon a2, b2, c2, d2, and e2 to appear. We see here that time first arises where the *essential being* of something comes to *outer manifestation* (*Erscheinung*). Time belongs to the phenomenal world. It does not yet have anything to do with the essential being itself. This essential being can only be grasped ideally. Only someone who cannot manage, in his train of thought, to go back from the phenomenon to the essential being will hypothesize time as something preceding the facts. Then, however, he needs a form of existence that endures beyond the changes. He conceives indestructible matter to be just such an existence. He has thereby created for himself a thing to which time supposedly can do nothing, something that abides amidst all change. Actually, however, he has only shown his inability to press forward, from the temporal phenomenon of the facts, to their essential being, which has nothing to do with time. Can I therefore say of the essential being of a fact that it arises or passes away? I can only say that one fact's content determines another and that this determining influence then appears as a sequence in time. The essential being of a thing cannot be destroyed; for, it is outside of all time and itself determines time. With this, we have shed light upon two concepts at the same time for which but little understanding is still to be found: upon *essential being* (*Wesen*) and *outer manifestation* (*Erscheinung*). Whoever grasps the matter correctly in our way cannot look for proof of the indestructibility of the essential being of something, because destruction includes within itself the time-concept, which has nothing to do with essential being.

In the light of these discussions, we can say: The sense-perceptible world picture is the sum total of metamorphosing perceptual contents without an underlying matter.

But our considerations have also shown us something else. We have seen that we cannot speak of a subjective character of perceptions. When we have a perception, we can follow the processes from the stimulator to our central organ: nowhere is there a point to be found where the jump can be demonstrated from the objectivity of the non-perceived to the subjectivity of the perception. This refutes the subjective character of the world of perception. The world of perception stands there as a content founded upon itself, which, for the moment, still has absolutely nothing to do with subject and object.

Our discussion, of course, applies only to that concept of matter upon which physics bases its observations and which it identifies with the old, equally incorrect substance-concept of metaphysics. Matter, as the actually real element underlying phenomena, is one thing; matter, as phenomenon, as outer manifestation, is something else. Our exposition applies solely to the first concept. The second one remains untouched by it. For if I call what fills space "matter," that is merely a word for a phenomenon to which no higher reality is ascribed than to other phenomena. I must only keep this character of matter always in mind.

The world of what presents itself to us as perceptions – i.e., extension, motion, state of rest, force, light, warmth, color, sound, electricity, etc. – this is the object of all science.

If now the perceived world picture were of such a kind that, in the way it arises before us for our senses, it could express itself in accordance with its nature, unobscured; or in other words, if everything that arises in outer manifestation were a complete, undisturbed image of the inner being of things, then science would be the most unnecessary thing in the world. For, the task of knowledge would already be fully and totally fulfilled in the perception. Indeed, we would not then be able to differentiate at all between essential being and outer manifestation. The two would completely coincide as identical.

This, however, is not the case. Let us imagine that element A, contained in the factual world, stands in a certain relationship to element B. Both elements, of course, according to our expositions, are nothing more than phenomena. Their relation also comes to manifestation as a phenomenon. Let us call this phenomenon C. What we can now determine within the factual world is the relationship of A, B, and C. But now, besides A, B, and C, there also exist infinitely many other such elements in the perceptible world. Let us take some fourth element or other D; it enters in, and at once everything presents itself in a modified form. Instead of A, in conjunction with B, resulting in C, an essentially different phenomenon, E, will arise from the entering of D.

That is the important point. When we confront a phenomenon, we see it determined by many factors. We must seek out all the interrelationships if we are to understand the phenomenon. But these relationships differ from each other; some are more intimate, some more distant. The fact that a phenomenon E confronts me is due to other phenomena that are more intimately or more distantly related. Some are absolutely necessary if such a phenomenon is to arise at all; other phenomena, by their absence, would not at all keep such a phenomenon from arising, but do cause it to arise in precisely *this* or *that* way. We see from this that we must differentiate between necessary and coincidental determining factors of a phenomenon. Phenomena that arise in such a way that only the necessary determining factors bring them about can be called *primary*, and the others *derivative*. When, from their determining factors, we understand the primary phenomena, we can then also understand the derivative ones by adding new determining factors.

Here the task of science becomes clear to us. It has to penetrate far enough through the phenomenal world to seek out the phenomena that are dependent only upon necessary determining factors. And the verbal-conceptual expression for such necessary relationships is *laws of nature*.

When a person is confronting a sphere of phenomena, then, as soon as he has gone beyond mere description and registering of these, he must therefore first of all ascertain those elements that determine each other necessarily, and present them as archetypal phenomena. One must then add those determining factors that stand in a more distant relationship to those elements, in order to see how they modify those primary phenomena.

This is the relationship of science to the phenomenal world: within the latter, the phenomena absolutely do arise as derivative ones and are therefore incomprehensible from the very beginning; in science, the archetypal phenomena arise in the forefront with the derivative ones following, whereby the whole connection becomes comprehensible. The system of science differentiates itself from the system of nature through the fact that in the system of science the interrelationships of the phenomena are ascertained by the intellect and are rendered comprehensible thereby. Science never has to bring something in addition to the phenomenal world, but rather has only to disclose the hidden interrelationships of this world. All use of the intellect must be limited only to this latter work. By taking recourse to something that does not manifest in order to explain the phenomena, the intellect and any scientific activity are exceeding their powers.

Only someone who sees the absolute correctness of our findings can understand Goethe's color theory. Any reflection about what a perception like light or color might be in addition to the entity as which it manifests was completely foreign to Goethe's nature. For he knew what the powers of intellectual thinking were. Light was given to him as sensation. When he then wanted to explain the connection between light and color, that could not occur through speculation, but only through an *archetypal phe-*

nomenon, by his seeking out the necessary determining factor that must join light in order for color to arise. Newton also saw color arise in connection with light, but he then only thought speculatively about how color arises out of light. It lay in his speculative way of thinking to do so; but not in Goethe's way of thinking, which was objective and rightly understood itself. Therefore, Newton's assumption that "light is composed of colored lights" had to appear to Goethe as the result of unrightful speculation. He considered himself justified only in expressing something about the *connection* between light and color when some determining factor joins in, and not in expressing something about the light itself by bringing in a speculative concept. Therefore his statement: "Light is the simplest, most undivided, most homogeneous being that we know. It is not a composite." Any statements about the composition of light are, indeed, only statements of the intellect about one phenomenon. The powers of the intellect, however, extend only to statements about the *connection* of phenomena.

This reveals the deeper reason why Goethe, as he looked through the prism, could not accept Newton's theory. The prism would have had to be the *first determining factor* for the coming about of color. But another determining factor, the presence of something dark, proved to be more primary to its coming about; the prism proved to be only the second determining factor.

With this exposition, I believe I have removed any hindrances that might lie in the way of readers of Goethe's color theory.

If this difference between the two color theories had not always been sought in two mutually contradictory forms of explanation that one then wanted simply to examine as to their validity, then the value of the Goethean color theory, in all its great scientific significance, would have been recognized long ago. Only someone who is filled with such fundamentally wrong mental pictures – such as that, through intellectual thinking, one must go from the perceptions back to the cause of the perceptions – can still raise the question in the way present-day physics does. But someone who has really become clear about the fact that explaining the phenomena means nothing other than *observing* them in a connection established by the intellect must accept the Goethean color theory *in principle*. For, it is the result of a correct way of looking at the relationship of our thinking to nature. Newton did not have this way of looking at things. Of course, it would not occur to me to want to defend every detail of the Goethean color theory. It is only the *principle* that I want to uphold. But it can also not be my task here to derive from his principle the phenomena of color theory that were still unknown in his day. If I should ever have the good fortune to possess the time and means for writing a color theory in Goethe's sense that is entirely on the high level of modern achievements in natural science, that would be the only way to accomplish such a task. I would consider that as belonging to my finest life tasks. This introduction could extend only to the scientifically strict validation of Goethe's *way of thinking* in his color theory. In what follows, light is also still to be shed upon the inner structure of this theory.

3. The System of Natural Science

It could easily seem as though, in our investigations that attribute to thinking only a power whose goal is to connect perceptions, we ourselves were now calling into question the independent significance of concepts and ideas for which we stood so energetically at first.

Only an inadequate interpretation of this investigation can lead to this view.

What does thinking accomplish when it carries out the connecting of perceptions?

Let us look at two perceptions A and B. These are given to us at first as entities without concepts. I cannot, through any conceptual reflection, transform into something else the qualities given to my sense perception. I can also find no thought-quality by which I could construct what is given in sense-perceptible reality if I lacked the perception. I can never create a mental picture of the quality "red" for someone blind to red, even though I paraphrase it conceptually for him by every conceivable means. *The sense perception therefore has a something that never enters into the concept, that must be perceived if it is to become an object of our knowledge at all.* What kind of a role does the concept play, therefore, that we connect with some sense perception or other? The concept must obviously bring to the perception a completely independent element, something new, which does belong to the sense perception, to be sure, but that does not come into view in the sense perception.

But it is now certain, indeed, that this new "something" that the concept brings to the sense perception is that which first expresses what can meet our need for explanation. We are first able to understand some element or other in the sense world when we have a concept of it. We can always simply point to what sense-perceptible reality offers us, and anyone who has the possibility of perceiving precisely this element to which we are referring knows what it is all about. Through the concept, we are able to say something about the sense world that cannot be perceived.

From this, however, the following immediately becomes clear. If the essential being of the sense perception consisted only in its sense-perceptible qualities, then something completely new, in the form of the concept, could not join it. The sense perception is therefore not a totality at all, but rather only one side of a totality. And it is that side, in fact, which can be merely looked upon. Through the concept it first becomes clear to us *what* we are looking at.

What we developed *methodologically* in the previous chapter can now be expressed in terms of the significance of its *content*. Through our conceptual grasp of something given in the sense world, the "*what*" of that which is given to our view first comes to manifestation. We cannot express the content of what we look at, because this content consists only in the "*how*" of what we look at, i.e., in the *form* of its manifestation. Thus, in the *concept*, we find the "what," the other content of that which is given in the sense world in an observed form.

The world first gains its full content, therefore, in the concept. But now we have discovered that the concept points us beyond the individual phenomenon to the interrelationship of things. Thus that which appears in the sense world as separated, isolated, presents itself to the concept as a *unified* whole. And so our natural-scientific methodology gives rise to a *monistic natural science* as its final goal; but it is not an abstract monism that already presupposes the unity and then forcibly includes in it the individual facts of *concrete* existence, but rather it is a concrete monism that, piece by piece, shows that the seeming manifoldness of sense existence proves ultimately to be only an ideal unity. The multiplicity is only a form in which the unified world content expresses itself. The senses, which are not in a position to grasp this unified content, hold fast to the multiplicity; they are born pluralists. Thinking, however, overcomes the multiplicity and thus, through a long labor, returns to the unified world principle.

The manner, now, *in which* the concept (the idea) expresses itself within the sense world constitutes the differences among the realms of nature. If a sense-perceptibly real entity attains only a kind of existence in which it stands totally outside the concept and is only governed in its transformations by the concept as by a *law*, then we call this entity *inorganic*. Everything that occurs with such an entity is to be traced back to the influences of another entity; and how the two act upon each other can be explained by a law standing outside them. In this sphere we have to do with phenomena and laws that, if they are primary, can be called *archetypal phenomena*. In this case, therefore, the conceptual element that is to be perceived stands outside of a perceived manifoldness.

But a sense-perceptible unity itself, in fact, can point beyond itself; it can compel us, if we want to grasp it, to go on to further determining factors than to those perceptible to us. Then, what is conceptually graspable appears as a sense-perceptible unity. The two, concept and perception, are, indeed, not identical, but the concept does not appear *outside* the sense-perceptible manifoldness as a law, but rather *within* the manifoldness as a principle. The concept underlies the manifoldness as something that permeates it, as something that is no longer sense-perceptible, as something that we call *typus*. *Organic* natural science has to do with this.

But here also the concept does not yet appear in the form particular to it as concept, but still only as *typus*. *Where*, now, the concept appears, not merely as *typus*, as permeating principle, but rather in its own conceptual form, there it appears as *consciousness*, there there finally comes to manifestation that which is present at the lower stages only in essence. There the concept becomes a perception. We have to do with the self-aware human being.

Natural law, typus, and *concept* are the three forms in which the ideal element expresses itself. The natural law is abstract, standing over the sense-perceptible manifoldness; it governs inorganic natural science. Here idea and reality separate from each other completely. The *typus* already unites the two within one entity. The spiritual becomes an active entity, but does not yet act as such; it is not there as such, but rather, if it wants to be viewed in accordance with its existence, it must be *looked at* as something sense-perceptible. This is the situation in the realm of organic nature. The concept is present in a perceptible way. In human consciousness, it is the concept itself that is perceptible. The observed and the idea coincide. It is precisely the ideal element that is observed. Therefore, at this level, the ideal cores of existence of nature's lower levels can also come to manifestation. With human consciousness the possibility is given that what, at the lower levels of existence, merely is, but does not manifest, now becomes also manifesting reality.

4. The System of the Color Theory

Goethe worked at a time when human spirits were filled by a powerful striving for an absolute knowledge that would find its satisfaction within itself. Man's activity of knowing once again dared, with holy fervor, to investigate every means of knowledge in order to draw nearer to a solution of the highest questions. The period of oriental theosophy, the period of Plato and Aristotle, and then the period of Descartes and Spinoza are the representatives, in previous epochs of world history, of a similar inner deepening. Goethe is not thinkable without Kant, Fichte, Schelling, and Hegel. If these thinkers possessed above all a vision into the depths and an eye for the highest, his gaze rested upon the things of immediate reality. But in his gaze there lies something of that depth itself. Goethe exercised this vision in looking at nature. The spirit of that time is poured out like a fluid over his contemplations of nature. Hence their power, which, in contemplating the details, always maintains the broad outlines. Goethe's science always goes after what is central.

We can see this in Goethe's color theory more than anywhere else. It alone, besides his attempts relative to the metamorphosis of the plant, was brought to a completed whole. And what a strictly complete system it does represent, such as is demanded by the nature of the thing itself!

Let us now consider this edifice according to its inner structure.

In order that something founded in the being of nature may come to manifestation, the necessary prerequisite is that a causal opportunity, an organ, be present in which this something can present itself. The eternal, iron laws of nature would, in fact, hold sway even if they never presented themselves within a human spirit, but their manifestation as such would not then be possible. They would then be present merely in essence and not in manifestation. This would also be the case with the world of light and color if no perceiving eye confronted them. Color, in its essential being, cannot be traced back in Schopenhauer's manner to the eye; but the possibility for color to manifest must very definitely be shown to lie within the eye. The color is not conditional upon the eye, but the eye is the cause of its manifestation.

Here is where color theory must therefore take its start. It must investigate the eye, must disclose its nature. This is why Goethe places *physiological* color theory at the beginning. But even there his conception is essentially different from what one usually understands this part of optics to be. He does not want to explain the functions of the eye by its structure, but wants rather to observe the eye under various conditions in order to arrive at a knowledge of its capacities and abilities. Here also his procedure is essentially an *observational* one. What happens when light and darkness act upon the eye; what happens when defined images enter into relationship with it, etc.? He does not ask, to begin with, what processes occur within the eye when one or another perception comes about, but rather he seeks to fathom what can come about through the eye in the *living* act of seeing. For his purpose, that is to begin with the only important question. That other question does not belong, strictly speaking, to the realm of physiological color theory, but rather to the science of the human organism, i.e., to general physiology. Goethe has to do with the eye only insofar as it sees, and not with the explanation of seeing that comes from the perceptions we can have of the dead eye.

From there, he then goes over to the objective processes that bring about the phenomena of colors. And here it is important to bear in mind that Goethe, with these objective processes, is by no means thinking of hypothetical processes of matter or of motion that are no longer perceptible, but rather that he absolutely remains within the perceivable world. His *physical color* theory, which constitutes the second part, seeks the conditions that are independent of the eye and are connected to the arising of the colors. But these conditions are still always perceptions. Here, with the help of the prism, of lenses, etc., he investigates how colors arise in connection with light. But for the time being, he does not go beyond tracing color as such in its development and observing how, in itself, separated from objects, it arises.

Only in a separate chapter on *chemical color theory* does he go on to colors that are fixed, that are connected with objects. If, in the *physiological* color theory, the question is answered as to how colors can come to manifestation at all, and, in the *physical* color theory, the question as to how the colors come about under external conditions, so Goethe responds here to the problem of how the corporeal world manifests as *colored.*

In this way, Goethe advances from contemplation of color as an attribute of the phenomenal world to this world itself as manifesting with that attribute. He does not stop there, but goes on finally to contemplate the higher relationship of the colored corporeal world to the human soul in that chapter on *"The sense-perceptible and moral Effect of Color." ("Sinnlich-sittliche Wirkung der Farbe")*

This is the strict, complete path of a science: from the subject as determining factor, back again to the subject as the being who satisfies himself in and with his world.

Who will not recognize here again the impulse of the time – from subject to object and back into the subject again – that led Hegel to the architectonics of his whole system.

In this sense then, the *Sketch of a Color Theory*,[72] appears as the actual optical main work of Goethe. The two essays, *Contributions to Optics*[73] and *The Elements of Color* Theory[74] must be considered as preliminary studies. *The Exposure of Newton's Theory*[75] is only a polemical addition to his work.

5. The Goethean Concept of Space

Since a complete understanding of Goethe's work in physics is possible only for someone with a view of *space* that is entirely consonant with his, let us describe this view here. Whoever wants to arrive at this view must have gained the following convictions from our considerations until now: 1. The things that confront us in experience as separate have an inner relationship to each other. They are, in truth, held together by a unified world bond. There lives in them all *one* common principle. 2. When our spirit approaches the things and strives to encompass what is separate with a spiritual bond, then the conceptual unity that our spirit establishes is not outside of the objects but rather is drawn from the inner being of nature itself. Human knowledge is not a process taking place outside of the things, not a process springing from mere subjective arbitrariness, but rather: what arises there in our spirit as a law of nature, what expresses itself within our soul, that is the heartbeat of the universe itself.

For our present purposes, let us take under consideration the most external of all relationships that our spirit can establish between the objects of experience. Let us consider the simplest case in which experience summons us to a spiritual activity. Let us assume that two simple elements of the phenomenal world are given. In order not to complicate our investigation, let us take something as simple as possible – two luminous points, for example. Let us completely disregard the fact that in each of these luminous points themselves we perhaps have before us something that is already immensely complicated, that sets our spirit a task. Let us also disregard the quality of the concrete elements of the sense world we have before us, and take into consideration purely and simply the fact that we have before us two separate elements, i.e., two elements that appear to the senses as separated. Two factors, each of which is able to make an impression upon our senses – that is all we presuppose. Let us assume further that the existence of one of these factors does not exclude that of the other. *One* organ of perception can perceive both.

If we assume, namely, that the *existence* of the one element is in any way dependent upon that of the other, we are then facing a different problem than our present one. If the existence of *B* is of such a kind that it excludes the existence of *A* and yet, in its being, is dependent upon it, then *A* and *B* must stand in a *temporal relationship*. For the dependency of *B* upon *A* requires – if one pictures to oneself at the same time that the existence of *B* excludes that of *A* – that *A* precedes *B*. But that is a separate matter.

For our present purposes, let us not assume any *such* relationship. Our presupposition is that the things with which we are dealing are not mutually exclusive in their existence, but rather are co-existing entities. When we disregard every relationship that their inner natures demand, then there remains only the fact that a relationship exists between the two separate qualities, that I can go from the one over to the other. I can move from the one element of experience over to the second one. No one can have any doubts about what kind of a relationship it is that I establish between things when I disregard their character and nature themselves. Whoever asks himself what transition can be found from one thing to another, if the thing itself remains a matter of indifference thereby, must absolutely give the answer: *space*. Every other connection must be based upon the qualitative character of that which appears as separate in world existence. Only space takes absolutely nothing else into consideration except the fact that the things are indeed *separated*. When I reflect that *A* is above and *B* is below, it is a matter of complete indifference to me what *A* and *B* are. I join no other mental picture to them at all other than that they are, indeed, separate factors of the world I grasp with my senses.

What our spirit wants to do when it confronts experience is this: it wants to overcome the separateness; it wants to show that, within the particular thing, the power of the whole is to be seen. In its spatial view, the human spirit does not want to overcome anything other than the separateness as such. It wants to establish the *most general relationship of all*. What the spatial way of looking at things states is that *A* and *B* are not each a world in itself, but rather belong to something in common. That is what *being beside one another* (*Nebeneinander*) means. If each thing were an entity in itself, then there would be no being beside one another. I could not establish any relationship at all between one entity and another.

Let us now investigate what else follows from this establishing of an outer relationship between two separate entities. I can think of two elements in only *one* way in this kind of relationship. I think of *A as beside B*. I can now do the same thing with two other elements of the sense world, *C* and *D*. I have thereby determined a concrete relationship between *A* and *B*, and the same one between *C* and *D*. Let us now entirely disregard the elements *A, B, C,* and *D* and only relate the two concrete relationships to each other again. It is clear that I can relate these, as two particular entities, to each other in exactly the same way as I did with *A* and *B* themselves. What I am here relating to each other are concrete relationships. I can call them *a* and *b*. If I now go a step further, I can again relate *a* and *b*. But now I have already lost all particularity. When I look at *a*, I no longer find any particular *A* and *B* that are being related to each other; and just as little when I look at *b*. In both, I find nothing else at all except that a relationship was made. But this conclusion is exactly the same for *a* and for *b*. What made it possible for me still to keep *a* and *b* apart was the fact that they pointed to *A, B, C,* and *D*. If I leave out its remaining elements of particularity and then relate only *a* and *b* to each other – i.e., relate together only the facts that relationships were being made at all (not the fact that something specific was being related) – then I have again arrived quite generally at the spatial relationship from which I took my start. I can go no further. I have achieved what I was striving for previously: *space* itself stands before my soul.

Herein lies the secret of the three dimensions. In the first dimension I relate two concrete phenomenal elements of the sense world to each other; in the second dimension I relate these spatial relationships themselves to each other. I have established a relationship between relationships. I have stripped away the concrete phenomena; the concrete relationships remain for me. I now relate these themselves spatially to each other. This means: I entirely disregard the fact that these are concrete relationships; then, however, I must find *exactly the same thing* again in the second relationship that I found in the first. I establish relationships between similar entities. Now the possibility of relating ceases because the difference ceases.

What I earlier took as the point of view for my considerations – the completely external relationship – I have now achieved again myself as a sense picture; from my spatial consideration, after I have carried out the operation three times, I have arrived at space, i.e., at my starting point.

Therefore space can have only three dimensions. What we have undertaken here with respect to the mental picture of space is actually only a specific case of the method always employed by us when we confront things in observation. We regard concrete objects from one general point of view. Through this, we gain concepts about the particulars; we then regard these concepts themselves again from the same point of view, so that we then have before us any longer only the concepts of the concepts; if we still join these also, then they fuse into that ideal unity which cannot any longer be brought under one point of view with anything other than itself. Let us take a specific example. I become acquainted with two people, *A* and *B*. I look at them from the point of view of friendship. In this case I will arrive at a quite specific concept, *a*, of the friendship between the two people. I now look at two other people, C and *D*, from the same point of view. I arrive at another concept, *b*, of this friendship. Now I can go further and relate these two concepts of friendship to each other. What remains for me, when I disregard the concrete element I have gained, is the *concept of friendship in general*. But I can arrive at this in an even more real way, when I look at two other people, *E* and *F*, from the same point of view, and likewise two people G and *H*. In this, as in innumerable other cases, I can obtain the concept of *friendship in general*. But all these concepts, in their essential nature, are identical to each other; and when I look at them from the same point of view, it then turns out that I have found a unity. I have returned again to where I took my start.

Space, therefore, is a view about things, a way in which our spirit draws them together into a unity. The three dimensions relate to each other thereby in the following way. The first dimension establishes a relationship between two sense perceptions. It is therefore a *concrete mental picture*. The second dimension relates two concrete mental pictures to each other and thus passes over into the region of *abstraction*. The third dimension, finally, establishes in addition only the ideal *unity* between the abstractions. It is therefore completely incorrect to take the three dimensions of space as though they were altogether of equal significance. The nature of the first dimension depends, of course, upon the perceived elements. But then the other two have a quite definite and *different* significance than this first one. Kant was quite wrong in his assumption when he conceived of space as the whole (*totum*), instead of as an entity conceptually determinable in itself.

Now we have hitherto spoken of space as a relationship, a connection. But the question now arises: Is there then only this relationship of "being beside one another"? Or is there an absolute place-determination for every thing? This last question is of course not touched upon at all by our above explanations. But let us consider whether there is, indeed, any such place-relationship, any quite specific "there." What am I actually indicating when I speak of such a "there"? Nothing else, in fact, than that I am referring to an object that is in immediate proximity to the actual object under consideration. "There" means in proximity to some object indicated by me. With this, however, the absolute place-indication is brought back to a *space relationship*. Our investigation is thus cancelled.

Let us now raise the question quite definitely: According to the preceding investigations, what is space? Nothing more than a necessity, lying within the things, of overcoming their separateness in an entirely outer way and without entering into their nature, and of joining them into a unity, even though of just such an outer kind. Space is therefore a way of grasping the world as a unity. *Space is an idea.* Not, as Kant believed, an observation (*Anschauung*).

6. Goethe, Newton, and the Physicists

As Goethe began his consideration of the being of colors, it was essentially an interest in art that brought him to it. His intuitive spirit soon recognized that the use of color in painting is subject to a deep lawfulness. Wherein this lawfulness consisted he could not discover as long as he only moved about theoretically in the realm of painting, nor could trained painters give him any satisfactory information about this. These painters knew very well, in a practical sense, how to mix and apply the colors, but could not express themselves in concepts about the matter. When Goethe, then, was confronted in Italy not only by the most sublime works of art of this kind, but also by the most magnificent colors of nature, the urge awoke in him with special force to know the natural laws of the being of color.

Goethe himself, in the *History of Color Theory*,[76] gives a detailed account of the historical aspect. Let us deal here only with the psychological and factual aspects.

Goethe's study of color began right after his return from Italy. This study became particularly intensive in the years 1790 and 1791, and then occupied the poet continuously until the end of his life.

We must picture to ourselves where the Goethean worldview stood at this time, at the beginning of his study of color. By this time he had already grasped his magnificent thoughts about the metamorphosis of organic entities. Through his discovery of the intermaxillary bone, a view had already arisen in him of the unity of all natural existence. Each individual thing appeared to him as a particular modification of the ideal principle that holds sway in the whole of nature. In his letters from Italy he had already stated that a plant is only a plant through the fact that it bears within itself the "idea of the plant." This idea was something concrete for him; it was the unity, filled with spiritual content, in all particular plants. It could not be grasped by the bodily eyes, to be sure, but could very well be grasped by the eye of the spirit. Whoever can see it, sees it in *every* plant.

Thus the whole realm of the plants and, with the further elaboration of this view, the whole realm of nature, in fact, appears as a unity that the human spirit can grasp.

But no one is able to construct, from the idea alone, the manifoldness that arises before the outer senses. The intuitive spirit is able to know the idea. The *particular* configurations are accessible to him only when he directs his senses outward, when he observes, looks. The reason why a modification of the idea arises in sense-perceptible reality in precisely this and not in another way cannot be thought up, but rather must be *sought* in the realm of reality.

This is Goethe's individual way of looking at things and can best be designated as *empirical idealism*. It can be summarized with the words: Underlying the things of a *sense-perceptible manifoldness*, insofar as they are of a similar kind, there is a *spiritual unity* that brings about their similar nature and relatedness.

Taking his start from this point, Goethe was confronted by the question: What spiritual unity underlies the manifoldness of color perceptions? What do I perceive in *every* modification of color? And there it soon became clear to him that *light* is the necessary basis for every color. No color without light. But the colors are the modifications of light. And now he had to seek that element within reality that modifies, specializes the light. He found that this element is lightless matter, active darkness – in short, that which is the opposite of light. Thus each color became for him light that is modified by darkness. It is completely incorrect to believe that with light Goethe meant the concrete sunlight that is usually called "white light." Understanding of the Goethean color theory is hindered only by the fact that one cannot free oneself from this picture of light and regards this sunlight, which is composed (*zusammengesetzt*) in such a complicated way, as the representative of light in itself. Light, as Goethe apprehends it, and as he contrasts it to darkness as its opposite, is a purely spiritual entity, is simply what all color sensations have in common. Even though Goethe has nowhere clearly expressed this, still his whole color theory is applied in such a way that it can only be interpreted thus. If he did experiment with sunlight in order to develop his theory, his only reason for doing so was that sunlight, in spite of its being the result of such complicated processes as those that occur in the body of the sun, does after all present itself to us as a unity that holds its parts within itself only in a state of abeyance. What we achieve for color theory with the help of sunlight is after all only an *approximation* of reality, however. One cannot apprehend Goethe's theory to mean that, according to it, light and darkness are contained in an outwardly real way in every color. No, it is rather that the outwardly real that confronts our eye is only a particular

210

nuance of color. Only the human spirit is able to take this sense-perceptible fact apart into two spiritual entities: light and non-light.

The outer arrangements by which this occurs, the material processes in matter, are not affected in the least by this. That is a completely different matter. I am not disputing that a process of oscillation occurs in the ether while "red" arises before me. But what brings about a perception *in an outwardly real way*, has, as we have already shown, nothing at all to do with the *essential nature of its content*.

Someone may object: But it can be proven that everything about the sensation is subjective and only the process of motion that underlies it really exists outside of our brain. Then one could not speak at all about a physical theory of perceptions, but only about a *physical* theory of the underlying processes of motion. The state of affairs with respect to this proof is about as follows: If someone in location A sends a telegram to me in location B, then everything given into my hands as this telegram, without exception, has come into existence in B. The telegraph operator is in B; he writes on paper that has never been in A, with ink that has never been in A; he himself does not know location A at all, and so on; in short, it can be proven that absolutely nothing from A has entered into what I now have before me. Accordingly, everything that comes from B is a matter of no significance for the content, for the essential nature, of the telegram; what matters to me is only communicated by B. If I want to explain the essential nature of the content of the telegram, I must entirely disregard what comes from B.

The state of affairs is the same with respect to the world of the eye. Thinking consideration must encompass what is perceptible to the eye and must seek the interrelationships within this area. The material, spatial-temporal processes might be very important for the *coming about* of the perceptions; but they have nothing to do with the *essential nature* of perceptions.

The state of affairs is the same with respect to the question often discussed today as to whether or not one and the same form of motion in the ether underlies the various phenomena of nature such as light, heat, electricity, etc. Hertz, for example, has shown recently that the transmission of electrical effects in space is subject to the same laws as the transmission of light-effects. One can infer from this that waves, such as those that are the bearers of light, also underlie electricity. One has also already assumed before now, indeed, that within the solar spectrum only *one* kind of wave motion is active which, according to whether it falls upon reagents sensitive to heat, light, or chemicals, produces heat, light or chemical effects.

But this is, in fact, clear from the very beginning. If one investigates what is occurring in that which has extension in space, while the entities we are discussing are being communicated, then one must arrive at a *homogeneous* motion. For, a medium in which *only* motion is possible, must react to everything with motion. And all the communicating that it must take over, it will also accomplish with motion. If I then investigate the forms of this motion, I do not then experience what the communicated element *is*, but rather how it was brought to me. It is simply nonsense to say that heat or light are motion. Motion is only the reaction to light of a matter that is capable of motion.

Goethe himself had already heard of the wave theory and had seen nothing in it that could not be brought into harmony with his convictions about the essential nature of color.

One must only free oneself of the picture that, for Goethe, light and darkness are real entities, and regard them, rather, as *mere* principles, as spiritual entities; then one will gain a completely different view of his color theory than one usually forms of it. If, as Newton does, one understands light to be only a mixture of all the colors, then any concept of the concrete entity "light" disappears. "Light" then evaporates completely into an empty general mental picture, to which nothing in reality corresponds. Such abstractions were foreign to the Goethean worldview. For him every mental picture had to have a *concrete* content. But for him, the "concrete" did not cease with the "physical."

Modern physics actually has no concept at all for "light." It knows only specific lights, colors, that in particular mixtures evoke the impression "white." But even this "white" cannot be identified with light in itself. "White" is actually also nothing other than a *mixed* color. Modern physics does not know "light" in the Goethean sense, any more than it knows "darkness." Thus

Goethe's color theory moves in a realm that makes no contact at all with what the physicists determine conceptually. Physics simply does not *know* any of the basic concepts of the Goethean color theory. Therefore, from its standpoint, it cannot judge this theory at all. Goethe, in fact, begins where physics ends.

It demonstrates a completely superficial grasp of the matter when one speaks continuously of the relationship of Goethe to Newton and to modern physics, and in doing so is completely unaware of the fact that two entirely different ways of looking at the world are being indicated.

We are convinced that someone who has grasped our expositions on the nature of sense impressions in the right sense can gain no other impression of the Goethean color theory than the one described. To be sure, someone who does *not* accept these considerations of ours that prepare the ground will remain at the standpoint of physical optics and will therefore also reject Goethe's color theory.

XVII

Goethe Against Atomism

1.

There is much talk nowadays about the fruitful development of natural science in the nineteenth century. I believe that one *can* rightfully speak of significant natural-scientific experiences that one has had, and of a transformation of our practical life by these experiences. But with respect to the basic mental pictures by which the modern view of nature seeks to *understand* the world of experience, these I consider to be unhealthy and, to an energetic thinking, inadequate. I have already expressed myself on this subject on pages 183ff. of this book. Quite recently a well-known scientist of the present day, the chemist Wilhelm Ostwald, has expressed the same view.[77] He says: "When asked how he thinks the world to be 'inwardly' constituted, every scientifically-thinking person, from the mathematician to the practical physician, will summarize his view in the direction that the things are composed of moving 'atoms,' and that these atoms, and the *forces* working between them, are the ultimate realities of which the individual phenomena consist. In hundreds of repetitions one can hear and read this statement, to the effect that no other understanding of the physical world can be found except by tracing it back to a 'mechanics of atoms'; matter and motion seem to be the ultimate concepts to which the manifoldness of the natural phenomena must be related. One can call this view *scientific materialism.*" On pages 183ff. of this book I have said that the basic views of modern physics are untenable. Ostwald (on page six of his lecture) says the same thing in the following words: *"that this mechanistic worldview does not fulfill the purpose for which it was developed; that it comes into contradiction with undoubted and universally known and recognized truths."* The agreement between Ostwald's expositions and my own goes still further. I say (on page 194 of this book): "The sense-perceptible world picture is the sum total of metamorphosing perceptual *contents without an underlying matter.*" Ostwald says (p. 12ff.): "But when we reflect upon the fact that everything we know about a particular substance is a knowledge of its characteristics, we then see that it is *not very far from pure nonsense to assert that a particular substance is indeed present but no longer has any of its characteristics.* In fact, this purely formal assumption serves only to unite the general facts of chemical processes, especially the stoichiometric laws of mass, with the *arbitrary concept of a matter that in itself is unchanged.*" And on page 182 of this book appears the statement: "It is these considerations that compelled me to reject as impossible any theory of nature that in a principle way goes *beyond* the realm of the perceived world, and *to seek the sole object of natural science exclusively within the sense world.*" I find the same thing expressed in Ostwald's lecture on page 25 and 22: "What do we experience then of the physical world? Obviously only that which our sense instruments allow to come to us from it." "The task of science is to bring *realities*, demonstrable and measurable magnitudes, into a definite relationship to each other, in such a way that when certain realities are given the others can be deduced; and this task cannot be accomplished by basing things on some hypothetical picture or other, but only *by demonstrating the reciprocal relationships of dependency between measurable magnitudes.*" If one disregards the fact that Ostwald is speaking in the sense of a natural scientist of the present day and therefore sees in the sense world nothing other than demonstrable and measurable *magnitudes*, then his view corresponds entirely with mine, in the way I have expressed it, for example, in the statement (p. 211): "Thinking consideration must encompass what is perceptible ... *and must seek the interrelationships within this area.*"

In my discussion of Goethe's color theory, I have carried on the same battle against the basic mental pictures of present-day natural science as Professor Ostwald does in his lecture "The Overcoming of Scientific Materialism." What I have put in the place of these basic mental pictures does not, to be sure, agree with what Ostwald has set up. For, as I will show later on, he takes his start from the same superficial presuppositions as do his opponents, the adherents of scientific materialism. I have also shown that the basic mental pictures of the modern view of nature are the cause of the unhealthy judgments that were, and continue to be, passed on Goethe's color theory.

I would now like to deal somewhat more exactly with the modern view of nature. I will seek to know, from the goal that this modern view of nature sets itself, whether this view is a healthy one or not.

It is not without justification that one has seen in the following words of Descartes the basic formula by which the modern view of nature judges the world of perceptions: "When I examine corporeal things more closely, I find that very little is contained in them that I can understand *clearly* and *definitely*, except: magnitude, or extension in length, depth, and breadth; shape, that results from the limits of this extension; location, that the variously shaped bodies have relative to each other; and motion, or change in this location; to which one may add substance, duration, and number. As for other things – such as light, colors, sounds, odors, sensations of taste, warmth, cold and the other qualities that the sense of touch experiences (smoothness, roughness) – they arise within my spirit in such an *obscure and confused way* that I do not know whether they are true or false, i.e., whether the ideas that I grasp of these objects are in fact the ideas of some real things or other, or whether they represent only chimerical entities that cannot exist." The adherents of the modern view of nature have become so habituated to thinking along the lines of this statement of Descartes that they find every other way of thinking to be scarcely worthy of their attention. They say: What is perceived as light is caused by a process of motion that can be expressed in a mathematical formula. When a color arises in the phenomenal world, they trace it back to an oscillating motion and calculate the number of oscillations in a specified time. They believe that the entire sense world will be explained when they have succeeded in tracing all perceptions back to relationships that can be expressed in such mathematical formulas. A mind that could give such an explanation would, according to the view of these natural scientists, have attained the utmost that is possible for man with respect to knowledge of natural phenomena. Du Bois-Reymond, a representative of these learned men, says of such a mind: for it, "the hairs of our heads would be numbered, and not a sparrow would fall to earth without its knowledge." (*Limits to Knowing Nature*)[78] To make the world into a mathematical problem is the ideal of the modern view of nature.

Since, without the presence of forces, the parts of their assumed matter would never come into motion, modern scholars of nature also include *force* among the elements by which they explain the world; and Du Bois-Reymond says: "Knowing nature is a tracing back of changes *within* the corporeal world to the motion of atoms that is caused by the atoms' central forces that are independent of time; or, in other words, knowing nature is a breaking down of nature processes into the *mechanics of atoms*." Through the introduction of the *concept of force*, mathematics passes over into mechanics.

Today's philosophers stand so much under the influence of nature scholars that they have lost all courage to think for themselves. They accept without reservation what nature scholars set up. One of the most respected German philosophers, W. Wundt, says in his *Logic*: "With reference to ... and in the employment of the basic proposition – that because of the qualitative changelessness of matter, all natural processes are, in the last analysis, motion – one regards the goal of physics to be its complete transference into ... *applied mechanics*."

Du Bois-Reymond finds that: "It is a psychological fact of experience that, where such a breaking down (of natural processes into a mechanics of the atoms) succeeds, our need for causality feels itself satisfied for the time being." That may be a fact of experience for Du Bois-Reymond. But it must be stated that there are other human beings as well who absolutely do not feel themselves satisfied by a banal explanation of the corporeal world such as Du Bois-Reymond has in mind.

Goethe belongs to these other human beings. Someone whose need for causality is satisfied when he has succeeded in tracing the processes of nature back to the mechanics of atoms lacks the organ by which to understand Goethe.

2.

Magnitude, shape, location, motion, force, etc., are perceptions in exactly the same sense as light, colors, sounds, odors, sensations of taste, warmth, cold, etc. Someone who isolates the magnitude of a thing from its other characteristics and looks at it by itself no longer has to do with a *real* thing, but only with an abstraction of the intellect. It is the most nonsensical thing imaginable to ascribe a different degree of reality to an abstraction drawn from sense perception than to a thing of sense perception itself. Spatial and temporal relationships have no advantage over other sense perceptions save their greater simplicity and surveyability. It is upon this simplicity and surveyability that the certainty of the mathematical sciences rests. When the modern view of nature traces all the processes of the corporeal world back to something that can be expressed mathematically and mechanically, it does so because the mathematical and the mechanical are easy and comfortable for our thinking to deal with. And human thinking does have an inclination toward being comfortable. One can see that precisely in the above-mentioned lecture of Ostwald. This nature scholar wants to set *energy* in the place of matter and force. Note what he says: "What is the determining factor needed for one of our (sense) instruments to become active? No matter how we look at this, we find no common element except that *the sense instruments react to differences in energy between themselves and their environment.* In a world whose temperature were everywhere the same as our body's, we would in no way be able to experience any warmth, just as we have no sensation at all of the constant atmospheric pressure under which we live; only when we establish spaces with different pressures, do we arrive at any knowledge of this pressure." (p. 25f. of his lecture) And furthermore (p. 29): "Imagine that you were struck by a stick! What would you feel then, the stick or its energy? There can be only one answer: its *energy*. For a stick is the most harmless thing in the world as long as it is not swung. But we can also hit against a motionless stick! Quite right; but as we have already emphasized, what we feel are differences in states of energy against our sense apparatus, and it therefore makes no difference whether the stick strikes us or we hit against the stick. But if we both have the same velocity and are moving in the same direction, then the stick no longer exists for our sensation, because it cannot come into contact with us and effect an exchange of energy." These statements prove that Ostwald isolates *energy* from the realm of the world of perceptions, i.e., abstracts it from everything that is not energy. He traces everything perceptible back to one single characteristic of the perceptible, to the manifestation of energy – to an abstract concept, therefore. Ostwald's entanglement in the natural-scientific habits of the present day is clearly recognizable. If asked, he could also not offer anything more in justification of his procedure than that it is a psychological fact of experience, that his need for causality is satisfied when he has broken down the processes of nature into manifestations of *energy*. Essentially it makes no difference whether Du Bois-Reymond breaks down the processes of nature into a mechanics of atoms or Ostwald breaks them down into manifestations of energy. Both spring from human thinking's inclination toward being comfortable.

Ostwald says at the end of his lecture (p. 34): "Is energy, as necessary and useful as it might be for understanding nature, also *sufficient* for this purpose (of explaining the corporeal world, namely)? Or are there phenomena that cannot be completely described by the laws of energy we know so far? I believe that I cannot meet the responsibility I have assumed toward you today through my presentation, better than by emphasizing that the answer to this question is *no*. As immense as the advantages are that the energistic worldview has over the mechanistic or materialistic one, still several points can already be indicated today, it seems to me, that are not covered by the known main principles of energistics, and that therefore point to the existence of principles that transcend them. Energistics will continue side by side with these new principles. But in the future it will not, as we must still regard it today, be the most comprehensive principle for mastering natural phenomena, but presumably will appear as a particular case of still more general conditions, *of whose form, to be sure, we hardly have an inkling today.*"

3.

If our nature scholars also read the books of people outside of their guild, Professor Ostwald would not have been able to make a statement like this. For in 1891, in the previously mentioned introduction to the Goethean color theory, I have already expressed how we in fact do have an inkling and more than an inkling of such "forms," and that the task of natural science in the future lies in the developing of Goethe's basic natural-scientific conceptions.

Just as little as the processes of the corporeal world can be "broken down" into a mechanics of atoms, so just as little into states of energy. Nothing further is achieved by this approach than that attention is diverted from the content of the real sense world and directed toward an unreal abstraction, whose meager fund of characteristics, after all, is also only drawn from the same sense world. One cannot explain one group of characteristics of the sense world – light, colors, sounds, odors, tastes, warmth conditions, etc. – by "breaking them down" into another group of characteristics of the same sense world: magnitude, shape, location, number, energy, etc. The task of natural science cannot be to "break down" one kind of characteristics into another kind, but rather to seek out the relationships and connections between the perceptible characteristics of the sense world. We then discover certain determining factors according to which one sense perception necessarily follows from the other. We find that a more intimate relationship exists between certain phenomena than between others. We then no longer connect phenomena in the way they present themselves to chance observation. For we recognize that certain relationships of phenomena are *necessary* ones. Other relationships, in contrast to them, are *coincidental*. Goethe calls the necessary relationships between phenomena "archetypal phenomena."

The expression of an archetypal phenomenon consists in the statement about a particular sense perception that it necessarily calls forth another one. This expression is what one calls a *law of nature*. When one says, "through heating, a body is expanded," one has given expression to a necessary relationship between phenomena of the sense world (warmth, expansion). One has recognized an *archetypal phenomenon* and expressed it in the form of a *natural law*. Archetypal phenomena are the forms Ostwald sought for the most general relationships of inorganic nature.

The laws of mathematics and mechanics are also only expressions of archetypal phenomena like the laws that bring other sense-perceptible relationships into a formula. When G. Kirchhoff says that the task of mechanics is "to describe, *completely* and in the *most simple way*, the motions occurring in nature," he is mistaken. Mechanics does not describe the motions occurring in nature merely in the simplest way and completely, but rather seeks certain *necessary* processes of motion that it lifts out of the sum total of the motions occurring in nature, and sets forth these necessary processes of motion as *fundamental laws of mechanics*. It must be regarded as the height of thoughtlessness that this statement of Kirchhoff is brought forward again and again as something quite significant, without any feeling for the fact that the statement of the simplest basic law of mechanics refutes it.

The archetypal phenomenon represents a necessary relationship between the elements of the perceptual world. One could hardly say something wider of the mark than what H. Helmholtz presented in his address to the Weimar Goethe Conference on June 11, 1892: "It is a pity that Goethe, at that time, did not know the undulation theory of light that Huyghens had already presented; this would have provided him with a far more correct and surveyable 'archetypal phenomenon' than the scarcely adequate and very complicated process that he finally chose to this end in the colors of turbid mediums."[79]

So, the unperceivable undulating motions that the adherents of the modern view of nature have *thought up and added* to the phenomena of light would supposedly have provided Goethe with a far more correct and surveyable "*archetypal phenomenon*" than the process – that is not at all complicated, but rather plays itself out before our very eyes – which consists in the fact that light, seen through a turbid medium, appears *yellow* and darkness, seen through an illuminated medium, appears *blue*. The "breaking down" of sense-perceptible processes into unperceivable mechanical motion has become so habitual to modern physicists that they seem to have no inkling at all of the fact that they are setting an abstraction in the place of reality. Statements like that of Helmholtz can be made only when all of Goethe's statements like the following have first been eliminated from the world: "The highest would be to grasp that everything factual is already theory. The blue of the heavens reveals to us the basic law of the science of colors. *Only do not seek anything behind the phenomena; they are themselves the teaching.*" Goethe remains within the phenomenal world; modern physicists gather up a few scraps from the phenomenal world and transfer them behind the phenomena, in order then to derive the phenomena of really perceptible experience from these hypothetical realities.

<h1 style="text-align:center">4.</h1>

Individual younger physicists maintain that they do not attach to the concept of moving matter any significance transcending experience. One of these, Anton Lampa, *Nights of the Seeker*[80] who accomplishes the remarkable feat of being an adherent of mechanistic natural science and of Indian mysticism at the same time, states, in opposition to Ostwald's expositions, that the latter is "waging a battle with wind mills like the brave Don Quixote of yore. Where then is the giant of scientific (Ostwald means natural-scientific) materialism? There is no such thing. There was at one time a so-called natural-scientific materialism of *Messieurs* Büchner, Vogt, and Moleschott – in fact there still is – but this does not exist in natural science itself, and has also never been at home in natural science. Ostwald overlooked this fact, otherwise he would have taken the field merely against the *mechanistic* view, which because of this misunderstanding, he only does incidentally, but which, without this misunderstanding, he would probably not have done at all. Can one believe then that an investigation in nature following the paths opened by Kirchhoff can grasp the concept of matter in the sense that materialism has done so? That is impossible; that is a contradiction lying clearly open to view. The concept of matter, just like that of force, can only have a meaning precisely determined by the demand for a simplest possible description, i.e., expressed in the Kantian way; it can only have a merely empirical meaning. And if any natural scientist attaches to the word "matter" a meaning that goes beyond this, then he does so, not as a natural scientist, but rather as a materialistic philosopher." (*Die Zeit*, Vienna, Nr. 61, Nov. 30, 1895).

According to these words, Lampa must be characterized as typical of the normal natural scientist of the present day. He applies the mechanistic explanation of nature because it is comfortable to deal with. But he avoids thinking about the true character of this explanation of nature, because he fears getting tangled up in contradictions before which his thinking feels inadequate.

How can someone who loves clear thinking attach any meaning to the concept of matter without going beyond the world of experience? Within the world of experience there are objects of certain magnitude and location; there are motion and forces; furthermore there are the phenomena of light, color, warmth, electricity, life, etc. As to whether magnitude, warmth, color, etc., are attached to some matter, experience says nothing. Matter is nowhere to be found within the world of experience. Whoever wants to think matter must think it up *and add it* to experience.

This kind of a thinking up of matter and adding it to the phenomena of the world of experience is apparent in the physical and physiological reflections that have found a home in modern natural science under the influence of Kant and Johannes Müller. These reflections have led to the belief that the outer processes that allow sound to arise in the ear, light in the eye, warmth in the sense for warmth, etc., have nothing in common with the sensations of sound, of light, of warmth, etc. Rather, these outer processes, supposedly, are certain motions of matter. The researcher of nature then investigates what sort of outer processes of motion allow sound, light, color, etc., to arise in the human soul. He comes to the conclusion that, outside of the human organism, red, yellow, or blue are nowhere to be found in all of world space, but rather that there is only a wave-like motion of a fine elastic matter, the ether, which, when it is sensed by the eye presents itself as red, yellow, or blue. The modern teacher about nature believes that if no sensitive eye were present, then there would also be no color present, but rather only moving ether. The ether is supposedly what is objective, and the color is merely something subjective, something created within the human body. The Leipzig professor Wundt, whom one sometimes hears acclaimed as one of the greatest philosophers of the present day, says therefore about matter that it is a substratum *"which never becomes visible to us itself, but always only in its effects."* And he finds that "an explanation of phenomena that is free of contradictions will be achieved only" when one assumes such a substratum (*Logic*, Vol. 2, p. 445). The Cartesian delusion about definite and confused mental pictures has become physics' fundamental way of picturing things.

5.

Someone whose ability to picture things has not been thoroughly ruined by Descartes, Locke, Kant, and modern physiology will never understand how one can regard light, color, sound, warmth, etc., to be merely subjective states of the human organism and yet still assert that there is an objective world of processes outside of this organism. Someone who makes the human organism into the creator of the happenings of sound, warmth, color, etc., must also make it the producer of extension, magnitude, location, motion, forces, etc. For, these mathematical and mechanistic qualities are, in reality, inseparably united with the rest of the content of the world of experience. The separating out of conditions of space, number, and motion, as well as manifestations of force, from the qualities of warmth, sound, color, and the other sense qualities, is only a function of our abstractive thinking. The laws of mathematics and mechanics relate to abstract objects and processes that are drawn from the world of experience and that therefore can find an application only within the world of experience. But if the mathematical and mechanistic forms and relationships are also explained as merely subjective states, then nothing remains that could serve as content for the concept of objective things and events. And no phenomena can be derived from an empty concept.

As long as modern scholars of nature and their train bearers, the modern philosophers, hold fast to the view that sense perceptions are only subjective states that are called forth by objective processes, a healthy thinking will always point out to them in reply that they are either playing with empty concepts, or are ascribing to what is objective a content that they are borrowing from that world of experience that they have declared to be subjective. In a number of books, I have demonstrated the absurdity of the assertion that our sense impressions are subjective.[81]

Still, let us turn from the question as to whether or not a different form of reality is ascribed to the processes of motion and to the forces that bring them forth – from which recent physics derives all the phenomena of nature – than to sense perceptions. Let me now merely ask what the mathematical-mechanistic view of nature can accomplish. Anton Lampa maintains (*Nights of the Seeker*, p. 92): "Mathematical methods and mathematics are not identical, for the mathematical method is applicable without the use of mathematics. The experimental research on electricity by Faraday, who hardly knew how to square a binomial, offers us a classic proof of this fact in physics. Mathematics, in fact, is nothing more than a means of abbreviating logical operations and therefore of proceeding in very complicated cases where ordinary logical thinking would let us down. But at the same time it accomplishes far more still: through the fact that every formula implicitly expresses its processes of development, it builds a living bridge back to the elementary phenomena that served as the starting point for the investigation. A method, however, that cannot make use of mathematics – which is always the case when the magnitudes that apply in an investigation are not measurable – must therefore, in order to match the mathematical method, not only be strictly logical, but also must be particularly careful in the business of tracing things back to the basic phenomena, since, lacking mathematical supports, it can precisely here make a false step; but if a method does achieve this, it can quite rightly lay claim to the title "mathematical," insofar as this is meant to express the degree of exactitude."

I would not concern myself with Anton Lampa at such length if he were not, in one respect, a particularly suitable example of a natural scientist of the present day. He satisfies his philosophical needs by Indian mysticism and therefore does not taint the mechanistic view of nature like others do with all kinds of supplementary philosophical conceptions. The theory of nature that he has in mind is, so to speak, the chemically pure view of nature of the present day. I find that Lampa left one main characteristic of mathematics completely out of consideration. Every mathematical formula does indeed build a "living bridge" back to the elementary phenomena that served as the starting point for the investigations. But those elementary phenomena are of the same kind as the non-elementary ones from which the bridge is built. The mathematician traces the characteristics of complicated numerical and spatial configurations, as well as their reciprocal relationships, back to the characteristics and relationships of the simplest numerical and spatial configurations. The mechanical engineer does the same thing in his field. He traces composite processes of motion and force-effects back to simple, easily distinguishable motions and force-effects. In doing so, he makes use of mathematical laws, to the extent that motion and manifestations of force are expressible through spatial configurations and numbers. In a mathematical formula that brings a mechanical law to expression, the individual parts no longer represent purely mathematical configurations, but rather forces and motion. The relationships in which these parts stand to one another are not determined by a purely mathematical lawfulness, but rather by characteristics of force and motion. As soon as one disregards this particular content of the mechanical formulae, one no longer has to do with a mechanical lawfulness, but solely with a mathematical one. Physics relates to mechanics in the same way that mechanics relates to pure mathematics. The task of the physicist is to trace complicated processes in the realm of color, sound, and warmth phenomena, of electricity, of magnetism, etc., back to simple happenings *within the same sphere*. He has, for example, to trace complicated color occurrences back to the simplest color occurrences. In doing so, he has to make use of mathematical and mechanical lawfulness, to the extent that the color processes occur in forms that can be determined spatially and numerically. What corresponds to the mathematical method in the realm of physics is not the tracing back of processes of color, sound, etc., to phenomena of motion and to relationships of force within a colorless and soundless matter, but rather the seeking out of relationships *within* the phenomena of color, sound, etc.

Modern physics skips over the phenomena of sound, color, etc., as such and considers only unchangeable attracting and repelling forces and motion in space. Under the influence of this way of picturing things, physics today has already become applied mathematics and mechanics, and the other fields of natural science are on the way to becoming the same thing.

It is impossible to build a "living bridge" from the one fact – that a particular process of motion of colorless matter is occurring at this location in space – and the other fact – that the human being sees red at this spot. From motion only other motion can be derived. And from the fact that a motion acts upon a sense organ and through it upon the brain, it follows only – according to the mathematical and mechanical method – that the brain is stimulated by the outer world into certain processes of motion, but not that the brain perceives the concrete phenomena of sounds, colors, warmth, etc. Du Bois-Reymond also recognized this. You can read on page 35f. of his book *Limits to Knowing Nature*: "What conceivable connection can exist between certain motions of certain atoms in my brain on the one hand, and the immediate, undefinable, and undeniable fact for me, on the other hand, that I feel pain, feel pleasure, taste something sweet, smell the fragrance of a rose, hear organ music, see red..." And, on page 34: "Motion can only produce motion." Du Bois-Reymond is therefore of the opinion that one must designate this as a limit to our ability to know nature.

The reason why the fact that I see red cannot be derived from a particular process of motion is, in my view, easy to indicate. The quality "red" and a particular process of motion are in reality an inseparable unity. The separation of the two occurrences can only be a conceptual one, carried out within the intellect. The process of motion that corresponds to the "red" has no reality in itself; it is an abstraction. To want to derive the fact that I see red from a process of motion, is just as absurd as deriving the real characteristics of rock salt, in its crystallized cube form, from the mathematical cube. It is not because a limit of knowledge hinders us, that we cannot derive any other sense qualities from motion, but rather because the demand that we do so makes no sense.

6.

The endeavor to skip over colors, sounds, warmth phenomena, etc., as such, and to consider only the mechanical processes corresponding to them can spring only from the belief that a higher degree of comprehensibility is attributable to the simple laws of mathematics and mechanics than to the characteristics and reciprocal relationships of the rest of the configurations of the perceptual world. But this is absolutely not the case. The simplest characteristics and relationships of spatial and numerical configurations are stated to be immediately comprehensible because they can be easily and completely surveyed. All mathematical and mechanical understanding is a tracing back to simple factual situations that are obvious the moment one becomes aware of them. The principle that two magnitudes which are equal to a third must also be equal to each other, is known the moment one becomes aware of the factual situation that this principle expresses. In the same sense, the simple occurrences of the world of sound and color and of the other sense perceptions are known the moment one looks upon them.

Only because modern physicists are led astray by the preconception that a simple mathematical or mechanical fact is more comprehensible than an elementary occurrence of a sound or color phenomenon as such, do they eliminate what is specifically sound or color from the phenomena, and consider only the processes of motion that correspond to the sense perceptions. And since they cannot conceive of motion without something that moves, they take matter, that has been stripped of all sense-perceptible characteristics, to be the bearer of these movements. Whoever is not caught up in this preconception of the physicists must see that the processes of motion are states that are bound up with the sense-perceptible qualities. The content of the wave-like movements that correspond to the occurrence of sound are the qualities of sound themselves. The same holds true for all the other sense qualities. We know the content of the oscillating movements of the phenomenal world through immediate awareness of this content and not by thinking up some abstract matter and adding it to the phenomena.

7.

I know that I am expressing something with these views that sounds completely impossible to physicists' ears of the present day. But I cannot take the standpoint of Wundt, who in his *Logic* (Vol. 2, Part 1) presents the thought-habits of modern natural scientists as binding logical norms. The thoughtlessness of which he is guilty there becomes particularly clear in the passage where he is discussing Ostwald's attempt to replace moving matter with energy in oscillating movement. Wundt presents the following: "From the existence of phenomena of interference there arises the necessity of presupposing some sort of oscillating movement. But since a movement is unthinkable without a substratum that moves, the unavoidable demand is therefore also made that one trace light phenomena back to a mechanical process. Ostwald, to be sure, has tried to get around this latter assumption by not tracing 'radiant energy' back to the vibrations of a material medium, but rather by defining it as energy existing in a state of oscillating movement. But precisely this double concept, which is composed of an observable component and of a purely conceptual one, seems to me to be striking proof that the concept of energy itself demands a division that leads back to elements of observation. A real movement can be defined only as the changing in location of a real substratum given in space. This real substratum can reveal itself to us merely through the force-effects that go forth from it, or through functions of force whose bearer we consider this substratum to be. But the demand that such merely conceptually established functions of force themselves move, seems to me something that cannot be fulfilled without *thinking up* some sort of substratum and *adding* it."

Ostwald's energy-concept stands much nearer to reality than the supposedly "real" substratum of Wundt. The phenomena of the perceptual world – light, warmth, electricity, magnetism, etc. – can be brought under the general concept of force-output, i.e., of energy. When light, warmth, etc., call forth a change in an object, an energy-output has thereby taken place. When one designates light, warmth, etc., as energy, one has disregarded what is specifically characteristic of the individual sense qualities, and is considering one general characteristic that they share in common.

This characteristic does not, indeed, include everything that is present in the things of reality; but it is a real characteristic of these things. The concept of the characteristics, on the other hand, that physicists and their philosophical defenders suppose their hypothetically assumed *matter* to have, includes something nonsensical. These characteristics are borrowed from the sense world and yet are supposed to belong to a substratum that does not belong to the sense world.

It is incomprehensible how Wundt can assert that the concept of "radiant energy," because it contains an *observable* and a *conceptual* component, is therefore an impossible one. The philosopher Wundt does not understand, therefore, that every concept that relates to something in sense-perceptible reality, must necessarily contain an observable and a conceptual component. The concept "rock salt cube" has, after all, the *observable* component of the sense-perceptible rock salt and the other *purely conceptual* component that solid geometry establishes.

8.

The development of natural science in the last few centuries has led to the destruction of any mental pictures by which this science could be a part of a world conception that satisfies higher human needs. This development has led to the fact that "modern" scientific heads call it absurd for anyone to speak as though *concepts* and *ideas* belong just as much to reality as the forces working in space and the matter filling space. Concepts and ideas, to such minds, are a product of the human brain and nothing more. The scholastics still knew how matters stand in this respect. But scholasticism is held in contempt by modern science. It is held in contempt but one does not know scholasticism. One especially does not know what is healthy and what is sick about it. What is healthy about it is a feeling for the fact that concepts and ideas are not only a chimera of the brain that the human mind thinks up in order to understand real things, but rather that they have something to do with the things themselves, more, in fact, than substance and force do. This healthy feeling that the scholastics had is our inheritance from the great worldview perspectives of Plato and Aristotle. The sick aspect of scholasticism is the mixing up of this feeling with mental pictures that entered into the medieval development of Christianity. This development finds the source of everything spiritual, including therefore also concepts and ideas, to lie in an unknowable, because otherworldly, God. It needs to believe in something that is not of this world. A healthy human thinking, however, keeps to this world. It does not bother about any other. But at the same time, it spiritualizes this world. It sees in concepts and ideas realities of this world just as much as in the things and events perceptible through the senses. Greek philosophy is an outflow of this healthy thinking. Scholasticism still took up into itself an inkling of this healthy thinking. But it sought to reinterpret this inkling in accordance with the belief in the beyond that is considered Christian. It was not concepts and ideas that were supposed to be the deepest thing that man beholds within the processes of this world, but rather God, the beyond. Whoever has grasped the idea of something is not compelled by anything to seek yet some further "origin" of that something. He has attained that which satisfies the human need for knowledge. But what did the scholastics care about the human need for knowledge? They wanted to rescue what they regarded as the Christian picture of God. They wanted to find the origin of the world in that God in the beyond, although their seeking for the inner life of things provided them only with concepts and ideas.

9.

In the course of centuries, the Christian picture took effect more than the dim feelings inherited from Greek antiquity. One lost the feeling for the reality of concepts and ideas. But one also lost therefore one's belief in the spirit itself. There began the worship of the purely material: the era of Newton began in natural science. Now it was no longer a question of the unity that underlies the manifoldness of the world. Now all unity was denied. Unity was degraded into a "human" mental picture. In nature, one saw only the multiplicity, the manifoldness. The general basic picture was what misled Newton to see in light not a primal unity, but rather something composite. In his *Data for the History of Color Theory*[82] Goethe has presented a part of the development of natural-scientific mental pictures. One can see from his presentation that recent natural science has arrived at unhealthy views in color theory through the general mental picture that it uses in grasping nature. This science has lost its understanding for what light is within the series of nature's qualities. Therefore, it also does not know how, under certain conditions, light appears colored, how color arises in the realm of light.

XVIII

Goethe's Worldview in His
Aphorisms in Prose

The human being is not content with what nature willingly offers to his observing spirit. He feels that nature, in order to bring forth the manifoldness of its creations, needs driving forces that it at first conceals from the observer. Nature does not itself utter its final word. Our experience shows us what nature can create, but does not tell us how this creating occurs. Within the human spirit itself there lies the means for bringing the driving forces of nature to light. Up out of the human spirit the ideas arise that bring clarification as to how nature brings about its creations. What the phenomena of the outer world conceal becomes revealed within the inner being of man. What the human spirit thinks up in the way of natural laws is not invented and added to nature; it is nature's own essential being, and the human spirit is only the stage upon which nature allows the secrets of its workings to become visible. What we *observe* about the things is only one part of the things. What wells up within our spirit when it confronts the things is the other part. It is the same things that speak to us from outside and that speak within us. Only when we hold the language of the outer world together with that of our inner being, do we have full reality. What have the true philosophers in every age wanted to do? Nothing other than to make known the essential being of things that the things themselves express when the human spirit offers itself to them as their organ of speech.

When man allows his inner being to speak about nature, he recognizes that nature falls short of what, by virtue of its driving forces, it could accomplish. The human spirit sees what experience contains, in its more perfect form. It finds that nature with its creations does not achieve its aims. The human spirit feels itself called upon to present these aims in their perfected form. It creates shapes in which it shows: This is what nature wanted to do but could only accomplish to a certain degree. These shapes are the works of art. In them, the human being creates in a perfected way what nature manifests in an imperfect form.

The philosopher and the artist have the same goal. They seek to give shape to the perfected element that their spirit beholds when it allows nature to work upon it. But they have different media at their command for achieving this goal. For the philosopher, a *thought*, an *idea*, lights up within him when he confronts a process in nature. This he expresses. For the artist, a *picture* of this process arises within him that manifests this process more perfectly than can be observed in the outer world. The philosopher and the artist develop the observation further in different ways. The artist does not need to know the driving forces of nature in the form in which they reveal themselves to the philosopher. When the artist perceives a thing or an occurrence, there arises directly in his spirit a picture in which the laws of nature are expressed in a more perfect form than in the corresponding thing or occurrence in the outer world. These laws do not need to enter his spirit in the form of thoughts. Knowledge and art, however, are inwardly related. They show the *potentialities* of nature that do not come to full development in merely outer nature.

When now, within the spirit of a genuine artist, not only the perfected pictures of things express themselves, but also the driving forces of nature in the form of thoughts, then the common source of philosophy and art appears with particular clarity before our eyes. Goethe is such an artist. He reveals the same secrets to us in the form of his works of art and in the form of thoughts. What he gave shape to in his poetic works, this he expresses in his essays on natural science and art and in his *Aphorisms in Prose*[83] in the form of thoughts. The deep satisfaction that emanates from these essays and aphorisms stems from the fact that one sees the harmony of art and knowledge realized in one personality. There is something elevating in the feeling, which arises with every Goethean thought, that here someone is speaking who at the same time can behold in a picture the perfected element that he expresses in ideas. The power of such a thought is strengthened by this feeling. That which stems from the highest needs of *one* personality must inwardly belong together. Goethe's teachings of wisdom answers the question:

What kind of philosophy is in accordance with genuine art? I will try to sketch in context this philosophy that is born out of the spirit of a genuine artist.

* * *

The content of thought that springs from the human spirit when it confronts the outer world is truth. The human being cannot demand any other kind of knowledge than one he brings forth himself. Whoever seeks something in addition behind the things that is supposed to signify their actual being has not brought to consciousness the fact that all questions about the essential being of things spring only from a human need: the need, namely, also to penetrate with thought what one perceives. The things speak to us, and our inner being speaks when we observe the things. These two languages stem from the same primal being, and man is called upon to effect their reciprocal understanding. It is in this that what one calls knowledge consists. And it is this and nothing else that a person seeks who understands the needs of human nature. For someone who has not arrived at this understanding, the things of the outer world remain foreign. He does not hear the essential being of things speaking within his inner life. Therefore he supposes that this essential being is hidden behind the things. He believes in yet another outer world in addition, behind the perceptual world. But things are outer things only so long as one merely observes them. When one thinks about them, they cease to be outside of us. One fuses with their inner being. For man, opposition between objective outer perception and subjective inner thought-world exists only as long as he does not recognize that these worlds belong together. Man's inner world is the inner being of nature.

These thoughts are not refuted by the fact that different people make different mental pictures of things for themselves. Nor by the fact that people's organizations are different so that one does not know whether one and the same color is seen by different people in exactly the same way. For, the point is not whether people form exactly the same judgment about one and the same thing, but whether the language that the inner being of a person speaks is in fact the language that expresses the essential being of things. Individual judgments differ according to the organization of the person and according to the standpoint from which one observes things; but all judgments spring from the same element and lead into the essential being of things. This can come to expression in different nuances of thought; but it is, nevertheless, still the essential being of things.

The human being is the organ by which nature reveals its secrets. Within the subjective personality the deepest content of the world appears. "When the healthy nature of man works as a whole, when he feels himself in the world as though in a great, beautiful, worthy, and precious whole, when his harmonious sense of well-being imparts to him a pure, free delight, then the universe, if it could experience itself, would, *as having achieved its goal, exult with joy and marvel at the pinnacle of its own becoming and being*." (Goethe, *Winckelmann*) The goal of the universe and of the essential being of existence does not lie in what the outer world provides, but rather in what lives within the human spirit and goes forth from it. Goethe therefore considers it to be a mistake for the natural scientist to want to penetrate into the inner being of nature through instruments and objective experiments, for "man in himself, insofar as he uses his healthy senses, is the greatest and most accurate physical apparatus that there can be, and that is precisely what is of the greatest harm to modern physics, that one has, as it were, separated experiments from man; one wants to know nature merely through what manmade instruments show, yes, wants to limit and prove thereby what nature can do." "But man stands at such a high level precisely through the fact that what otherwise could not manifest itself does manifest itself in him. For what is a string and all its mechanical divisions compared to the ear of the musician? Yes, one can say, what are the elemental phenomena of nature themselves compared to man who must first tame and modify them all in order to be able to assimilate them to some extent?"

Man must allow the things to speak out of his spirit if he wants to know their essential being. Everything he has to say about this essential being is derived from the spiritual experiences of his inner life. The human being can judge the world only from out of himself. He must think anthropomorphically. One brings anthropomorphism into the simplest phenomenon, into the impact of two bodies, for example, when one says something about it. The judgment that "one body strikes another" is already anthropomorphic. For if one wants to go beyond the mere observation of the process, one must bring to it the experience our own body has when it sets a body in the outer world into motion. All physical explanations are hidden anthropomorphisms. One humanizes nature when one explains it; one puts into it the inner experiences of the human being. But these subjective experiences are the inner being of things. And one cannot therefore say that, because man can make only subjective mental pictures for himself about nature, he does not know the objective truth, the "in-itself" of things.[84] There can absolutely be no question of anything other than a subjective human truth. For, truth consists in putting our subjective experiences into the objective interrelationships of phenomena. These subjective experiences can even assume a completely individual character. They are, nevertheless, the expression of the inner being of things. One can put into the things only what one has experienced within oneself. Thus, each person, in accordance with his individual experiences, will also put something different, in a certain sense, into things. The way I interpret certain processes of nature for myself is not entirely comprehensible for someone else who has not inwardly experienced the same thing. It is not at all a matter, however, of all men having the same thoughts about things, but rather only of their living within the element of truth when they think about things. One cannot therefore observe the thoughts of another person as such and accept or reject them, but rather one should regard them as the proclaimers of his individuality. "Those who contradict and dispute should reflect now and then that not every language is comprehensible to everyone." A philosophy can never provide a universally valid truth, but rather describes the inner experiences of the philosopher by which he interprets the outer phenomena.

* * *

When a thing expresses its essential being through the organ of the human spirit, then full reality comes about only through the flowing together of the outer objective and the inner subjective. It is neither through one-sided observation nor through one-sided thinking that the human being knows reality. Reality is not present in the objective world as something finished, but rather is only first brought forth by the human spirit in connection with the things. The objective things are only a part of reality. To someone who extols sense experience exclusively, one must reply like Goethe "that experience is only half of experience." "Everything factual is already theory"; that means, an ideal element reveals itself in the human spirit when he observes something factual. This way of apprehending the world, which knows the essential being of things in ideas and which apprehends knowledge to be a living into the essential being of things, is not mysticism. But it does have in common with *mysticism* the characteristic that it does not regard objective truth as something that is present in the outer world, but rather as something that can really be grasped within the inner being of man. The opposite worldview transfers the ground of things to behind the phenomena, into a region lying beyond human experience. This view can then either give itself over to a blind *faith* in this ground that receives its content from a positive religion of revelation, or it can set up intellectual hypotheses and theories as to how this realm of reality in the beyond is constituted. The mystic, as well as the adherent of the Goethean worldview, rejects both this faith in some "beyond" and all hypotheses about any such region, and holds fast to the really spiritual element that expresses itself within man himself. Goethe writes to Jacobi: "God has punished *you* with *metaphysics* and set a thorn in your flesh, but has blessed *me,* on the other hand, with *physics.* ... I hold more and more firmly to the reverence for God of the atheist (Spinoza) ... and leave to you everything you call, and would have to call, religion. ... When you say that one can only believe in God ... then I say to you that I set a lot of store in *seeing.*" What Goethe wants to *see* is the essential being of things that expresses itself within his world of ideas. The mystic also wants to know the essential being of things by immersing himself in his own inner being; but he rejects precisely that innately clear and transparent world of ideas as unsuitable for attaining higher knowledge. He believes he must develop, not his capacity for ideas, but rather other powers of his inner being, in order to *see* the primal ground of things. Usually it is unclear feelings and emotions in which the mystic wants to grasp the essential being of things. But feelings and emotions belong only to the subjective being of man. In them nothing is expressed about the things. Only in ideas do the things themselves speak. Mysticism is a superficial worldview, in spite of the fact that the mystics are very proud of their "profundity" compared to men of reason. The mystics know nothing about the nature of feelings, otherwise they would not consider them to be expressions of the essential being of the world; and they know nothing about the nature of ideas, otherwise they would not consider them shallow and rationalistic. They have no inkling of what people who really have ideas experience in them. But for many people, ideas are in fact mere words. They cannot acquire for themselves the unending fullness of their content. No wonder they feel their own word husks, which are devoid of ideas, to be empty.

* * *

Whoever seeks the essential content of the objective world within his own inner being can also regard the essential being of the *moral world order* as lying only within human nature itself. Whoever believes in the existence of a reality in the beyond, behind human reality, must also seek the source of morality there. For, what is moral in a higher sense can come only from the essential being of things. The believer in the beyond therefore assumes moral commandments to which man must submit himself. These commandments reach him either via revelation, or they enter as such into his consciousness, as is the case with Kant's categorical imperative. As to how this imperative comes into our consciousness from out of the "in-itselfness" of things in the beyond, about this nothing is said. It is simply there, and one must submit oneself to it. The philosopher of experience, who looks for his salvation in pure sense observation, sees in what is moral, only the working of human drives and instincts. Out of the study of these, norms are supposed to result that are decisive for moral action.

Goethe sees what is moral as arising out of man's world of ideas. It is not objective norms and also not the mere world of drives that directs moral action, but rather it is ideas, clear within themselves, by which man gives himself his own direction. He does not follow them out of duty as he would have to follow objective moral norms. And also not out of compulsion, as one follows one's drives and instincts. But rather he serves them out of love. He loves them the way one loves a child. He wants to realize them, and steps in on their behalf, because they are a part of his own essential being. The *idea* is the guideline and *love* is the driving power in Goethean ethics. For him duty is "where one loves what one commands oneself to do."

Action, in the sense of Goethean ethics, is a *free* action. For, the human being is dependent upon nothing other than his own ideas. And he is responsible to no one other than himself. In my *Philosophy of Spiritual Activity* I have already refuted the feeble objection that a moral world order in which each person obeys only himself would have to lead to a general disorder and disharmony in human action. Whoever makes this objection overlooks the fact that human beings are essentially alike in nature and that they will therefore never produce moral ideas which, through their essential differentness, would cause discord.[85]

* * *

If the human being did not have the ability to bring forth creations that are fashioned in exactly the same sense as the works of nature and only bring this sense to view in a more perfect way than nature can, there would be no art in Goethe's sense. What the artist creates are nature objects on a higher level of perfection. Art is the extension of nature, "for inasmuch as man is placed at the pinnacle of nature, he then regards himself again as an entire nature, which yet again has to bring forth within itself a pinnacle. To this end he enhances himself, by imbuing himself with every perfection and virtue, summons choice, order, harmony, and meaning, and finally *lifts himself to the production of works of art.*" After seeing Greek works of art in Italy, Goethe writes: "These great works of art have at the same time been brought forth by human beings according to *true* and *natural* laws, as the greatest works of nature" (*Italian Journey*, September 6, 1787). For the merely sense-perceptible reality of experience, works of art are a beautiful semblance; for someone who is able to see more deeply, they are "a manifestation of hidden laws of nature that without them would never be revealed."

It is not the substance the artist takes from nature that constitutes the work of art; but only what the artist puts into the work of art from out of his inner being. The highest work of art is one that makes you forget that a natural substance underlies it, and that awakens our interest solely through what the artist has made out of this substance. The artist forms things naturally; but he does not form things the way nature itself does. These statements to me express the main thoughts that Goethe set down in his aphorisms on *art*.

Notes

1.   Whoever declares from the very beginning that such a goal is unattainable will never arrive at an understanding of the Goethean views of nature; on the other hand, whoever undertakes to study them without preconceptions, and leaves this question open, will certainly answer it affirmatively at the end. Doubts could very well arise for many a person through several remarks Goethe himself made, such as the following one, for example: "... *without presuming to want to discover the primal mainsprings of nature's workings,* we would have directed our attention to the manifestation of the forces by which the plant gradually transforms one and the same organ." But with Goethe such statements never direct themselves against the possibility, in principle, of knowing the being of things; he is only cautious enough about the physical-mechanical conditions underlying the organism not to draw any conclusions too quickly, since he knew very well that such questions can only be resolved in the course of time.

2.   We do not mean in any way to say that Goethe has never been understood at all in this regard. On the contrary, we repeatedly take occasion in this very edition to point to a number of men who seem to us to carry on and elaborate Goethean ideas. Belonging among them are such names as: Voigt, Nees von Esenbeck, d'Alton (senior and junior), Schelver, C.G. Carus, and Martius, among others. But these men in fact built up their systems upon the foundation of the views laid down in the writings of Goethe, and, precisely about them, one cannot say that they would have arrived at their concepts even *without Goethe,* whereas to be sure, contemporaries of Goethe – Josephi in Göttingen, for example – did come independently upon the intermaxillary bone, and Oken upon the vertebral theory.

3.   See *Poetry and Truth,* part 2, book 6

4.   *Faust* quotations are from George Madison Priest's translation

5.   *Poetry and Truth,* Part 2, Book 8

6.   *Poetry and Truth,* Part 3, book 11

7.   *Das Neueste aus dem Reiche der Pflanzen,* (Nürnberg 1764)

8.   *Auserlesene mikroskopische Entdeckungen bei Pflanzen, Blumen und Blüten, Insekten und anderen Merkwürdigkeiten,* (Nürnberg 1777-81)

9.   *Ideen zur Philosophie der Geschichte*

10.   "I would gladly send you a little botanical essay, if only it were already written." (Letter to Knebel, April 2, 1785)

11.   *Geschichte meines botanischen Studiums*

12.   *Italian Journey,* October 8, 1786

13.   *Italian Journey*, September 8, 1786

14.   It is certainly unnecessary to state that the modern theory of evolution should not at all be placed in doubt by this, or that its assertions should be curtailed by it; on the contrary, only it provides a secure foundation for them.

15.   What we have here is not so much the theory of evolution of those natural scientists who base themselves on sense-perceptible empiricism, but far more the theoretical foundations, the principles, that are laid into the foundations of Darwinism; especially by the Jena school, of course, with Haeckel in the vanguard; in this first-class mind, Darwin's teachings, in all their one-sidedness, have certainly found their consequential development.

16.   We will have occasion at various places to demonstrate in what sense these individual parts relate to the whole. If we wanted to borrow a concept of modern science for such working together of living partial entities into one whole, we might take for example that of a "stock" in zoology. This is a kind of statehood of living entities, an individual that itself further consists of independent individuals, an individual of a higher sort.

17.   *Physiognomische Fragmente zur Beförderung der Menschenkenntnis und Menschenliebe*

18.   "A troublesome service of love that I have undertaken is bringing me closer to my passion. Loder is explaining all the bones and muscles to me, and I will grasp a great deal within a few days."

19.   "He (Loder) has demonstrated osteology and myology for me during these eight days, which we have used almost entirely for this purpose; as much, in fact, as my attentiveness could stand."

20.   *Lehrbuch der Naturphilosophie*

21.   In: *Natural Scientific Discussions on the Orangutan* ("*Natuurkundige verhandelingen over den orang outang*")

22.   An animal, see page 39-Ed.

23.   "An exquisite pleasure has been granted me; I have made an anatomical discovery that is important and beautiful."

24.   "I have found – not silver or gold, but something that gives me inexpressible joy – the os intermaxillare in man!"

25.   "*Morphologische Hefte*"

26.   Until now, one has assumed that Camper received the treatise anonymously. It came to him in a roundabout way: Goethe sent it first to Sömmerring, who sent it to Merck, who was supposed to get it to Camper. But among the letters of Merck to Camper (which are not yet published, and whose originals are to be found in the Library of the Netherlands Society for the Progress of Medicine in Amsterdam), there is one letter of January 17, 1785 containing the following passage (I quote it verbatim): "Mr. Goethe, celebrated poet, intimate counselor of the Duke of Weimar, has just sent me an osteological specimen that is supposed to be sent to you after Mr. Sömmerring has seen it. It is a small treatise on the intermaxillary bone that teaches us among other things, the truth that the manatee has four incisors and that the camel has two of them." A letter of March

10, 1785, in which the name Goethe is again expressly present, states that Merck will shortly send the treatise on to Camper: "I will have the honor of sending you the osteological specimen of Mr. von Goethe, my friend ... " On April 28, 1785, Merck expressed the hope that Camper received the thing and again the name "Goethe" is present. Thus there is no doubt that Camper knew who the author was.

27. *Anatomie der Säugetiere*

28. *Vom Baue des menschlichen Körpers*

29. *Handbuch der vergleichenden Anatomie*

30. *"Versuch, die Metamorphose der Pflanze zu erklären"*

31.   A few philosophers maintain that we can indeed trace the phenomena of the sense world back to their original elements (forces), but that we can explain these just as little as we can explain the nature of life. On the other hand, one can say that those elements are *simple, i.e.,* cannot themselves be composed of still simpler elements. But to trace them, in all their simplicity, further back, to explain them, is an impossibility, not because our capacity for knowledge is limited, but rather *because these elements rest upon themselves;* they are present for us in all their immediacy; they are self-contained, cannot he traced back to anything else.

32.   This is precisely the contrast between an organism and a machine. In a machine, everything is the interaction of its parts. Nothing real exists in the machine itself other than this interaction. The unifying principle, which governs the working together of the parts, is lacking in the object itself, and lies outside of it in the head of its builder as a plan. Only the most extreme short-sightedness can deny that the difference between an organism and a mechanism lies precisely in the fact that the principle causing the interrelationship of the parts is, with respect to a mechanism, present only externally (abstractly), whereas with respect to an organism, this principle gains real existence within the thing itself. Thus the sense-perceptible components of an organism also do not then appear out of one another as a mere sequence, but rather as though governed by that inner principle, as though resulting from such a principle that is no longer sense-perceptible. In this respect it is no more sense-perceptible than the plan in the builder's head that is also there only for the mind; this principle is, in fact, essentially that plan, only that plan has now drawn into the inner being of the entity and no longer carries out its activities through the mediation of a third party – the builder – but rather does this directly itself.

33.   Readers familiar with German philosophy in English will remember that the conventional translation of *Verstand* is "understanding." – Ed.

34.   Critique of Judgment (Kritik der Urteilskraft)

35.   Certain attributes of God within the things.

36.   *Von den göttlichen Dingen und derer Offenbarung* (1811)

37.   The fruit arises through the growth of the lower part of the pistil, the ovary (l); it represents a later stage of the pistil and can therefore only be sketched separately. With the fruiting, the last expansion occurs. The life of the

plant differentiates itself into an organ – the actual fruit – that is closing itself off, and into the seeds; in the fruit, all the factors of the phenomenon are united, as it were; it is mere phenomenon; it estranges itself from life, becomes a dead product. In the seed are concentrated all the inner essential factors of the plant's life. From it a new plant arises. It has become almost entirely ideal; the phenomenon is reduced to a minimum in it.

38.   *Italian Journey,* December 1, 1786.

39.   In modern natural science one usually means by "archetypal organism" *(Urorganismus)* an archetypal cell (archetypal cytode), i.e., a simple entity standing at the lowest level of organic development. One has in mind here a quite specific, actual, sense-perceptibly real entity. When one speaks in the Goethean sense about the archetypal organism, then one does not have this in mind but rather that essence (being), that formative entelechical principle which brings it about that this archetypal cell is an organism. This principle comes to manifestation in the simplest organism just as in the most perfect one, only differently developed. It is the animalness in the animal; it is that through which an entity is an organism. Darwin presupposes it from the beginning; it is there, is introduced, and then he says of it that it reacts in one way or another to the influences of the outer world. For him, it is an indefinite X; Goethe seeks to explain this indefinite X.

40.   Goethe often experienced this unconscious behavior of his as dullness.

41.   *Von der Weltseele*

42.   *Entwurf eines Systems der Naturphilosophie*

43.   *Grundzüge der philosophischen Naturwissenschaft*

44.   *Über die Spiraltendenz der Vegetation*

45.   *Wissenschaftslehre*

46.   *The Science of Knowing. Outline of an Epistemology Implicit in the Goethean World View* (*Grundlinien einer Erkenntnistheorie der Goetheschen Weltanschauung*), also translated as *Theory of Knowledge*.

47.   *Kritik der Urteilskraft*

48.   *Bedeutende Fördernis durch ein einziges geistreiches Wort*

49.   *Kants Erkenntnistheorie nach ihren Grundprinzipien analysiert*

50.   *Die Philosophie als Denken der Welt gemäss dem Prinzip des kleinsten Kraftmasses. Prolegomena zu einer Kritik der reinen Erfahrung.*

51.   *Vorstellung* is often translated as "representation" in philosophical works. – Ed.

52.   This separation is indicated by the solid lines.

53.   This is represented by the dotted lines.

54.   Meaning: *that* it exists – Ed.

55.   *Der Versuch als Vermittler von Subjekt und Objekt*

56. Later footnote of the author: "In my introduction to the thirty-fourth volume, I said that the essay appears, unfortunately, to have been lost that could serve as the best support to Goethe's views on experience, experiment, and scientific knowledge. It has not been lost, however, and has come to light in the above form in the Goethe archives. It bears the date January 15, 1798, and was sent to Schiller on the seventeenth. It represents a continuation of the essay *The Experiment as Mediator between Subject and Object*. I took the train of thought of his essay from the correspondence between Goethe and Schiller and presented it in the above-mentioned introduction in exactly the same way in which it is now found to be in the newly discovered essay. With respect to content nothing is added by this essay to what I expressed there; *on the other hand, however, the view I had won from Goethe's other works about his method* and way of knowing was confirmed in every respect.

57. *Entwurf einer Farbenlehre*

58. *Zur Naturwissenschaft*

59. *Die ethische Freiheit bei Kant* (*Philosophische Monatshefte*). Published by Mercury Press as *Spiritual Activity in Kant.*

60. *Geisteswissenschaften,* literally: "spiritual sciences" – Ed.

61. *Bilder aus der deutschen Vergangenheit*

62. All quotations in this paragraph are from *Aphorisms in Prose.*

63. *Erster Entwurf eines Systems der Naturphilosophie*

64. An essay quite worth reading is Dr. Adolf Harpt's *Goethe and Schopenhauer* (Philosophische Monatshefte, 1885). Harpf, who has also already written an excellent treatise on *Goethe's Principle of Knowledge (Goethes Erkenntnisprinzip,* Philos. Monatshefte, 1884), shows the agreement between the "immanent dogmatism" of Schopenhauer and the objective knowledge of Goethe. Harpf, who is himself a follower of Schopenhauer, did not discover the principle difference between Goethe and Schopenhauer that we characterized above. But his reflections are quite worthy of attention.

65. *Vorstellungen*: Usually translated as "representations" in English versions of Schopenhauer's work – Ed.

66. *Philosophie des Unbewussten*

67. *Philosophische Fragen der Gegenwart* (Leipzig, 1885)

68. This does not mean to say that the concept of *love* receives no attention in Hartmann's ethics. He dealt with this concept both phenomenologically and metaphysically (see *The Moral Consciousness, Das sittliche Bewusstsein).* But he does not consider love to be the last word in ethics. Self-sacrificing, loving devotion to the world process does not seem to Hartmann as something *ultimate* but rather only as a *means* of deliverance from the unrest of existence and of regaining our lost, blissful peace.

69. *Geologische Probleme und Versuch ihrer Auflösung*

70. See the essay: *"Significant Help from One Single Intelligent Word"* (*"Bedeutende Fördernis durch ein einziges geistreiches Wort"*)

71. *Das Unbewusste vom Standpunkte des Darwinismus und der Deszendenztheorie* (1872)

72. *Entwurf einer Farbenlehre*

73. *Beiträge zur Optik*

74. *Elemente der Farbenlehre*

75. *Enthüllungen der Theorie Newtons*

76. *Geschichte der Farbenlehre*

77. *"The Overcoming of Scientific Materialism"* (*"Die Überwindung des Wissenschaftlichen Materialismus"*); a lecture held in the third general session of the meeting of the Society of German Scientists and Physicians in Lübeck on September 20, 1895. (Leipzig 1895)

> **78.** *Über die Grenzen des Naturerkennens,* p. 13.

> **79.** H.L.F. v. Helmholtz, *Goethe's Pre-inklings of Future Scientific Ideas* (*Goethes Vorahnungen kommender wissenschaftlicher Ideen usw.*), p. 34. (Berlin 1892)

80. *Nächte des Suchenden* (Braunschweig 1893)

81. *The Science of Knowing, Outline of an Epistemology Implicit in the Goethean World View with Particular Reference to Schiller* (1886) (*Grundlinien einer Erkenntnistheorie der Goetheschen Weltanschauung mit besonderer Rücksicht auf Schiller*); *Truth and Science, Prelude to a Philosophy of Spiritual Activity* (1892) (*Freiheit und Wissenschaft, Vorspiel einer Philosophie der Freiheit*); *Philosophy of Spiritual Activity, Basic Features of a Modern Worldview* (1894) (*Philosophie der Freiheit, Grundzüge einer modernen Weltanschauung*).

82. *Materialien zur Geschichte der Farbenlehre*

83. *Sprüche in Prosa*

84. Goethe's views stand in the sharpest possible opposition to Kantian philosophy. The latter takes it start from the belief that the world of mental pictures is governed by the laws of the human spirit and that therefore everything brought from outside to meet this world can be present in this world only as a subjective reflection. Man does not perceive the ˝in-itself˝ of things, but rather the phenomenon that arises through the fact that the things affect him and that he connects these effects according to the laws of his intellect and reason. Kant and the Kantians have no inkling of the fact that the essential being of the things speaks through this reason. Therefore the Kantian philosophy could never hold any significance for Goethe. When he acquired for himself some of Kant's principles, he gave them a completely different meaning than they have in the teachings of their originator. It is clear, from a note that only became known after the opening of the Goethe archives in Weimar, that Goethe was very well aware of the antithesis between his worldview and the Kantian one. For him, Kant's basic error lies in the fact that he "regards the *subjective* ability to know as an *object* itself and, sharply indeed but not entirely correctly, he distinguishes the point where *subjective* and *objective* meet." Subjective and objective meet when man joins together into *the unified* being of things what the outer world expresses and what can be heard by his inner being. Then, however, the antithesis between subjective and objective entirely ceases to exist; it disappears in this unified reality. I have already indicated this on page 164ff. of this book. Now K. Vorländer, in the first number of "Kant Studies," directs a polemic against what I wrote there. He finds that my view about the antithesis between the Goethean and the Kantian world conception is "strongly one-sided at best and stands in contradiction to Goethe's own statements," and is due to a "complete misunderstanding on my part of Kant's transcendental methods." Vorländer has no inkling of the worldview in which Goethe lived. It would be utterly pointless for me to enter into polemics with him, because we speak a different language. The fact that he never knows what my statements mean shows how clear his thinking is. For example, I make a comment on the following statement of Goethe: "As soon as the human being becomes aware of the objects around him, he regards them with respect to himself, and justifiably so. For, his whole destiny depends upon whether he likes or dislikes them, whether they attract or repel him, whether they help or harm him. This entirely natural way of looking at things and of judging them seems to be as easy as it is necessary....Those people take on a far more difficult task whose active drive for knowledge strives to observe the objects of nature *in themselves* and in their relationships to each other; they seek out and investigate what is and not what pleases." My comment on this is as follows: "This shows how Goethe's worldview is the exact polar opposite of the Kantian one. For Kant, there is absolutely no view of things as they are in themselves, but only of how they appear with respect to us. Goethe considers this view to be a quite inferior way of entering into a relationship with things." Vorländer's response to this is: "These words of Goethe are not intended to express anything more than, in an introductory way, the trivial difference between what is pleasant and what is true. The researcher should seek out 'what is and not what *pleases.*' It is advisable for someone like Steiner – who dares to say that this latter, in fact *very* inferior, way of entering into a relationship with things is Kant's way – to first make clear to himself the basic concepts of Kant's teachings: the difference between a subjective and an objective sensation, for example, which is described in such passages as section three of the *Critique of the Power of Judgment.*" Now, as is clear from my statements, I did not at all say that that way of entering into a relationship with things is Kant's way, but rather that Goethe does not find Kant's under-standing of the relationship between subject and object to correspond to the relationship in which man stands toward things when he wants to know how they are in themselves. Goethe is of the view that the Kantian definition does not correspond to human knowing, but only to the relationship into which man enters with things when he regards them with respect to his pleasure or displeasure. Someone who can misunderstand a statement the way Vorländer does would do better to spare himself the trouble of giving advice to other people about their philosophical education, and first acquire for himself the ability to learn to read a sentence correctly. Anyone can look for Goethe quotes and bring them together historically; but Vorländer, in any case, cannot interpret them in the spirit of the Goethean worldview.

85.   The following story shows how little understanding is present in professional philosophers today both for ethical views and for an ethic of inner freedom and of individualism in general. In 1892, in an essay for *Zukunft* (No. 5), I spoke out for a strictly individualistic view of ethics. Ferdinand Toennies in Kiel responded to this essay in a brochure: *Ethical Culture and its Retinue. Nietzsche Fools in the Future and in the Present* (Berlin 1893). He presented nothing except the main principles of philistine morality in the form of philosophical formulas. Of me, however, he says that I could have found "no worse Hermes on the path to Hades than Friedrich Nietzsche." It struck me as truly humorous that Toennies, in order to condemn me, presents several of Goethe's *Aphorisms in Prose*. He has no inkling of the fact that if I did have a Hermes, it was not Nietzsche, but rather Goethe. I have already shown on page 146ff. of this book the connections between the ethics of inner freedom and Goethe's ethics. I would not have mentioned this worthless brochure if it were not symptomatic of the misunderstanding of Goethe's world view that holds sway in professional philosophical circles.